Young Workers of the Industrial Age

Young Workers of the Industrial Age

Child Labour in the 18th and 19th Centuries

Sue Wilkes

PEN & SWORD
HISTORY

First published in Great Britain in 2011 as
'The Children History Forgot' by Robert Hale Ltd
Now republished in 2024 by Pen & Sword History
An imprint of Pen & Sword Books Limited
Yorkshire – Philadelphia

ISBN 978 1 03611 383 4

A CIP catalogue record for this book is
available from the British Library

Typeset by Mac Style
Printed in the UK by CPI Group (UK) Ltd, Croydon, CR0 4YY.

MIX
Paper | Supporting
responsible forestry
FSC® C013604

Pen & Sword Books Limited incorporates the imprints of After
the Battle, Atlas, Archaeology, Aviation, Discovery, Family History,
Fiction, History, Maritime, Military, Military Classics, Politics,
Select, Transport, True Crime, Air World, Frontline Publishing, Leo
Cooper, Remember When, Seaforth Publishing, The Praetorian Press,
Wharncliffe Local History, Wharncliffe Transport, Wharncliffe True
Crime and White Owl.

For a complete list of Pen & Sword titles please contact

PEN & SWORD BOOKS LIMITED
47 Church Street, Barnsley, South Yorkshire, S70 2AS, England
E-mail: enquiries@pen-and-sword.co.uk
Website: www.pen-and-sword.co.uk
or
PEN AND SWORD BOOKS
1950 Lawrence Rd, Havertown, PA 19083, USA
E-mail: uspen-and-sword@casematepublishers.com
Website: www.penandswordbooks.com

For Mum and Dad, with love.

Contents

Acknowledgements

Many people have helped me write and research 'Young Workers of the Industrial Age'. I am very grateful to Martin Brayne, editor of the Parson Woodforde Society Journal for his help with Woodforde's diaries. I would like to thank Jennifer Kelly, librarian at the North of England Institute of Mining and Mechanical Engineers, for permission to quote from *A Letter from the Dead to the Living*. I would also like to thank Cheshire West and Chester Libraries staff, and Alice Lock and staff at Tameside Local Studies and Archives Centre.

The text has been extensively corrected and revised for this new edition. Any errors in the book are, of course, my own.

Many thanks are also due to the editors and production staff at Pen & Sword. I am extremely grateful to Amy Jordan and Lori Jones who have helped and encouraged me with my work.

The biggest thanks of all, as ever, are for my much-loved husband Nigel and children Lizzie and Gareth. I could never have written this book without their help, patience, and support at all times of the day and night.

Illustrations

Images are from the author's collection unless otherwise credited.

Chapter 1
Forging the Fairytale

Once upon a time, in Queen Victoria's reign, a fairytale palace of glass and iron was built. The Great Exhibition of 1851 displayed the wonders of Britain's industry and empire.

Lustrous silks, innovative cotton machinery, shining steel blades, and giant lumps of coal were emblematic of the country's many great manufactures. Fortunes had been made, and world-wide fame won, by Victoria's captains of industry. But there was a dark truth behind the Crystal Palace's glittering façade. Britain's industrial might was forged with the blood, sweat and tears of the most vulnerable members of society.

Children of all ages worked by day and by night. Workers as young as four years old crawled underground in coal mines, far from the light of day. They toiled in factories and print-works. Boys sweated with effort in the dark heart of glasshouses, lit only by the blaze of the furnaces. Youngsters drudged for long hours in squalid workshops. Hundreds were killed or injured by unguarded machinery; others died early deaths from breathing in poisonous metal or pottery dust.

Social historians the Hammonds have commented that in the early stages of industrialism: '…the employment of children on a vast scale became the most important social feature of English life.'[1] This is rather an over-simplistic view. Amongst the working classes, children had always been expected to earn their keep from an early age. It was a fact of life.

The use of children as cheap labour is an emotive and contentious issue in modern times. The harsh realities of the past cast long shadows into our own century. In 2023, the International Labour Organisation estimated that there are 160 million child workers worldwide.[2] Many of these occupations potentially endanger their physical and mental health, or affect their social development. Children are trafficked, sexually exploited, or work in sweatshops, mines, and quarries.

Can we learn from the way the Victorians approached the problems associated with child workers in Britain? The story of reform in factory and workshop is not a neat progression of success stories but a catalogue of missed opportunities, punctuated by small advances in the right direction.

In the early eighteenth century, child labour was not considered controversial. Since time immemorial, children helped their parents in the family business, or followed them into the same trade, or learnt a handicraft. Daniel Defoe, who toured Britain during the 1770s, beamed with national pride at the sight of four-year-old children busily earning a living in Halifax. Statesman William Pitt the Younger (1759–1806) considered child workers a national asset. They played a key role in the country's economic success.

The sheer scale of child labour during this period can be difficult to comprehend. Children worked in an amazing variety of industries across Britain. Employment opportunities depended on the work available in a particular area and how labour-intensive it was.

Each region had its own specialist trades and industries. Lancashire, birthplace of the Industrial Revolution, was famous for its cotton mills and coal mines. 'Boom' cotton towns such as Ashton-under-Lyne employed thousands of child workers. In 1794, Ashton had just ten small cotton-spinning mills. By 1839, there were thirty-three spinning-mills. Eighty-two cotton firms in the town employed over 4,300 children and young people below the age of eighteen: over one-third of the factory workforce.[3]

Cheshire had the lion's share of Britain's silk mills. Yorkshire had flourishing woollen and worsted factories. The north-east was famed for its coal and glass. The eponymous Potteries were renowned for earthenware; Sheffield and Birmingham were home to metal manufactures. Scotland exported cotton and linen; Ireland was also famed for its linen.

Great cities like London harboured the sweated trades: millinery, tailoring, and so on. Child scavengers or 'mud-larks' grubbed along the banks of the Thames, looking for saleable garbage. Children helped manufacture bricks, paper, lucifer matches and tobacco. Little boys were forced up chimneys to clean them.

Children worked on the land, too. Their work, like helping bring in the harvest, was regulated by the seasons. Agriculture was the largest employer at the turn of the nineteenth century, providing work for over a third of Britain's labourers. By the early 1840s, agriculture and domestic service were still the two largest single occupations. Crafts like lace-making and straw-plaiting helped families eke out a living in some rural districts.

How many children were at work at a given time? Unfortunately, it is very difficult to give precise figures, especially before 1851, because we lack reliable census data. The first complete official census did not take place until 1801, and the returns from the first three ten-yearly censuses were destroyed before the First World War.

Frustratingly, children's occupations did not need to be recorded by enumerators for the 1841 census. Information on children's work was collected for the 1851 census, but there are problems with the way that data was recorded. The number of child workers was under-reported, particularly in rural areas. The occupations of farmers' wives and children were not recorded, even if they worked on the farm. Young farm servants who 'lived-in' with their master were sometimes mistakenly listed as domestic workers, further skewing the statistics.

Professor Hopkins has estimated there were at least 423,000 boys under fifteen (including 120,000 in agriculture), and 237,000 girls under fifteen at work in Britain in 1851.[4]

Why were so many child workers needed? It was partly a consequence of demographics: young people formed a much higher proportion of the population than today. According to the 2011 Census, there were just over 10.5 million children aged fifteen and below in England and Wales – approximately one in five of the population.[5]

The population picture was very different in the nineteenth century. A time traveller would be amazed by the vast numbers of children and youngsters everywhere. In 1821, thirty-nine per cent of England's population was below the age of fifteen, with roughly similar figures for Scotland, Ireland, and Wales.

Twenty years later, the proportion of young people (below the age of fifteen) in England and Wales had reduced only very slightly, to thirty-six per cent of the population.[6] People died at a much younger age than today, too; cotton workers, miners and metal grinders were considered 'old' at forty.

The Industrial Revolution had an immense impact on working-class children. Horrific abuses were discovered in factories in Lancashire and Derbyshire at the turn of the nineteenth century. Children as young as seven were sent far from home to work in the early textile mills. They lived, ate and slept in appalling conditions.

However, it would be a mistake to assume that extremely young children formed a high proportion of the factory workforce. In 1816, the busy cotton town of Manchester contained forty-three working mills, which employed 12,940 people. Of these, just under 800 child workers (six per cent) were under the age of ten years; 5,460 (forty-two per cent) were aged ten to eighteen. The largest employer was McConnel & Kennedy's mill (1,020 workers), with thirty-four child workers under ten, and 464 youngsters aged ten to eighteen.[7]

It is tricky comparing statistics for child factory workers in later decades because the age at which they started work changed when factory legislation was introduced, but we can get a rough idea.

In 1835, children under thirteen comprised roughly sixteen per cent of the total textile workforce of 354,700 people. Most textile workers were female: 167,000 adult women plus girls aged thirteen to eighteen. (Women and girls were counted together for statistical purposes). Only 44,500 children aged thirteen to eighteen in textile mills were boys.[8]

We also need to put the factory workforce into context nationally. The children employed in textile mills formed only a small fraction of the total working population of Britain. Most child workers never stepped through a factory gate.

One problem we face is how to define 'childhood' during this time period. Can we fix the end of 'childhood' as the age when a youngster enters the world of work?

In general, children started full-time work when they were about ten years old, but there was no definitive starting age. It was not unusual for them to begin part-time work at a much younger age, depending on their strength, the jobs available, and parental income.

At one Somerset silk mill in 1816, children as young as six worked an eight-hour day during the summer (six hours in winter). When they reached the age of nine, they worked an eleven-and-a-half hour day, beginning work before breakfast. During the early 1840s, Warrington children began pin-making from the age of five or six.

As late as the 1860s, Bedfordshire children who were only three or four years old were employed at straw-plaiting, and it would seem intuitively obvious that 'childhood' was not yet over for these tiny workers.

Poverty was the most important factor determining when, and how many, children in a family started work. Families with several dependent children were keen to send them to work as soon as they could bring in a wage. Ten-year-old William Russell and his four brothers hewed coal in a pit in eastern Scotland in 1842. They were forced to earn their own living after their father died of lung disease when he was forty, and their mother died in childbed.

Children who lost one or both parents were more likely to enter the workplace when very young. Mary Weldon made spools (paper tubes) for worsted yarn-spinning at Bingley in the West Riding of Yorkshire in 1862: 'I am going eight… Three of us are dead. Father is dead. Mother is not well, and cannot work'.[9] (Mary was probably seven, not eight years old. Children said they were 'going seven', or whatever age was appropriate, rather than admit they were younger than their avowed age, in case they got their parents or master in trouble).

Having both parents at work did not guarantee that a young child's earnings could be dispensed with. Joseph Corbett, a Birmingham mechanic, was one of eleven children. His father's drinking habits meant that money was always tight. Joseph's mother worked full-time in a workshop, and returned to work after the birth of each child. The baby was brought to her at dinnertime so she could feed it. Meanwhile, Joseph's father wanted to be waited on hand and foot, even though his wife sat up nearly all night washing and mending her children's clothes. The children all went out to work.

In the 1840s, Corbett looked back to his childhood. His memories were dominated by: 'cold and hunger', and an unhappy home atmosphere: 'the frightful poverty; the constant quarrelling; the pernicious example to my brothers and sisters…one and all of us being forced out to work so young that our feeble earnings would only produce 1s a week'.[10]

If the mother of a family went out to work, she might leave her oldest child in charge of the younger siblings: a full-time 'job' in itself. If no child or grandparent was available, she hired a child to act as baby-minder or 'nurse'. Ellen Moore, a twelve-year-old button-sorter at Birmingham in 1864, previously worked as a 'nurse' when she was 'going…seven' years old.[11] Children like Ellen indirectly helped build Britain's industrial might because they freed parents or older siblings to go to work.

Hard times could tip a relatively affluent family's finances from a comfortable living into penury with terrifying speed. Charles Dickens (1812–1870) had a very happy early childhood. He loved going to school at Chatham, where his family lived for several years, and his father John enjoyed a regular salary as a naval pay-officer. But John got into debt, compounded by a reduction in salary, and in 1821 the family moved to Camden Town, one of London's poorest suburbs.

As John's creditors closed in, the family moved to Gower St, hoping his wife Elizabeth could earn a living by teaching. Soon afterwards, John was arrested for debt, and imprisoned at Marshalsea. One by one, the Dickens family's possessions were pawned to raise money, including Charles's treasured storybooks.

Dickens's mother had no success as a teacher. His older sister Fanny was studying at the Royal Academy of Music. His younger sister and brothers were too young to work, so Charles was the only one with earning potential. When a relative offered twelve-year-old Charles a job in a blacking-factory warehouse at old Hungerford Stairs for six shillings a week, his parents jumped at the chance.

In a 'secret agony' of despair, Charles sealed and labelled pots of blacking in a tumbledown building over-run with rats. He was deeply ashamed of his family's fall from grace, and constantly fretted that he would forget all he had previously learnt at school. He never forgave his parents for sending him out to work. They did not even try to get him a place in a common day-school: 'It is wonderful to me that I could have been cast away at so early an age'.[12]

His mother and siblings moved into Marshalsea prison for a time, while Charles lived alone in lodgings. Eventually, the family fortunes revived when a relative left a legacy to John Dickens, and he was released from prison. Charles got his dearest wish and went to school. But the memory of his time at the blacking-factory haunted Dickens to his dying day and inspired his later work.

If we instead define the end of childhood as the age of independence, when youngsters left home and its parents ceased to have any responsibility for them, this varied by region and by trade.

In rural areas during the 1850s, children commonly began farm work as early as six years old; they usually lived at home with their parents. When they were ten years old, many children left their parents to become farm servants, 'living-in' with a farmer and his wife all year round.

Age ten was also a common milestone for a child to be apprenticed into a trade like shoe-making or weaving. But for apprentices, 'adulthood' was not achieved until the age of twenty-one. As legislation on employment and education impacted on children's lives during the nineteenth century, the age when a child entered the world of work rose.

When parliament eventually agreed to protect factory children against exploitation, those below the age of thirteen were classed as 'children', and those aged thirteen to eighteen were classed as 'young persons'. Both age groups were seen as needing protection because they were not 'free agents'. They were not yet adults capable of making their own decisions. Accordingly, this work looks at the experiences of children and youngsters under eighteen in the world of work during Georgian and Victorian times.

Child workers can be divided into two main groups: 'free labour' children, and apprentices. 'Free labour' children contributed to the household income by going out to work, or helping their parents at home in the family business. Perhaps they accompanied their parents to the factory, mine, or workshop where they were employed, or helped them in the fields if they were agricultural labourers.

Apprentices in their turn comprised two different groups: the first were apprenticed to masters, either formally or informally by their parents. The second group were pauper apprentices.

Parish overseers had long-established and draconian powers under the Poor Laws. They had a statutory duty to apprentice out the children in their care. There were humane masters who treated pauper apprentices reasonably well, but far too many children were ruthlessly exploited. Some of the most horrific cases of abuse relate to the parish apprentice system, as we shall see presently.

Philanthropist Jonas Hanway (1712–86) was greatly interested in the welfare of poor children and successfully campaigned for legislation to help safeguard them. He firmly believed that children 'had better be dead than in idleness or vice'. Little children should be placed with a master as early in life as possible, so they could learn industrious habits: 'train a child up in the way he should go'.[13]

This view of child labour taken by Hanway and many other well-meaning people was rooted in religious and moral conviction. The human race was weak, sinful, and easily tempted by evil. The devil 'found work for idle hands to do.' Families who did not use every means possible to support themselves, for example by making their children work, were considered feckless and improvident. They were a burden on the poor rates.

The best path to true happiness and prosperity for the children of the poor was through 'habits of industry'. William Hogarth's famous series of moralistic engravings on 'Industry and Idleness' was first published in 1747.

Hogarth told the story of two boys. The industrious apprentice, Francis Goodchild, works hard and follows the path of virtue. When he grows up, he marries his master's daughter, and eventually becomes mayor of London. But Thomas Idle, the other apprentice, follows a very different path. Thomas neglects his work. His life of wickedness and idleness ends at Tyburn, where he suffers a felon's death by hanging. Hogarth deliberately made his prints as affordable as possible so they could reach a wide audience. 'Industry and Idleness' was still used as a teaching aid for children over half a century later.

Educational writers like Sarah Trimmer (1741–1810) and Hannah More (1745–1833) advocated work for young children to stop them falling into slothful habits. Like Hogarth, they believed that indolence inevitably led to vice, and probably an untimely end via the hangman's noose.

Trimmer urged the establishment of schools of industry where children could learn a trade, so that they did not spend: 'seven days of the week in idleness and dirt... there are in this kingdom thousands of idle children, who might be employed, not only to the advantage of the families...but for the benefit of the community'.[14] Sarah thought that a school of industry at Lewisham (1796), which taught children spinning and knitting, was a good example of how to set children's feet on the right path.

Hannah More used children's stories to get her message across. Farmer White, a character in More's tale *Tom White the Postboy*, said sternly: 'Those who do not set their young children to work on week days, and send them to school and church on Sundays, deserve little favour'.[15]

In the late eighteenth century, the Sunday school movement, pioneered by Robert Raikes and others, gave a little education to child workers like pin-headers and framework (stocking) knitters. Children like these worked all week and had no opportunity to go to day schools. The Sunday school movement was controversial; some people considered it blasphemous to teach children anything other than the Bible on the Sabbath. Others felt there was no point teaching working-class children to read and write at all; their time should be spent in honest labour. This was all part of God's plan for society.

The experiences of working-class children were worlds apart from those of upper- and middle-class children, who went to a good school, or were taught at home. James Watt (1736–1819), whose amazingly efficient steam-engines later made him famous, was taught the three 'Rs' by his parents at his Greenock home before he attended a commercial school, and later, the nearby grammar school.

Novelist Jane Austen (1775–1817) and her sister Cassandra had some education at home in Steventon. Later they were sent away from home to a school at Southampton, and the Abbey House School in Reading. The girls learnt history and geography, as well as feminine accomplishments like needlework and dancing.

The upper- and middle-classes regarded 'the poor' as a problem society was permanently lumbered with, as ordained by heaven. William Cobbett commented acidly that it was as if: 'paupers were a distinct race amongst human beings, as wolves and asses are amongst four-footed animals'.[16]

Parson Malthus's controversial ideas were hugely influential in the debate on how much help should be given to 'the poor', and how much they should do for themselves. Thomas Robert Malthus (1766–1834) first published his *Essay on the Principle of Population* in 1798. His view of humanity and its future was deeply pessimistic.

Malthus believed that population would always out-run the food sources available to it for subsistence. Population growth was only held in check by natural disasters such as war, famine and so on, or by preventative checks, e.g., people having fewer children. 'Misery, and the fear of misery' was the 'grinding law' of economic 'necessity' which stopped the population spiralling out of control.

He argued that poor families should have no state help whatsoever. Families should fend for themselves. Poor Law institutions like workhouses, and payments of 'outdoor relief' (money, food, blankets) to paupers living at home, should be gradually abolished.

If poor families were given aid, they were more likely to marry early and have babies. Hence there would be more hungry mouths to feed, and the drain on society would increase. Illegitimate children should not be entitled to any parish relief, but 'left entirely to the support of private charity. If parents desert their children, they ought to be made answerable for the crime. The infant is, comparatively speaking, of little use to society, as others will immediately supply its place.'[17]

Malthus's theories outraged Radical critics like William Cobbett, William Hazlitt and others. They denounced his work as inhuman, hard-hearted and un-Christian. But Malthus's ideas gained great ground.

Stockbroker David Ricardo, another influential economist, believed that wages, prices and rents were governed by market forces. They must not be hindered in any way by state interference. The theories of Adam Smith (*Wealth of Nations*), Malthus, Ricardo and other economists underpinned the gospel of laissez-faire.

Laissez-faire or 'leave well alone' economics, put simply, taught that industry should determine its own progress. Masters and men in a particular industry (cotton, say) knew best how to govern their affairs. They should strike their own bargains regarding wages and hours. A manufacturer naturally wanted to make a profit: his efforts to prosper provided employment for his workforce, which in turn added to society's prosperity. Any attempts by government to regulate wages and hours would be at best, clumsy, and at worst, disastrous.

If Britain's trade and industry was to reign supreme, individuals must follow their own best interests. This economic doctrine held sway amongst upper- and middle-class thinkers for many years, and stalled attempts to help working-class children. If a young child was brutally exploited in a tiny workshop, then it was no-one else's business. Or was it? Others felt it was time for change. Something must be done to 'rescue' children.

The massive social changes wrought by the Industrial Revolution coincided with new ways of thinking pioneered by Jean-Jacques Rousseau and his followers. Rousseau believed that childhood was a special time of life. (Although he was not exactly a good role model for parenthood. He put all his children in a foundling hospital). Rousseau's ideas inspired the Romantic poets such as William Wordsworth, Samuel Taylor Coleridge, and Robert Southey, to question society's values.

They pointed accusingly at the factory system. Had the Industrial Revolution really brought such great benefits to society? The Romantics likened child labour in factories to slavery. They looked back wistfully to a so-called 'golden age' before the mills opened their gates.

Wordsworth lamented the Industrial Revolution's impact on Westmorland cottagers; the spinning-wheels which once gave them employment now lay gathering dust. Coleridge said that if he were forced to work in a factory for twelve hours, his soul would be enslaved. He would cease to be a rational, thinking being and sink into a mere animal existence.

Poet Laureate Robert Southey wrote of the operatives' children being 'literally worked to death…murdered by inches'.[18] He painted an idealised picture of the olden days, when proud, independent labourers worked busily in their cottages, with children playing happily by the fireside.

The Romantics' vision was rose-tinted, however. Thomas Babington Macaulay, for one, ridiculed Southey's vision of peasant life in a trenchant essay. Working-class housing before and after the advent of cotton factories in the 1770s was hardly idyllic. Families in the towns and countryside lived in overcrowded, damp, insanitary homes.

As the Industrial Revolution gathered pace, people flocked into the cities looking for work in the new factories. They needed somewhere to live, and entrepreneurs took advantage of this, running up poorly-built slums to accommodate them. Few people had access to clean water. Sanitation was primitive in some areas and non-existent in others.

One Manchester street in 1832 had just one privy shared by over 380 people. Houses in Leeds had broken windows and 'filth and vermin in every nook… with the walls un-whitewashed for years, black with the smoke of chimneys', and no 'out-offices' (privies). The town's streets were covered with the accumulation of years of muck and human waste, 'unpaved, undrained, unventilated… such places are the hot-beds of disease'.

Rural labourers enjoyed the benefits of fresh country air as they worked in the fields, but at night they slept in hovels with earth floors and leaking roofs. A family and its belongings were typically crammed into a 'miserable dwelling' of just two rooms: the living space used during daylight hours was shared with cooking utensils, farm tools, and washtub. The windows were broken and stuffed with rags to keep out draughts.

All the family slept in one room, sometimes with a lodger. Commonly, the only bedroom had no window: 'the openings in the half-thatched roof admit light, and subject the family to every vicissitude of the weather'. Clean water, proper sanitation and drainage were at a premium here, too. 'Filth of every description' ran in gutters near the houses; cesspools lurked close by.[19] A few enlightened factory owners and rural landowners built model housing for their workers, but these were the exception rather than the rule.

The appalling state of housing and sanitation left people exposed to diseases such as typhus, tuberculosis and cholera, and this was reflected in the mortality statistics. In London parishes between 1823 and 1824, a shocking 6,476 infants under two years old perished, plus another 2,900 children between two and ten years old.[20]

The gentry, who enjoyed a higher standard of living conditions than the working classes, were no strangers to early death, either. A terrifying cholera visitation from 1831 to 1832 left tens of thousands of people dead. Neither the 'rich man in his castle' nor the 'poor man at his gate' was spared.

Politicians became alarmed when cholera, typhus and other horrific diseases wreaked deadly havoc in upper- and middle-class homes as well as the slums of the poor. In 1840, the government launched investigations into the health of towns and working-class living conditions.

Sanitary reformer Edwin Chadwick's landmark report (1842) discovered that in towns like Liverpool and Manchester, one in three working-class children died before they were five years old. The average age of death for rural labourers in Wiltshire was thirty-three years; for Liverpool townsfolk it was just fifteen years.

Despite damning evidence from reports like these, and another cholera epidemic in 1848–9, the government found it virtually impossible to persuade local ratepayers to shoulder the massive burden of cleaning up their towns.

A few enlightened local authorities, notably Liverpool and London in the late 1840s, took tentative steps to clean up their act. But little was done over the country as a whole. Townsfolk and rural labourers endured squalor, overcrowding and rampant disease throughout Victoria's reign and beyond. In the 1870s, a doctor in County Tyrone described the homes of flax workers in Cookstown: 'The use of the bath is almost unknown, and dirt and squalor are common in their houses; and in my visits among them I am often shocked at the state of their bed-clothes, and at the want of suitable healthy ventilation'.[21]

The Romantics' cosy vision of artisans' working life in their own homes was also flawed. In theory, workers set their own hours, but in practice, this depended on piecework rates. The children of workers in textile and metal manufacturing industries endured long hours toiling under their parents' watchful eyes. Greedy or impoverished parents were often brutal taskmasters, and their children suffered accordingly.

It is not difficult to find apologists for child labour in contemporary literature. Social commentators such as William Cooke Taylor argued that 'juvenile labour' in the factories was 'a national blessing' because without their children's wages, parents could not afford to feed and clothe them. Surely it was much better for young people to work than starve, or beg on the streets, or steal food? Here we come to the crux of the child labour debate.

Cooke Taylor brushed aside lurid tales of tiny child workers: 'To talk of infant labour is sheer nonsense, and nothing else. What master would be insane enough to employ an infant or a child incapable of performing the task for which he pays wages?' Cooke Taylor's observations appear at first glance to be common sense, but as we shall see presently, 'infant labour' was all too real.

Cooke Taylor did make one good point: 'If it were true that cruelties are practised on children in the mills, or that tasks are imposed on them injurious to health or life, such a fact would only prove that the physical or moral destitution of the parents must be of the most frightful kind, or else they would never, for such trifling wages, expose their offspring to such sufferings.' His comments apply equally to children's work in the mines or metal workshops.

The 'physical and moral destitution' of parents *was* truly appalling. Poverty and ignorance were the engine drivers of child labour.

Perhaps more surprisingly, some recent historians have argued the use of child workers was regrettable but necessary during the rise of industrialism. They made a significant contribution to Britain's economic success. Historians like Clark Nardinelli, echoing Cooke Taylor, believed that the new factories gave families fresh opportunities to boost their income and raise their living standards by employing children. However, some authors have tended to gloss over the extremely early age at which some children began productive work.

Was factory work really as awful as its detractors claimed? Like many other contemporaries, Cooke Taylor believed that factory work was 'not laborious', although admittedly 'monotonous and fatiguing'. He argued: 'the mill is a better place than the mine, the ship, the forge, and very many private workshops'.[22]

Physical correction was considered acceptable, but children were treated in an unbelievably callous way, even if we put their treatment in its historical context. Young metal workers in the Black Country were horse-whipped. At Sedgley, children were burnt with red-hot irons. The collier master of one young Rochdale apprentice starved and beat him with a piece of wood spiked with a nail. The boy was sent home to his widowed mother in a state of collapse, covered in wounds.

The issue of child poverty in the era before the modern welfare state was very real, and here opponents of factory and workshop reform were on firmer ground. Many everyday items were taxed, including bread, soap, salt, tea, sugar and paper. Taxation pressed especially hard on the working classes, eroding their buying power. Parents had little option but to send their children out to work.

People knew only too well that working-class families could not survive without their children's wages. The earliest supporters of factory and workshop reform (on both sides of the class divide) did not want to abolish child labour. They wanted excessively long working hours curbed, and children protected from brutality in the workplace.

But campaigners for change were constantly thwarted by vested interests in parliament. When proposals for reform were put before the Houses of Parliament, opponents used time-honoured delaying tactics. They would request a commission to gather evidence and then report back to the honourable members.

The wide-ranging Commissions on Children's Employment of the nineteenth century gathered thousands of pages of detailed evidence on children's working conditions in trade, industry and agriculture. Tellingly, in some areas, both adults and children referred to any time not spent in work as 'play'. Edward Lomax, a ten-year-old ironworker at Willenhall in the 1860s, said: 'I played [was off sick] for a week when I burnt my foot. I did not play for the burns on my arm'.[23]

Months passed while evidence was amassed by investigators. Protective legislation often took years to successfully reach the statute books. Laws were repealed or made toothless following lobbying by factory owners and peers with industrial interests. One writer called the struggle for factory and mines reform: 'one long chronicle of the crimes of Christian England'.[24]

But this is no fairytale, with sharply defined heroes and villains. As Cooke Taylor pointed out, not all mill-owners were like the 'ogres and giants of our nursery tales'.[25] Nor was it a simple fight between humanitarians and factory owners driven by sordid profit motives.

Factory owners, philanthropists, politicians and writers straddled both sides of the child labour debate. Mill-owners Robert Owen and John Fielden were leading lights in the crusade to improve children's working conditions. When Lord Ashley (later the seventh earl of Shaftesbury) campaigned for factory and mine reform, his opponents pointed to the workers on his family estates living in appalling squalor.

It was a clash of ideals, a battle between opposing economic and political theories. The dead weight of 'laisser-faire' policies mesmerised politicians. When confronted by evidence of excessive working hours, they believed their hands were tied, and took a fatalistic view. No matter how bad conditions were, politicians genuinely believed any interference with the labour market would make matters infinitely worse.

Society had to be re-educated before reformers overcame some of the hideous abuses of their day. Over half a century of Victoria's long reign passed before men like Lord Ashley and Charles Dickens changed public and political attitudes on child labour.

When Charles Dickens was born in 1812, the early years of working-class children were spent in the world of work: typically from age seven, often younger. Education was considered an unnecessary luxury by many working-class parents. In June 1870, a few weeks after Dickens's death, Forster's Elementary Education Act became law. This Act put education within reach of the very poorest children in society. Young children were now expected to go to school, although attendance was still not compulsory. The story of this sea-change in society's attitudes forms the main theme of this book.

When so many children's working conditions were so dire, and thousands of young workers suffered death and injury, the author runs the risk of writing a 'misery memoir' for the masses. But there are tales of heroism amidst the gloom.

There is no shortage of documentary evidence of hard-hearted parents profiting from the labour of their young children. Many parents, however, cared for their children to the best of their ability. They complained if their children were ill-treated at work, or found them employment elsewhere. When a Birmingham boy had his arm burnt with red hot screws by the man he worked for: 'Father said I shouldn't go to be "munched" no more like that, and I left and went to a cooper's'.[26] The workman was sacked by the firm's owner.

Not all children were passive victims. They displayed considerable ingenuity and resilience under pressure. They ran away if they saw an opportunity. A master chimney sweep commented of the climbing boys: 'The boys can always run away if they like'.[27] Pauper apprentices in the early factories who absconded faced the risk of being caught and taken back to a brutal master, but they knew they were valuable workers. If they were fortunate, they found another job, and if they were really lucky, a kinder master. Pauper apprentices who survived the 'theft' of their childhoods made new lives for themselves and had children of their own.

These children's lives may seem unimaginably hard to modern readers, but we know that some skipped and sang in their workplace. 'Cheerfulness' was said to be characteristic of many young miners in the West Riding of Yorkshire. Boys working at Platt Brothers' forge in Oldham played leap-frog while metal was heating in the furnace. Annie Holt, a brick-works girl at Brierley Hill, sang at her work 'many a time.'[28]

The first major issue to attract the attention of reformers was the way in which pauper apprentices in the cotton industry were exploited. The controversy over these children's treatment gave the first impetus to legislative reform.

Chapter 2

Learning a Trade

Since medieval times, if parents wanted their child to enter a trade or manufacture, in theory, they had to find a master willing to take on the youngster as an apprentice.

The Statute of Artificers and Apprentices, which dated back to the reign of Elizabeth I, said that no-one could practise a 'craft, trade or mystery' without first serving an apprenticeship.[1] Some masters demanded extremely high apprenticeship premiums, for example, Leicester hosiers charged one hundred guineas or more during the eighteenth century. Only wealthy families could afford this kind of money.

In general, premiums ranged from a few pounds to a hundred pounds depending on the trade: twenty pounds for a butcher, or seventy pounds for a plumber. High premiums meant that children from poor families were most unlikely to join a skilled trade unless they could find someone willing to take them on without one.

The apprenticeship contract or 'indenture' specified length of service, whether the youngster received any wages, and if he or she was to 'live in' with his or her master. The child's clothes were sometimes included as well as board and lodging. Once the apprentice had served his term, he worked alongside his master as a journeyman, or perhaps set up his own business. An apprenticeship normally lasted for seven years. Scotland had its own apprenticeship laws: three years was a more common term.

When seventeen-year-old James Watt arrived in London, hoping to apprentice himself to a mathematical instrument-maker, he was shocked to find he was expected to serve seven years. (Watt later famously produced steam-engines with business partner Matthew Boulton). A friend of the family pulled some strings and got him a place in Cornhill for a year, but James had to pay a twenty-guinea premium.

In the skilled trades, corporation bye-laws determined the number of apprentices a master was allowed, and the number of years of service. The law varied from place to place: in Sheffield, a master cutler was only allowed one apprentice. At Norfolk and Norwich, a master weaver was only allowed two apprentices, and was fined five pounds a month (a very large sum) if he had more than two. Similar rules applied to master hatters and the Spitalfields silk-weavers in London.

Apprentices did not always 'live in' with their master. In 1816, John Debell Tuckett estimated that most of the 150,000 apprentices 'bound to mechanical employment' in London boarded out. (These were young persons, not small children). These apprentices received a sum of money from their master towards food and lodging.

Contemporaries considered this a bad system. Apprentices were not as strictly supervised as when they 'lived in'. Shocking to relate, apprentices spent their Sundays 'in all kinds of pleasure, such as excursions in the country, water, parties, etc., where they frequently mix with low company…'

Unsupervised apprentices acquired pert manners and dissolute habits. Their masters turned them adrift 'without a character, and consequently without the means of obtaining employment' at the end of their term. With no job prospects in store, they spent their time at the local pub, home to the 'most depraved characters' where 'vice becomes familiar to them'. Their fate was soon sealed – apprentices joined the ranks of the 'gamblers, cheats and paupers' infesting the towns.[2]

The Industrial Revolution blew the wind of change through the 'traditional' apprenticeship system. The new manufactures in Manchester, Birmingham and the Midlands weren't covered by the Elizabethan statute, because these industries didn't exist when the law was framed. The Statute of Artificers, with its limits on the number of apprentices allowed to each master, was considered increasingly old-fashioned, and fell into disrepute. Employers and politicians felt the statute was a 'drag' on free trade, and in 1814, its apprenticeship clauses were repealed.

Traditional apprenticeships could prove a stepping-stone to success for young people. The luckiest ones had the opportunity to 'better themselves' after their time was up, especially if apprenticed to a family member or friend. Jacob Bright, father of orator and politician John Bright (who will appear later in our story), was apprenticed to a prosperous fustian-weaver at New Mills, Derbyshire. Like Hogarth's industrious apprentice, Jacob married his master's daughter. He later set up his own cotton-spinning business at Rochdale, and his sons followed him into the family firm.

It was a wise move for the Bright family. Men like Sir Richard Arkwright had shown that fortunes could be made in cotton. The industry was the vanguard of the Industrial Revolution, and new innovations led to giant leaps in productivity.

One of the first major technological breakthroughs was John Kay's flying shuttle (1733), which greatly speeded up the weaving process. This in turn created a demand for more yarn, and great efforts were made to quicken the spinning process so spinners could keep pace with weavers.

A succession of inventions followed: James Hargreaves' 'spinning-jenny' (c.1764); the 'water-frame' developed by Richard Arkwright, John Wyatt, Lewis Paul and Thomas Highs (patented by Arkwright in 1775); and the 'mule' invented by Samuel Crompton (1779). As cotton-spinning machinery grew in size and complexity, it became too cumbersome for ordinary homes or small workshops. Cotton-masters built factories to house their new cotton-spinning machinery.

The example of apprentice Samuel Slater is one of the archetypal 'rags to riches' stories from the cotton industry. Slater (1768–1835) was a pioneer of the American industrial revolution. Samuel, the fifth son of a Derbyshire farmer, was born at Holly House, Belper. His father William was a farmer and timber merchant. Slater senior was acquainted with local cotton-spinner Jedidiah Strutt.

Strutt (1726–1797) was a business partner with famous cotton-spinner Richard Arkwright, and entrepreneur Samuel Need of Nottingham. In 1758, Need and Strutt patented an improvement to the stocking-frame for the manufacture of ribbed stockings: the revolutionary 'Derby rib' hose. Samuel's father helped Strutt purchase water rights for his mills.

William, knowing that Samuel was mechanically minded, asked Strutt if he would take his son as an apprentice. Samuel went to Strutt's cotton factory at Milford 'on trial', as was customary.

Tragedy struck before Samuel's trial period was up. His father William fell from a load of hay and was fatally injured. Before his father died, Samuel asked if he could be formally apprenticed to Strutt, as he was very happy at the mill. William had immense faith in his son's abilities, and asked him to sort out the apprenticeship himself.

Accordingly on 8 January 1783, when Samuel was fourteen-and-a-half years old, he apprenticed himself to Strutt until he was twenty-one. In his indenture, Slater promised to 'faithfully serve' his master, keep his secrets and obey his 'lawful commands'.

The young apprentice was not allowed any fun. He promised not to 'commit fornication nor contract Matrimony within the said Term', nor to 'play at Cards Dice Tables or any other unlawfull [sic]) Games' without his master's permission. There was no question of him being allowed to: 'haunt Taverns or Play Houses' or 'absent himself from his said Master's Service day or night'. In return, Strutt promised to teach Samuel 'the Art of Cotton Spinning' and find him 'Sufficient Meat Drink Washing and Lodging.'[3]

Slater was highly motivated and quickly learned the trade. Although he was only about a mile from home, he didn't visit his mother and brothers, but spent his Sundays experimenting with machinery. Strutt gave him a guinea for inventing an improvement to the spinning-machines.

Samuel was very ambitious and longed for his own factory. During the last few months of his apprenticeship, rumours reached England that the American authorities in several states had offered a reward to anyone who would help perfect cotton manufacture over there. At that time, to safeguard British industry, there were very strict laws against taking sensitive commercial information abroad.

Slater, now an expert on cotton-spinning, decided to seek his fortune in America. He kept his idea a dark secret to protect himself and his family. Samuel had a highly retentive memory, so did not carry any technical drawings in case he was searched by customs officers. The only documentation he took was his apprenticeship indenture to prove he knew the 'art' of cotton-spinning. When he called home to collect clothes for his journey, he didn't even tell his own mother he planned to emigrate. Slater just told her he was going to London on the stage-coach. But he posted her a letter before he sailed for New York.

Samuel's confidence in himself was soon justified. He found some financial partners, and opened a mill. By the time he was fifty, Slater was worth half a million dollars. His canny use of trade secrets was good news for the American cotton industry, but it raised the spectre of serious competition for British textile interests. Samuel was regarded as a turncoat in his native land.

However, the outlook for poor children whose families could not support them was far from rosy. They were at the mercy of the parish authorities. Pauper children were made to work in houses of industry, or were compulsorily bound as apprentices. Overseers could legally bind children as apprentice to a master, even if they still had a parent alive. Officials did not need the consent of the child's family.

Pauper children were apprenticed to many different occupations: domestic service, coal-mining, metal manufacture, millinery, farming, factory work and so on. Once apprenticed, they became their master's legal property. Rewards were offered for runaway apprentices like nineteen-year-old Thomas Swan, who went missing from his work at the Logographic Press in Printing House Square, Blackfriars in September 1789. His master, Mr Hibbert, offered a guinea for his return.[4]

Overseers were not very particular when indenturing 'their' children. All too often, once a child was bound to a master or mistress, it was a case of 'out of sight, out of mind'. There was great scope for abuse.

The handicraft trades were no exception. *Dodsley's Annual Register* for 1762 reported the horrific murder of pauper apprentices Anne Naylor (13) and her eight-year-old sister Mary. In 1758, haberdasher Sarah Metyard of Bruton St, Hanover Square, had five girl apprentices, including the Naylor children, from

Tottenham High Cross parish. The apprentices made silk purses and mittens in a tiny upstairs room with no ventilation. Metyard and her daughter (another Sarah) gave them little food. To ensure the girls couldn't complain to anyone about their treatment, they were only allowed out of the house once a fortnight, and never on their own.

Anne Naylor ran away, but was recaptured. Metyard punished her more savagely still, and gave her even less to eat. One September morning, when the milkman came, the child saw her chance and ran into the street. The younger Sarah shouted to him to stop her. He grabbed Anne and returned her to her legal owners, despite her piteous plea: 'Pray milkman, let me go, for I have had no victuals for a long time, and if I stay here, I shall be starved to death.'[5]

Anne's prediction came true all too soon. She died after being beaten, tied up and kept without food or water for three days. Her body was hidden in the garret of the house, and her sister Mary met the same fate shortly afterwards.

The murders came to light a few years later. Sarah junior, who did nothing to help the children, and concealed the crime, was considered an accessory to her mother's foul deeds. On 19 July 1768, mother and daughter were hanged at Tyburn.

Charities for orphaned and poor children also provided for children in their care by finding them apprenticeships. Elizabeth Monk was one of seven apprentices from the 'Asylum' (probably the Female Orphan Asylum) bound to button-maker Theophilus Bridges of Temple St, St George's Fields.

Bridges was indicted for Elizabeth's murder at Surrey Assizes in July 1796. Only three of the original apprentices had lived to tell the tale. They testified that Bridges was 'a very passionate and severe man, and had frequently beat and kicked the deceased…' The apprentices said that Elizabeth died from ill usage, hard work, and little food. Bridges was acquitted of murder because the surgeon who saw Elizabeth just before she died only checked her pulse. Bridges told him that Elizabeth was ill from 'consumption'.[6]

The Foundling Hospital (founded by Captain Coram in 1739) gave its children a sound education before apprenticing them out. The Hospital, one of the better charities, diligently cared for its children. Unlike some parish authorities, it took swift action once it realized there was a problem with a child's placement.

The trial of Elizabeth Brownrigg was one of the notorious most court cases of the eighteenth century. The overseers of White Friars parish, London, apprenticed Mary Mitchell to house painter James Brownrigg in 1765, when Mary was fourteen years old. Brownrigg's wife Elizabeth was a 'respectable' mother and midwife. Three months later, Mary Jones, who was the same age as Mary Mitchell, was apprenticed to Brownrigg by the Foundling Hospital.

Brownrigg and his wife Elizabeth whipped and tortured their apprentice girls. Elizabeth was the chief tormentor. An example of her cruelty was when Mary Jones scrubbed the floors. If Mrs Brownrigg found fault with her work, she plunged Mary's head in the bucket of water used for cleaning. One day, Mary Jones escaped and made her way back to the Foundling Hospital. She was covered in cuts and bruises, and almost blind in one eye.

The Hospital's solicitor wrote to James Brownrigg and demanded he make amends to the girl, or he would be prosecuted. Mary Jones was released from her indentures; she was lucky to escape with her life.

Unfortunately, parish apprentice Mary Mitchell was still in the Brownriggs' clutches. She managed to escape, but a son of the Brownriggs found her in the street, and she was dragged back again. In February 1766, White Friars parish apprenticed another girl, Mary Clifford, to the Brownriggs. One would have thought they would check carefully on Mary Mitchell's condition before they committed another child to the Brownriggs' tender care, as she had already been there several months. If this was done, it was not done carefully enough.

Mary Clifford's first month with the Brownriggs was 'on liking,' as was the custom. At first she was treated well. Once formally apprenticed, however, it was not long before she was used 'with great cruelty'. Whilst sparing the reader the most distressing details, the two Marys were repeatedly left in rags, starved, whipped and beaten. They were confined in a filthy cellar without any bedding.

In the meantime, Mary Clifford's stepmother, who was away when the girl was indentured, came in search of her to see how she was getting on. The Brownriggs swore Mary was not there, and threatened to send for a constable. However, Clifford's stepmother was a determined woman, and when the Brownriggs' neighbour told her she believed the girls were being mistreated, she returned to the house, accompanied by the White Friars overseer. The Brownriggs did everything they could to stop them seeing Mary Clifford, but at last she was found, and both girls rescued.

Sadly, it was too late for Mary Clifford. She died from her injuries shortly afterwards. The truly sadistic way these girls were treated caused much comment in the press, as did the jury's verdict.

Elizabeth Brownrigg was found guilty of murder and hanged at Newgate on 14 September 1767. But her husband and son were acquitted of their part in her crimes, even though both admitted beating the girls. Strictly speaking, the children were apprenticed to James Brownrigg; they mixed his paints for him. But it seems the jury felt that Elizabeth was chiefly in charge of the girls, and as a wife and mother, she should have adopted a maternal attitude to her young servants. James Brownrigg and son were convicted of assault, and spent six months in prison for their 'misdemeanour'.[7]

This was an age when it was common for children to be physically disciplined, so it was not the fact that the Brownriggs beat the girls which caused a public outcry. It was because they took the girls' punishments to extremes. The Brownrigg case did not stop parish overseers apprenticing out their pauper children. They still needed to provide for them somehow. What little protection pauper children had under the law was rarely enforced, however, so horror stories continued to surface throughout the eighteenth and nineteenth centuries.

Why did parishes have so many poor children on their hands? Under the 'old' Poor Law, which dated back to Elizabethan times, poorhouses and workhouses were, in theory, a refuge for the poor and most indigent members of society. In practice, they were used as a dumping-ground for old and young, sick and healthy, and mentally ill people or 'lunatics'.

In former times, pauper children were not a major problem for overseers, because they did not last long under the parish's tender care. Mortality rates for infant paupers were terrifyingly high.

Jonas Hanway campaigned for more humane treatment for pauper children. He discovered that in some crowded London parishes over a twelve-month period, not one of the children admitted to the workhouse survived. Hanway estimated that over 1,000 children died unnecessarily every year because they were not properly cared for. Children who were 'put out to nurse' outside London and had the benefit of fresh country air were far more likely to survive their early years.

Hanway's Act of 1767 made it compulsory for all parish infants within the bills of mortality in London to be sent out of town until they were six years old. The infants were boarded out with foster parents. In 1778, the law was extended to cover pauper children from outside London. The poor called Hanway's Act 'the Act for keeping children alive'.[8] Contemporaries believed that thousands of children were saved from an early grave thanks to his efforts.

Workhouse children were not necessarily orphans like Robert Blincoe, who we shall meet presently. Impoverished parents were forced to let their children be apprenticed out, even if the children were sent far away. If they protested, and refused to let their children be 'bound,' the parish could (and did) withdraw the family's relief.

If cases such as those of the Brownriggs and Metyards occurred in a big city, with neighbours all around, the reader can imagine how vulnerable pauper children were when apprenticed hundreds of miles from home, in the early factories.

One of the most heartbreaking aspects of pauper apprenticeship was the sheer length of time children were 'bound.' Unlike 'traditional' trade indentures of seven years, male parish children were apprenticed from age nine or ten until they were twenty-four. Girls were apprenticed until they were twenty-one, or until they were married, whichever came first. (Hanway's Act of 1767 reduced parish apprenticeships for London children to seven years, or a maximum age of twenty-one. But the law did not change for children outside London parishes until 1778, when the end of parish apprenticeship was fixed at age twenty-one).

Economist Adam Smith disapproved of very long apprenticeships. Workers who were paid by the piece had an incentive to work hard, whereas: 'A young man naturally conceives an aversion to labour, when for a long time he receives no benefit from it. The boys who are put out apprentices from public charities are generally bound for more than the usual number of years, and they generally turn out very idle and useless.'[9]

The cost of feeding and clothing pauper children mounted up over the years unless some kind of provision was made for them. Saving money was a priority for parish overseers, but was not the sole reason for apprenticing pauper children.

It was the overseers' public duty to arrange industrial training for a child with a suitable master in the hope that he or she would one day earn their own living and be independent of the parish. Parishes paid the master a sum of money ('premium') to take the apprentice; it was customary to give the child a new set of clothes as well.

Even allowing for these initial costs, apprenticeship was cost-effective for parishes over the long-term. If a master refused to take an apprentice for some reason (perhaps because he had insufficient work), he was fined by the parish. Some parishes raffled off children as if they were 'booby' prizes to disgruntled parishioners; other parishes used a rota system. Since the ratepayer then faced the cost of maintaining this unwanted child for several years, many preferred to pay the fine instead. Parishes like Leeds made a handsome profit by deliberately trying to force children on unwilling masters.

Another key benefit for a child's 'home' parish was that once apprenticed, after forty days he was no longer legally 'chargeable': overseers had no further responsibility for him. The apprentice gained a 'settlement' in his new parish, which entitled him to parish relief there. This was a vital consideration for Poor Law officials. When the child grew up, the new parish was responsible for the upkeep of any spouse and children he acquired in the future (if he could not support them). His original parish potentially saved not just one lifetime of expense, but that of the child's descendants. The apprenticeship system was a 'win-win' situation for parish overseers.

There were many instances of children being bound to unsuitable masters. An unscrupulous master accepted a child for the sake of the premium (from two to ten pounds, depending on the parish), then deliberately ill-treated the apprentice until they ran away. To put a stop to this practice, some parishes kept back part of the apprentice premium as an 'insurance policy' until the child had lived with its new master for forty days.

Before we condemn parish overseers completely out of hand, we must consider the alternatives for a pauper child who stayed in the workhouse. Their outlook was pretty grim. Conditions in many workhouses were dirty and insanitary. Children mixed with the worst dregs of society. Instead of 'habits of industry and virtue', children learnt to lie and steal. They became 'pests to society'.[10]

During the late seventeenth and eighteenth centuries, parishes tried to profit from workhouse inmates by setting up 'Houses of Industry' where the residents, including young children, were set to work. In the parish of St Giles and St George in Bloomsbury, 200 children (aged six to fourteen) wound silk or picked oakum from six in the morning until six at night, with two hours for dinner and supper.

A much-publicised House of Industry at Shrewsbury set up a woollen factory which was successful for a few years. Its paupers learnt to card, spin and weave wool into cloth. The youngest children attended a schoolroom where they learnt to read and write, and recite the catechism. When they were five years old, they learnt to spin yarn and began earning a wage. The children had evening classes after finishing work.

For meals, the children had meat four times a week, and broth or porridge for breakfast. Supper was broth again, or mashed potato washed down with half a pint of beer (the youngest children drank water). They were reportedly 'contented and happy', and played in the dinner hour after finishing their meal. A singing-master was hired to teach the children 'short moral songs'. They had several holidays per year.

The children kept one-sixth of their earnings. Girls saved up for a 'plain, decent Sunday dress' more attractive than workhouse uniform, so they could go to church in a nice dress and straw hat. The girls were given hatbands inscribed: 'THE REWARD OF DILIGENCE'.[11] The boys' savings were used to kit them out with whatever they needed when they left to become apprentices. Not all the children worked in the wool factory. Some boys learnt shoe-making, tailoring or nail-making. The older girls learnt to cook, wash and scrub so they would make useful domestic servants.

Houses of industry fell from favour when parish overseers discovered that they ran at a loss. The cost of materials (wool, hemp, etc.), teaching, and organising the paupers' work outweighed any earnings produced by selling the finished article. The public did not want to pay top prices for workhouse goods. However, many overseers kept workhouse inmates hard at work to teach them industrious habits, and generate a little income to offset the poor rates. Children spun hemp or cotton, manufactured fishing-nets, made lace, sewed sacks, and so on.

Pauper children had little schooling. Few parishes could afford proper tuition. A workhouse 'schoolmaster' was most likely another uneducated pauper. One at Gravesend was a 'very ignorant, ill-conducted man.'[12] Often, children learnt nothing useful and grew up with very bad habits. They were unemployable as domestic servants, as people did not want to take an illiterate, dirty, foul-mouthed child into their home.

In the 1820s and early 1830s, escalating parish poor rates led to loud demands for reform from rate-payers. The government grasped the nettle and instituted root and branch 'reform' of the system. The 1834 Poor Law Commission condemned the controversial 'Speenhamland system' (named after the parish where it first originated). This system was very costly: parishes 'topped up' labourers' wages from the poor rates and gave families an allowance for each child. Rural wages plummeted, because farmers knew that the parish would supplement people's income. This scheme was more widespread in southern than northern counties.

The Commissioners, weaned on Parson Malthus's dismal economics, believed that hand-outs would foster ever-increasing numbers of poor people, leading to ruinously high poor-rates. They did not enquire into the root causes of poverty.

The Poor Law Amendment Act of 1834 had a major impact on working-class children. More workhouses were built. (Workhouses or 'poorhouses' were an old idea, but formerly not every parish had one). If a man wanted relief from the parish, and was capable of work, he was refused help unless his wife and children entered the workhouse with him.

The 1834 Poor Law Commission recommended separate workhouses for the young, elderly and sick. However, this was not enforced. Penny-pinching parishes herded them all under one roof, but kept them in separate wards. Once inside its doors, the family was split up and segregated by sex. Husbands and wives only met once or twice a week. Parents did not have the right to visit their children.

The Commission also cracked down on able-bodied people receiving parish relief. To discourage people from coming to the workhouse when they needed help, the diet inside was kept lower than the worst-paid labourer could earn outside, which might be a pitifully small amount.

The commission's worst and most unjustifiable mistake was to ignore the make-up of the pauper population: the old, the sick, mentally ill, orphans and babies. Previously, unmarried mothers could ask the parish to make the father of their child to contribute to its upkeep, or make the father marry them. Now they had to enter the workhouse with their baby if they wanted help.

The Commission wanted to make pauperism a badge of shame, and it succeeded. People went to any lengths to avoid the workhouse (nicknamed the 'Bastille' or prison), even if it meant sending their youngest children to work. In rural areas, as we shall see later, parents tried to get jobs for children formerly considered too small to contribute to the family income. However, if families could not get any work, or wages were too low, or there was no breadwinner, they had no choice but to enter the workhouse. In 1840, over 22,300 children – one fifth of the workhouse population – were children aged nine to sixteen. [13] An apprenticeship was often their only chance to escape a life inside the workhouse.

However, an apprenticeship was not always a prerequisite for entering a trade. By tradition, if a worker was already established in a trade (nail-making, for example), his wife and children could work alongside him without being formally apprenticed. And if a trade needed unskilled labourers for odd jobs, such as silk-winding, they did not need formal indentures. Many chimney-sweeps took children as 'apprentices' without a premium or indentures, which was a boon for poor parents.

Children did not necessarily learn anything useful while an apprentice. Like young William Hutton, they drifted from one trade to another, never learning enough to become a skilled journeyman.

Hutton (1723–1815) was a young apprentice at Sir Thomas Lombe's silk-throwing mill at Derby. In the silk-throwing process, thread from silk-moth cocoons was wound onto bobbins, then 'thrown' or twisted into yarn. Lombe's mill at Derby was founded in 1721, long before cotton-spinning moved into factories. It was the first commercially viable water-powered silk-throwing mill in England. Hutton published an account of his time there in his *History of Derby* (1791), and in his later autobiography.

Hutton liked to spin a good yarn, and wasn't always historically accurate, but his recollections of his early years have the ring of truth about them. His 'days of play' came to an end when he was seven. His parents: 'through mere necessity, put me to labour before Nature made me able.'

William said the seven years he spent at this 'wretched place' were 'the most unhappy of my life.' He got up at five o'clock every morning; the mill started work at six. Unfortunately, Hutton was too tiny to reach the machinery, so a 'pair of high pattens' was fastened to his feet until he had grown sufficiently. (A patten was a type of overshoe on an iron ring; women wore them to stop their shoes getting muddy).

Hutton didn't find the long hours or duties troublesome, but he endured terrible beatings from the overseer: 'the marks of which I yet carry, and shall carry to the grave.'[14] As soon as Hutton's term at the silk mill ended, his parents apprenticed him to a stocking-weaver for another seven years. Their anxiety to find him any sort of apprenticeship was understandable, though, if they could not afford to keep him.

Children like young Hutton found the factory regime very difficult to cope with. And for domestic workers accustomed to working in their own homes or workshops, it was a brave and unwelcome new world.

Formerly, they were their own bosses. It was the custom in many industries (metal trades as well as textiles) for people to down tools on Saturday afternoon. Then they enjoyed two rest days, Sunday and Monday (nicknamed 'Saint' Monday, a kind of mock holy day). Workers laboured at full pelt for the rest of the week, even if it meant staying up late or all night, to ensure they earned enough money to live on. Their children, if helping, worked the same hours.

The factory system changed all that. Workers lost their independence and became operatives or 'hands', not skilled workers in their own right. The factory bell or whistle dictated when they started and finished work. Many early mills were often small, cramped and poorly ventilated.

Masters were keen to employ women and children like Hutton. Economists such as Andrew Ure noticed the tendency of the factory system to increase the number of child workers: 'It is ...the constant aim and tendency of every improvement in machinery to supersede human labour altogether, or to diminish its cost, by substituting the industry of women and children for that of men, or that of ordinary labourers for trained artisans'.[15]

In other words, women and children were cheaper to employ than men. They were more tractable and docile than men, and tolerated factory discipline better. Tending machinery in spinning-mills was not a skilled task, and was easily learnt. Children's tiny fingers were ideal for this work. In fact, early mill machinery may even have been specially designed for child workers.

The early water-powered textile factories were, by necessity, constructed by rivers in country districts. However, some pioneering mills were built in towns, too. Sir Richard Arkwright's first cotton-spinning mill at Nottingham, founded in April 1768, was powered by horses, but proved too expensive to run. When he built another cotton mill three years later at rural Cromford in Derbyshire, this mill's machinery was water-powered

The problem with building mills in remote districts was their sparse population. Few people were available to tend the machinery. Mill-owners had major recruitment issues because factory work was deeply unpopular. Masters were forced to import labour from other areas. Arkwright brought workers from Manchester and Nottingham to man his mills in the Derwent valley.

The cotton masters enticed families into their workforce by offering them low-rent, purpose-built houses with gardens close to the mill. The Evans family, cotton-spinners at Darley Abbey, offered each family of workers a cow so their children could have milk. Even if masters succeeded in recruiting workers, turnover was extremely high. Workers just did not like the factory regime. Fortunately for manufacturers, a cheap labour supply was available.

Hanway's Act of 1767 had wrought a transformation in poorhouses. The survival rate of pauper children had greatly increased, thanks to the new regime of placing infants with foster parents during their earliest years. By the mid-1780s, parishes were over-run with young children, and poor rates had reached crisis levels. What on earth could parish overseers do with all these surplus children?

Chapter 3

Unknown, Unprotected and Forgotten

The factory system made it possible to exploit pauper children on a large scale. Cotton masters advertised for child workers, and parish overseers quickly took advantage of this golden opportunity. Factory discipline was considered character-building for young people. Children from cities like London and Bristol were sent in cartloads to textile mills in more northerly counties – Lancashire, Yorkshire, Cheshire, Derbyshire and Nottinghamshire – even as far away as Glasgow. Parish apprentices also worked in textile mills in southern counties like Kent, Hertfordshire and Middlesex. Children were sent to flax-spinning mills, silk, linen, woollen, worsted, and cotton factories.

Parish apprentice labour had a lot to offer a fledgling mill-owner who had sunk a lot of capital into mill buildings and machinery, and was on a tight budget. Since the master received a premium for every child he accepted, this amounted to a tidy sum if he took a whole batch of children. Next, although he promised to feed and house the children, he didn't pay them a wage while their indentures were in force, which could be many years if apprenticed when very young. 'Free' children required wages, and had a nasty habit of shopping around for better pay once they learnt how to tend the machinery.

Mill-owners used local pauper children, if any were available, as well as importing labour from faraway parishes. The masters sent representatives to bang on the doors of nearby workhouses to see if they had any surplus families or children to dispose of.

Working conditions depended on the mill-owner's character. Some manufacturers like Sir Robert Peel admitted that despite good intentions, in practice they knew very little about the day-to-day running of their factories. They relied on their overseers to get the job done. The wages of the overseer who ran the business were profit-dependent. The more money they spent on children's housing, food and clothing, the less profit they made.

This should not have prevented these gentlemen from treating children with basic humanity. As a general rule of thumb, children working in large, well-run enterprises were more likely to receive better treatment than those in small firms with precarious finances, where every penny counted.

If you explore the picturesque Wye valley in Derbyshire today, you can see a cotton-spinning mill, Cressbrook Mill, cradled in the arms of the dale. The wind howls down the valley even on a sunny day. Wildfowl play on the stream which once powered the mill's wheel. The white building near the mill was once home to over three hundred parish apprentices. The site of another old factory, Litton Mill, which burned down in the 1870s, lies just a short walk along the dale from Cressbrook. The apprentices who worked in these mills, however, had little time to enjoy the beauties of the scenery, …

Children were nice and small, just the right size to crawl under the spinning-mule to clean up any waste cotton. These workers were called 'scavengers'. 'Piecers' fastened together any cotton threads which broke on the spinning machinery. 'Doffers' took away full bobbins of cotton and replaced them with empty ones.

It was not 'heavy' labour, but the sheer length of time children were on their feet was exhausting. There was nowhere to sit down. The atmosphere in the mills was hot (over 70°F), and humid, to make it easier to spin the cotton. No talking was allowed in some firms. If children did not work quickly enough, or spoiled the goods, or fell asleep, they faced a beating by the overlooker or spinner they worked for. (Free labour children who were late for work had their wages docked).

Girls at Cressbrook mill near Tideswell had their hair cut off if caught talking to the boy apprentices, or if they tried to run away. A former girl apprentice said, 'This head-shaving was a dreadful punishment. We were more afeard of it than any other punishment, for girls are proud of their hair'.[1]

Samuel Oldknow (1756–1828) was known as a good master. This 'spirited' muslin manufacturer owned mills in Derbyshire and Cheshire in the 1780s. His working life began as an apprentice to his uncle Thomas, who owned a draper's shop at Nottingham. After Samuel was twenty-four and had served out his time, he was made a partner in the business.

Oldknow set up his own firm making cotton and fustians at his birthplace of Anderton in Lancashire. In 1790 he established an 'extensive muslin manufactory' in Stockport. That same year he began work on a new mill at Mellor, Derbyshire for 'spinning cotton on the banks of the Goyt'.

Oldknow employed between fifty and 100 apprentices at Mellor, where he built an apprentice house. Some apprentices came from the Royal Military Asylum at Chelsea (its patron was the Duke of York). The Asylum cared for the children of soldiers: orphans or those without a mother to care for them while their father was on active service. Boys and girls were taught to read and write at the Asylum as well as being given industrial training. Many boys went into the army, but others were apprenticed into trade or industry.

Ashford (Kent) and Clerkenwell parishes also supplied Mellor with apprentices. The Clerkenwell parish overseers originally offered him forty to fifty boys and the same number of girls. They met an unexpected hitch, however, when some of the children's parents got wind of what was intended. Anxious parents came in tears to the overseers, saying they would rather take their children back than have them sent so far away. In the end, Clerkenwell sent Oldknow seventy children, a smaller batch than hoped for.

The Mellor apprentices were extremely well-fed (probably much better fare than in the workhouse). They had meat every day, and enjoyed fresh fruit from trees specially planted by Oldknow near the factory for his workers.

Parish apprentices only received their bed and board, not wages, as they were 'learning a trade'. Sometimes their master gave them a few pennies or halfpennies for working overtime. It must have been very demoralising for apprentices when they worked alongside 'free' children receiving a wage for doing exactly the same work. The children of local labourers also worked at Oldknow's Mellor mill, and girl spinners earned 2s 6d to 3s per week.

Samuel regarded his apprentices as 'part of his family…whilst habits of industry were strongly enforced, the most scrupulous care and attention was paid to their health and comforts, and to their religious and moral habits.'[2]

He employed a doctor, Peter Hibbert, to look after the children when they became ill. Hibbert said: 'it is a great pride with him (Oldknow) to see his Work-people look well and do well'.[3]

When Samuel Oldknow died in September 1828, his apprentices from the Royal Military Asylum formed a line of honour at the church, each wearing: 'a scarlet spencer, and black band around the arm'.[4]

Another well-run factory which employed apprentices was Quarry Bank Mill at Styal, Cheshire, owned by the Greg family. These children were apprenticed when they were about ten to twelve years old (occasionally as young as nine). They worked a sixty-nine-hour week, and slept in a purpose-built apprentice house. The apprentices received decent food and clothing. Samuel Greg employed local surgeon Peter Holland (1766–1855), the uncle of novelist Elizabeth Gaskell, to care for the children.[5]

Unfortunately for pauper apprentices, there were some tight-fisted, uncaring masters. Their mills ran night and day. To maximise profits, the children worked in shifts. The night shift children slept in the beds just vacated by the day shift. Cotton manufacturer John Fielden later wrote: 'It is a common tradition in Lancashire that the beds *never got cold*'.[6]

William 'Black' Douglas was a notorious master. His mill at Pendleton, Lancashire, was a regular customer of London workhouses in the 1780s and 1790s. Samuel Jones was apprenticed to Douglas's Pendleton factory when he was eight years old. The mill never stopped, so he ate all his meals while the machinery was running: 'I just got a bit when I could; we used to take it with us.' The children never got a proper rest. As they worked, their food became covered by the cotton dust or 'fly' which filled the air in the mills. Children were often given emetics because they swallowed too much cotton fibre.

Lawrence Gardner was an overlooker at a Douglas-owned mill in Lancashire. He began working in cotton-spinning at the age of nine, and was apprenticed until he was eighteen. The children worked nights from six o'clock in the evening until six o'clock the next day, even on Saturday night.

Eventually the local Sunday school teachers complained to Mr Douglas when the children kept falling asleep in class. Douglas shortened the Saturday night shift to six hours so the children finished at midnight.

Gardner said his limbs became 'crooked' after he'd worked in the factory for several years, and the same was true for many other children in the mill. When his indentures finished, he went to sea, and served in a man o' war. At the end of the Napoleonic wars Gardner was discharged from the navy. Like many other servicemen, he couldn't get a job, as peace brought a trade slump and poverty in its wake. Gardner was forced back to the cotton mills, but only because that was the trade he knew best, not from preference.[7]

Douglas was also part-owner of the Holywell Twist Co. (with the Smalley family) in the Greenfield valley, North Wales. Three to four hundred parish apprentices worked at Holywell.

Travel writer and historian Thomas Pennant gave a glowing description of life there in the 1790s. The apprentices slept in 'commodious houses'; boys and girls were segregated into separate buildings. The apprentice houses were white-washed twice a year, and 'fumigated' three times a week with tobacco smoke. The bedrooms were cleaned twice a week. Pennant was told the children enjoyed good health.

The mill employed over three hundred apprentices, and over seven years 'they have only buried seven'. The children slept three to a bed, or two to a bed when they were older and bigger. There was no 'hot-bunking' here, though, with children occupying beds still warm from the previous occupant.

Food was plentiful, and of good quality. For dinner the children enjoyed: 'beef or pork and potatoes three or four times a week, the other days herrings and potatoes, or soup and bread and cheese, as much as they please to eat.'[8] During the summer they had milk and bread for breakfast and supper. In winter, when milk was scarce, they had porridge or broth with bread and cheese. A doctor cared for the children, and they regularly attended Sunday school.

One wonders if Pennant inspected the mill in person, or got all his information from the mill-owner. Local surgeon Llewellyn Jones reported in 1819 that the children were 'undergrown, and their appearance in many cases pallid and meagre'.[9] They regularly worked a thirteen-and-a half-hour day, including meal-times.

Flintshire poet John Jones (1788–1858) had unhappy memories of his time at Holywell as a young apprentice. He wrote a vivid poem, 'Holywell', in which he remembered: '… how in early years, I toiled therein, with unavailing tears.' Jones began a seven years' apprenticeship at Holywell when he was eight years old. He never forgot the sobs of the children being beaten:

> '…orphan girls and boys!
> Whose cries – which mercy in no instance found
> Were by the din of whirling engines drowned.'[10]

Jones served in the merchant navy after his apprenticeship ended. When war broke out, like Lawrence Gardner, he joined the Royal Navy to fight against Napoleon. After Napoleon was defeated, Jones returned to Holywell as a spinner before making a new home in Cheshire.

Now, life in Nelson's navy was no bed of roses. Press-gangs were needed to help crew the ships, which were ruled with iron discipline and floggings aplenty. But the navy was a real magnet for boys. Youthful volunteers who turned up in port anxious to join the navy when press-gangs were active were closely questioned by the officers in charge, just in case they were runaway apprentices.

When pauper apprentices were bound for years at a time far from home, common sense should have dictated that regular checks on the children were needed. Some charities and parishes like Leeds diligently followed up their children after they were apprenticed, but this was not always the case.

The more diligent parish overseers were fussy about how they placed 'their' children. They chose trades where children had a reasonable prospect of long-term employment afterwards, so they were less likely to rely on the poor rates. In Derbyshire at the turn of the nineteenth century, plenty of local 'free' children worked in cotton mills, but local magistrates refused to allow any pauper children to be apprenticed there: 'We cannot consider cotton-spinning as a trade… the learning of which can secure an independent provision when the apprentice is out of its time.'[11] They preferred to apprentice the children to craftsmen like carpenters or blacksmiths.

The Foundling Hospital, however, supplied child apprentices to firms such as William Toplis's mill at Cuckney (Nottingham), founded in 1785. The Hospital inspected mill premises and working conditions prior to binding its children, and periodically assessed their welfare afterwards.

Historian Katrina Honeyman has calculated that kind treatment made good economic sense. Masters who treated their child workers humanely were likelier to make a profit in the long term. A fit and healthy child was more productive and worked more efficiently than a sickly, exhausted one.

However, when a mill-owner faced financial difficulties, it was tempting to economise by making his apprentices work harder and give them less food. Toplis's Cuckney mill took on 780 apprentices over a nineteen-year period until it switched to free labour children in April 1805. Most apprentices were parish children; over 100 came from St Margaret's, Westminster.

This cotton-spinning mill had a clean bill of health in its early days. Visitors from St Margaret's parish gave Cuckney a glowing report regarding the care of their apprentice children in 1797. But by 1802, the firm had huge money worries, and when visitors from St Margaret's returned, they were shocked to find that children were badly fed, beaten and overworked. During the years that pauper apprentices were used at Cuckney, over 110 apprentices (on average, six children per year) ran away, and sixty-five children died.[12] These statistics are a strong indication that Cuckney apprentices were unhappy with their 'home'.

If parish overseers complained about their children's treatment, then mill-owners simply offered to return them. Parishes did not want the children back on their hands again, so they left them where they were.

A few masters, like Samuel Oldknow, sent home their young workers if they believed their health was affected. The children of Derbyshire man Charles Bond worked at the Mellor factory. When they became lame, Oldknow told them 'they had had factory enough.'[13] The Bond family were given relief by the parish, because their children were now too poorly to work. Workers sacked by Mr McConnel at Manchester ascribed more ignoble motives to Oldknow; they were not much use to him once they became ill.

Observers began to doubt whether the factory system was really such a wonder of the age. There were early warning signs all was not well. In Lancashire, a group of doctors was asked by magistrates to investigate conditions in Radcliffe mills after an outbreak of 'malignant fever' which lasted for months. Local residents were convinced that the fever originated in the factories.

When the doctors visited the mills, they were horrified to find that children were overworked, and night work was common. Youngsters were crammed together in filthy premises with little ventilation, which kept the fever in circulation. The doctors wrote to local magistrates recommending factories should be regularly cleaned, better ventilation provided, and the privies scrubbed daily. They added kindly: 'It may also be advisable to bathe the children occasionally' to keep them healthy.

Most importantly, they recommended a longer meal break, and a shorter working day, particularly for children under fourteen: 'We deem this indulgence essential for the present health, and future capacity for labour...the rising generation should not be debarred from all opportunities for instruction, at the only season of life, in which they can be properly improved.'[14]

Following the doctors' report, Manchester magistrates passed a resolution in 1784 to protect children. In future, no local pauper children could be apprenticed to cotton factories where children worked more than ten hours per day, or where night work was permitted. The Manchester magistrates' action was emulated by West Riding magistrates in May 1800.

These praiseworthy efforts, however, were nullified by the actions of their counterparts down south. It was pointless for Lancashire and Yorkshire magistrates to stop mill-owners taking local parish children if justices of the peace (JPs) and parish overseers in Middlesex and Surrey sent them 'scores or even hundreds of children'.[15]

Dr John Aikin condemned the traffic in children 'of a very tender age' transplanted far away from their home parishes and parents. They served out their time 'unknown, unprotected and forgotten'.[16]

Humanitarian Thomas Gisborne (prebendary of Durham) said cotton-mills which forced children to work all night were a 'disgrace'. A visitor to Whitaker & Merryweather's mill at Burley, Yorkshire, in 1802 discovered its apprentices did not even take turns to work nights. The night-work children stayed on that shift for four or five years at a time.

Gisborne was one of the earliest writers to argue that the government should protect child factory apprentices. Local JPs had no power to enter the factories or apprentice houses where children were housed, or check on their health.

In theory, apprentices could complain to a local magistrate if ill-treated. But when children protested, their master gave them 'most cruel punishments'.[17] Gisborne suggested that parish overseers should keep accurate returns of all children apprenticed out. Factories should regularly report on children's health to their home parish, and JPs must have powers to inspect factories.

Lancashire minister Thomas Whitaker also questioned the wholesale apprenticeship of parish children into factories. He believed this practice broke up family life: 'all domestic habits, parental ties, filial affection, and the bonds of subordination, are either loosened or destroyed' and 'a spirit of infant independence' was nurtured instead.[18]

Surprisingly, it was a cotton factory-owner who pioneered efforts to protect parish apprentices in mills. Sir Robert Peel (1750–1830) was the son of Robert 'Parsley' Peel, originally a small farmer near Blackburn. The town was famous for the manufacture of 'Blackburn greys', a type of cloth made from linen and cotton. Peel senior began cotton-weaving and experimented with calico-printing by rollers, a process then in its infancy. His first design was a parsley leaf (hence his nickname). With his sons' help, Peel built up a highly successful calico-printing business. The Peels owned mills in Lancashire and Burton-on-Trent in Staffordshire.

'Parsley' Peel's eldest son Robert (the first baronet) went into business on his own account in 1773. Peel became a highly successful cotton-spinner and calico-printer. It was his mills at Radcliffe, which employed nearly a thousand children, where the putrid fever had run amok. He was a very busy man, and rarely had time to visit cotton factories. When he did, he 'was struck with the uniform appearance of bad health, and stinted [stunted] appearance of the children.'[19]

The tragedy set Peel thinking, and he probed into his own mills and those of other owners. He was shocked to discover the overlookers who supervised the children regularly overworked them, and that many mill buildings were dirty and poorly ventilated. He successfully persuaded parliament that parish factory children needed protection, and his Health and Morals of Apprentices Act became law in 1802.

The new Act banned apprentices in cotton factories from working more than twelve hours per day. Night work was phased out by June 1804. Every apprentice must have a new suit of clothes every year. Provision was made for education: children must learn the three 'R's and attend church at least once a month.

Boys and girls must be segregated in the apprentice houses, with no more than two children sleeping in a bed. Every factory (not just those using parish apprentices) must be well-ventilated, and white-washed every six months. To ensure the Act was being complied with, each mill must register with the local clerk of the peace. Magistrates were empowered to appoint two visitors (one a clergyman, one a JP) to inspect the factories. Masters found breaking the regulations could be fined.

The Health and Morals of Apprentices Act did not (and was never intended to) apply to free labour children in factories. The new law tried to mend a perceived imperfection in the Poor Laws, and was therefore highly restricted in its scope. No protection was given to pauper apprentices outside cotton-mills, such as those indentured to coal miners or masters in the metal trades.

Peel estimated that 20,000 pauper children were covered by the new law. He claimed that: 'a visible improvement in the health and general appearance of the children soon became evident'.[20] There were fewer outbreaks of disease.

Some mill-owners obeyed the Act, but others flagrantly flouted the law. Magistrate James Watkins reported on Gortons & Roberts' Bolton factory, which had fifty apprentices in 1819: 'Most filthy; no ventilation; the apprentices and other children ragged, puny, not half clothed, and seemingly not half fed; no instruction of any sort; no human beings can be more wretched'.[21]

Many of the children that Peel's Act was designed to help, like Robert Blincoe, never heard of the law until years afterwards, when it was far too late.

Orphan Robert Blincoe's story is one of the most famous of the early industrial age. A 'Memoir' of his life first appeared in 1828 in *The Lion*, a

Radical publication. It was reprinted four years later in another newspaper, the *Poor Man's Advocate*, at a time of heated debate about factory labour. In 1833, Blincoe gave evidence to a parliamentary commission about the horrors he endured in his time as a pauper apprentice.

Robert Blincoe (c.1792–1860) had no idea who his parents were. He was not even sure of his own name: 'I used to be called, when young, Robert Saint, but when I received my indentures I was called in them Robert Blincoe, and I have gone by that name ever since'. When Robert was just seven years old, he was apprenticed for fourteen years to Lowdham Mill, near Nottingham, owned by the Lambert family.

Blincoe was one of a job lot of eighty children sent from St Pancras parish to Lowdham mill. The parish overseers regaled Robert and the other children with tales of the roast beef and plum pudding, fine clothes, and money they would enjoy if they 'volunteered' to go.

When they arrived at Lowdham the children quickly discovered that porridge, black bread and potatoes were their daily fare, not plum pudding. The food was so poor they could hardly swallow it. The children worked a fourteen-hour day, except Sunday. They received a halfpenny if they worked through their dinner hour to clean the machinery. Robert was beaten if he did not work quickly enough. The children were always hungry, and sneaked out at night to steal vegetables from the farmers' fields nearby.

The Lowdham children were given better food and housing after two girl apprentices, who were sisters, smuggled a letter to their mother in London. When the mother heard that her daughters were being made ill from poor food and overwork, she travelled up to Lowdham, and quietly observed what was going on. She returned to London and complained to the St Pancras parish officials, who sent a deputation to the mill without warning the Lamberts. This was roughly around the time when Peel's Apprentices Bill was going through parliament, which may have helped spur the overseers into action. They made a stiff complaint to the Lamberts, who built a new apprentice house, and gave the children a more plentiful diet.

But the Lamberts' business fell on hard times, and the mill closed. Robert and several of his fellow apprentices were sent to their next 'home': Litton Mill in the beautiful Wye valley in Derbyshire.

Blincoe felt that conditions at Lowdham were harsh, but they paled in comparison with the regime at Litton. Factory owner Ellice Needham and his sons kept the apprentices so short of food, they stole food from the pig-trough (the pigs were fattened up to feed the master, not the apprentices).

The children worked sixteen-hour shifts. Blincoe's knees began to 'bend in' when he was fifteen as a result of the long hours. The Litton overlookers kept the apprentices at work with a horrific system of beatings and more creative tortures. Robert had scars behind his ears where 'two hand vices of a pound weight each, more or less' were 'screwed behind my ears' to punish him.

He recalled another cruel punishment in which: 'three or four of us have been hung at once on a cross-beam above the machinery, hanging by our hands, without shirts or stockings'. The children risked being badly injured unless they kept lifting up their legs out of the way as the machine moved forwards and back. 'Mind, we were apprentices, without father or mother to take care of us; I don't say that they often do that now. Then we used to stand up, in a skip, without our shirts, and be beat with straps or sticks; the skip was to stop us running away from the strap'.[22] The Needhams knew what was going on, and often joined in the cruelty.

Girls who tried to run away were fettered with irons fastened to them by a local blacksmith. One girl was freed from Litton after throwing herself into the mill dam. Luckily, someone spotted her shoes, and dragged her from the water before she drowned. She was resuscitated 'with some difficulty'. Needham was 'afraid the example might be contagious' and sent her back to her family.[23]

Blincoe survived his servitude at Litton. He held down several different mill jobs, saved hard and set up his own business as a sheet-wadding manufacturer. He settled down in Manchester, where he married and started a family, and kept a grocer's shop for a short time. All his children went to school. But Robert never lost the mental and physical scars left by his early years.

However, Blincoe's claims have long been argued over by contemporaries and historians. His 'Memoir' was published during a period of intense campaigning by reformers for factory legislation, leading some historians to dismiss his account as sensationalist propaganda.

There is some supporting evidence for Blincoe's story, though. St. George's parish in London, which supplied children to Litton, brought some apprentices back home when they discovered they were being badly treated.

We also have the testimony of 'John', another orphan. His sufferings as a parish apprentice were reported in the *Ashton Chronicle* in the summer of 1849. John was unlucky enough to serve not one, but two, apprenticeships in mills supposedly regulated by Peel's Act.

John, born in 1805, was 'very kindly treated' at Bethnal Green workhouse, where he learnt to read. When he was twelve years old, John and nine other children from Bethnal were apprenticed to Litton Mill. They worked from five in the morning until 'nine or ten at night'. The children lived on porridge and oatcakes. 'It was very seldom we missed a day without being beaten in the most wanton and cruel manner. Old Needham was as bad as any of the rest...' John tried to write to the workhouse to get help, but his letter was opened, and he was beaten until he 'could scarcely crawl'.

Blincoe and 'John' both alleged the overlookers at Litton were guilty of sexually abusing the girl apprentices. They would 'take up the petticoats of big girls, and beat them most unmercifully'.

The Litton mill failed when Ellice Needham went bankrupt. The children had to make their own way home. John and some of his fellow apprentices begged their way back to London. He went to see his grandmother and sister, who cried when they saw his 'ragged and wretched state'. But his grandmother could not afford to look after him, so back to the workhouse he went. John was found a job helping a silk weaver, Mr Dubbs, who was kind and treated him well.

If the parish overseers' first priority was John's care, he should have stayed put. Mr Dubbs offered to take John as his apprentice. He was now earning a wage of five shillings and sixpence a week, which went to the parish towards his upkeep. The parish would not allow it, however. If John stayed, he would get a new settlement at Bethnal Green, and become chargeable there again.

The parish overseers insisted that John must return to Derbyshire. At first one of the magistrates hesitated over signing the indentures: 'I thought you were to send no more children into the country in that way'.[24] The overseers persisted, however. John told them how badly he and his fellow apprentices were treated, but there was no escape. John went back to the same valley in Derbyshire, this time to Cressbrook mill near Tideswell, very close to Litton.

The first mill on the Cressbrook site was founded by Richard Arkwright circa 1779, but was destroyed in a disastrous fire a few years later. It was replaced by a new mill, managed by William Newton (1750–1830). Newton, like Samuel Oldknow, took apprentices from the Royal Military Asylum.

Newton had a good reputation amongst contemporaries. He was a poet (the 'Minstrel of the Peak') and a friend of popular poetess Anna Seward. Visitors who came to admire the beauties of the dale were offered hospitality by Newton.

The *Gentleman's Magazine* reviewed an account of Cressbrook and the 'beneficent and kind-hearted Mr Newton', whose 'orphans of humanity' were 'provided for most comfortably; and are taught to chaunt in melodious lays the hallelujahs of Handel, and to participate in the heavenly science of music'. The writer was relieved to hear that not all cotton mills were 'scenes of unnatural labour or harsh severity'.[25]

John was now one of these 'orphans of humanity': apprentice number 253. All his clothes and shoes were numbered and labelled: 'every button was stamped "Cressbrook Mills"'. The children's food was 'cleaner and better, and more of it, than at Litton': they had potato pie or hash as well as porridge. They slept close to the mill, in Apprentice Row: 'a large building three stories [sic] high, very lofty… There was no fireplace in any part of the building. We never saw a fire either summer or winter'.

The Cressbrook apprentices were not regularly tortured like the Litton children, but were savagely punished if they transgressed. Boys who went nutting in the woods were flogged with hazel sticks. Retribution was swift when John and another boy, Henry Gilbert, picked some roses from the master's garden. Mr Newton beat John: 'till he was tired. Stiff and bloody, I was ordered to button up and go to my work'.[26]

After John had been at Cressbrook for a few years, he wondered when his indentures would finish, and asked Newton about it, but a beating was the only answer he received. He wrote to the Bethnal Green overseers, who wrote back with the correct date. When his time was up, John used their letter as proof he should be set free.

John's tale of woe was corroborated by another Cressbrook apprentice, Sarah Carpenter, who told her story to the *Ashton Chronicle*. When Sarah was eight years old, her brother and 'cart-loads' of other children from the Bristol workhouse were sent to Cressbrook by the parish overseers. 'My mother did not know where he was of [sic] two years. He was taken off in the dead of night without her knowledge, and the parish officers would never tell her where he was gone to'.

Sarah's mother frantically tried desperately to discover what had happened to her son. Sarah recalled: 'I think it was Joseph Livesey who first found out where the children were, and told my mother'. Mrs Carpenter and her daughter Sarah walked all the way from Bristol to see him: 'We were many days in the road… we were sadly tired'.

The mill owner's wife, Mrs Newton, convinced Mrs Carpenter that her son was in good hands. Sarah was so pleased to see her brother, she insisted on staying, but the only way they would let her stay was as an apprentice. She was offered a shilling 'binding money', which she thought was a huge sum. Her brother tried to warn Sarah she would be 'very ill off', but she would not listen. Sarah was apprenticed until she was twenty-one. Her mother went home without her. It must have been a long, lonely walk.

Once her mother had gone, Sarah found her brother's warnings were all too true. She was at the mercy of brutal overseers who beat and abused the children. When Sarah was hit by the overlooker, she threatened to write to her mother and complain. Mr Newton 'started beating me over the head with a stick till it was full of lumps and bled. He said, "Damn thee, thou may let thy mother know now, if thou can"'. Sarah never got over this beating: 'My head was so bad that I could not bide down nor sleep for a long time, and I have never been a sound sleeper since'.

The apprentices were terrified of the 'master carder', nicknamed 'Tom-the-Devil'. Thomas Birks: 'was a very bad man – and was encouraged by the master in ill-treating all the hands, and particularly the children. I have often seen him pull up the clothes of big girls seventeen or eighteen years of age, and throw them across his knee, and then flog them with his hand in the sight of both men and boys…We wished he might die'.

The children were allowed two annual outings. They were given fourpence each to spend at the wakes (a traditional holiday in the northern counties), and fourpence for the fair. 'If we had done the slightest thing amiss we must not have it, and must not go to the fair or the wakes'.

Sarah escaped from Cressbrook when her brother, who had served out his time, crept back and 'stole me away. But I was so feared and dateless with the punishment I had received, that for a long time I was like a person who had no wits'.[27] ('Dateless' – she literally did not know what day it was).

As more reports surfaced of ill-treatment in the mills, a select committee was set up in 1815 to discover what happened to parish apprentices sent far from home. The committee tried to trace apprentices from parishes inside the London bills of mortality, which included part of Middlesex and Surrey. (They confined their research to London pauper children because it was impossible to track down every single parish apprentice in England).

During 1802 and 1811, a total of 5,815 London parish children were indentured: 3,446 boys and 2,369 girls. Over 3,700 of these children were bound locally: as domestic servants, or to tradesmen, fishermen, watermen and the navy, but mostly to trades and professions.

Another 2,026 children were apprenticed outside their home parishes, and it was these children who aroused most concern. They were sent away in batches of between five to fifty children at a time. Three-quarters of the children were apprenticed into the cotton, silk and worsted industries. The committee wrote to the children's masters to check on the apprentices' whereabouts. If they did not get a reply, they wrote to the local parish overseer, who was responsible for looking after pauper apprentices if their master's firm failed.

Their findings make disquieting reading. Only 644 children (thirty-one per cent) were still serving under their original indentures. Another 108 had served out their time and stayed with their master. Eighty children had died; 166 had run away. The committee were most worried by the 433 children who were not 'satisfactorily or intelligibly accounted for' either by their masters or by parish overseers.

Was it really necessary to send these children so far away from home? A few parishes in the survey, such as Shadwell, Newington and Islington, had never felt the need.

The committee did not want to take away parishes' right to dispose of 'their poor children' but condemned the 'highly objectionable' practice of sending them hundreds of miles away. Some children were only six or seven years old, and could not be 'set free' for fourteen or fifteen years, when they reached twenty-one. These children had little chance of seeing their parents, and could not be supervised by their home parish.

With a 'trifling' effort by overseers, masters could be found for pauper children: 'without the violation of humanity, in separating children forcibly, and conveying them to a distance from their parents, whether those parents be deserving or undeserving'.[28]

These pauper apprentices' childhoods were effectively 'stolen'. They were forcibly taken away from the only home they had ever known, and transported in carts like criminals. They had little hope of redress.

Another select committee in 1816, headed by Sir Robert Peel, investigated working conditions for all factory children: parish apprentices and free labour. It soon discovered that the 1802 Act was a 'dead letter'. Local magistrates were not properly supervising apprentice children as required by the Act.

One of the witnesses was William David Evans, a Manchester magistrate and barrister. Evans received a salary of a thousand pounds a year for his duties as a magistrate.

However, Evans told astonished committee members that although he knew of the 1802 Act's existence, 'he had never read' it until the day he was asked to speak to them, when he hastily thumbed through the legislation. Cotton was Manchester's most important industry, and Evans was responsible for enforcing the Act's provisions, but formerly he 'had not had the curiosity' to look into the Act. Evans said the Act was 'not in operation' in Lancashire or Cheshire. He 'had never heard of such a thing' as appointing visitors to inspect mills.[29]

The select committee evidence on factories for this decade follows a common theme. Factory owners and their managers swore that their child workers did not come to any harm. Some mill-owners like Sir Robert Peel and Robert Owen, who we shall meet presently, begged to differ. The medical fraternity was divided on whether factory work was inherently unhealthy.

However, reformers who visited the mills, like magistrate Theodore Price at Warwick, drew attention to the miserable life led by child workers. Price visited a spinning-mill at Emscote. He was very distressed to learn that children worked for up to thirteen hours with just an hour for lunch, and no time for recreation. Price thought it 'extraordinary' that children had to eat their breakfast while working. He refused to sign any apprenticeship indentures for cotton mills, and said that if forced to choose between sending his four daughters to a mill, or the local Bridewell (house of correction), he would rather send them to Bridewell.

Peel's 1816 committee highlighted the dreadful conditions at one of the darkest of the 'dark satanic mills': Backbarrow.

John Birch, owner of Backbarrow mill at Cartmel, Lancashire, employed over 150 parish apprentices. Most children arrived in groups from St Clement Danes, St James's, and Whitechapel; some came from Liverpool workhouse.

When Birch's business failed, no-one at the mill cared what happened to the apprentices. The children were dumped on the highway and left to fend for themselves instead of being returned to their home parish. William Travers, overlooker at the mill, admitted: 'to be sure, they would not be well off; they would have to beg their way, or something of that sort.'[30] Some apprentices made their way to Lancaster workhouse, but were later sent back to Backbarrow.

The mill was then acquired by Ainsworth, Catterall & Co. They hired John Moss as 'master of the apprentices' at Backbarrow from February 1814 to March 1815.

Moss gave evidence to Peel's committee. Backbarrow's apprentices regularly worked a fifteen-hour day: from five o'clock in the morning until eight at night, with just half an hour for breakfast and thirty minutes for dinner. If the mill stopped for repair, or there was insufficient water for the mill-wheel, the children worked overtime to make up the loss, sometimes until ten o'clock at night, for weeks at a time. On Sundays, some apprentices cleaned the machinery from six in the morning until mid-day.

John Moss checked the children's beds in the apprentice house each night in case they had run away. Sometimes he found them still in the mill, fast asleep on the floor from exhaustion. Their housing was extremely poor. These children did not even have sheets to sleep on, just a blanket underneath, a thin blanket on top, and a 'horse-cover'.[31] After Moss and a parish officer from Liverpool workhouse (who visited the mill) complained about the children's bedding, they were given sheets and better coverings. Moss, disgusted with conditions at Backbarrow, left for a less well-paid job as manager of Preston workhouse.

Local worthies wrote to the committee in support of Ainsworth, Catterall & Co. They disputed Moss's allegations regarding the children's poor care. Surgeon John Redhead felt the children were very well treated; the number of deaths was 'very few.'

The minister for nearby Finsthwaite, Henry Seatle, said the children attended church whenever the weather permitted, and were very clean and orderly. There was nothing to worry about: 'I beg leave to state that out of 150 children, the number employed, there have only been six deaths in the seven last years:

and three of these came to the place in a sickly state, and one was drowned by accident'.[32]

The system of inspection under Peel's Act had clearly failed. Even if a magistrate or parish overseer visited a mill to inspect it, the children were often too frightened of their master to complain of ill-treatment.

Some visitors from London went to Litton Mill to check on the apprentices, but Ellice Needham was warned in advance they were coming. John and his fellow apprentices were washed and made presentable, and ordered to tell the visitors that 'we were very well treated. Needham and his sons were in the room the whole time'. John and the other children did as they were told: 'because we knew what we would catch if we told them the truth'.[33]

Assuming for a moment that an apprentice was brave enough to speak to a JP, it was very difficult to persuade him to break the indentures. In Lancashire, local magistrates were often mill-owners themselves, or friends of factory owners.

Public anger at the horrors of life at Backbarrow and other mills led to the first steps towards protective legislation. An 1816 Act of Parliament banned London pauper children from being apprenticed more than forty miles away from their home parish. This was a move in the right direction.

However, it was a case of shutting the stable door after the horse had already bolted. The use of pauper apprentices in mills was already less popular with masters, although some employed them as late as the 1860s.

Free labour children were increasingly preferred. The advent of steam-power meant that mills no longer had to be sited by fast-flowing streams. Factories were now built anywhere with good transport links (so it was easy for the mill to be supplied with coal). Parish apprentice labour was no longer necessary when mills were constructed in more densely populated areas.

Socialist pioneer Robert Owen (1771–1858) vowed to end the use of parish apprentices when he began running the New Lanark mills, near the Falls of the Clyde. Owen knew the cotton industry inside and out. He was convinced that factory workers would be healthier and produce better quality work if they worked shorter hours.

Robert, born in Newtown, Montgomeryshire, was a precocious child and an avid reader. When he was ten years old, he was apprenticed for three years to a linen draper at Stamford. (This was a really good way of learning the trade and the immense variety of different fabrics sold. Robert worked without wages for his first year except for his board, lodging and washing. He received eight pounds salary for the next year, and ten pounds for his final year).

When he was eighteen, Robert went to Manchester, and joined a cotton firm using the revolutionary 'new and curious' mule-spinning machinery. The young man saved hard, and was amazingly successful. Before long he became manager of Mr Drinkwater's spinning mill. Owen greatly improved the quality of the yarn and was made a partner in the firm before he was twenty. As he worked, Robert was struck by the great care taken of the machines, but the 'neglect and disregard of the living machinery': the factory hands.

Owen pondered ways to improve workers' lives. He did not get the opportunity to put his ideas more fully into practice until he became a partner in New Lanark Mills, owned by Mr Dale. Dale wanted to retire, and sold his mills to Owen and his Manchester partners. Owen married Mr Dale's daughter soon afterwards.

When Owen became manager of New Lanark, he put a great social experiment in place. He used 'justice and kindness', not punishments, to govern his workers.

When Owen arrived there were: 'between 400 and 500 pauper children, procured from parishes, whose ages appeared to be from five to ten – but said to be from seven to twelve'.[34] Many had come from Edinburgh poorhouses. Formerly, Mr Dale had been unhappy about employing infants only five and six years old. He tried to get older children, but soon found: 'if he did not take them at those ages, he could not obtain them at all'.[35]

Owen said: 'These children were, by Mr Dale's directions well-lodged, fed and clothed'. After the children finished work, a kindly schoolteacher gave them reading and writing lessons, but they were exhausted, and it 'only tormented them, without doing any real good'. Owen found: 'none of them understood anything they attempted to read, and many of them fell asleep'.[36]

Mr Dale knew nothing about the day-to-day running of his mills. He left all that to his managers. The children worked a thirteen-hour day, including mealtimes. Their 'limbs were generally deformed' and their growth 'stunted'. Owen was convinced this was owing to the early ages at which they began work, and long hours, because in every other respect: 'they were as well taken care of, and as well looked after, as any children could be'.[37]

Owen phased out the use of parish apprentices at New Lanark. He built new, sanitary housing in the village in the hope of attracting families to take the apprentices' places.

Some mills functioned perfectly well without parish apprentices. There were none at James Finlay & Co' s cotton mill at Catrine, Ayrshire in 1816, even though over 300 children were employed there, including fifty-nine children under ten years old. The mill children went to school (paid for by the factory owners) in the village for an hour after work every day, and there was a Sunday school.

The Cromford mills run by Richard Arkwright's son (another Richard) in 1816 did not have any apprentices. And at W.G. and J. Strutt's mills at Belper and Milford, the only apprentices were mechanics. Unlike apprentice Samuel Slater thirty years earlier, these young people lived with their parents, and received a weekly wage. The Strutts employed 1,494 people, including over 700 children (just 100 were younger than ten). On average, the children earned 2s 6d per week.[38]

As the expense of feeding and housing parish apprentices escalated, they became less economic to employ than free labour children. At Quarry Bank Mill, the cost of maintaining the parish apprentice workforce doubled between the 1820s and 1840s.

Another reason why fresh 'batches' of parish apprentices were no longer required was that the previous generation of children had grown up and were now earning a living. In spite of all their hardships, for some apprentices, the mill and area where they grew up gradually became thought of as 'home.'

At William Douglas's infamous Pendleton cotton-mill at Douglas Green (Lancashire) in 1819, ninety-one former apprentices stayed in the district after serving out their time. Sixty-three former apprentices still worked in the mill; twenty-nine of these had married. Another eighteen former apprentices also lived nearby, but no longer worked in the mill because they were now wives and mothers.[39] The apprentices' own children found jobs in the factories. A new generation of mill-workers had been created.

Chapter 4
Battle Begins

'Father, I'm up, but weary,
I scarce can reach the door,
And long the way, and dreary,
Oh, carry me once more!
To help us we've no mother,
And you have no employ,
They killed my little brother –
Like him I'll work and die!'
(*The Factory Girl's Last Day*, 1832).

Should the state regulate working conditions for free labour children? Peel's 1802 Act was passed with relatively little opposition because parish apprentices were seen as a 'special case.'

The state was, in effect, the 'parent' of workhouse children, so politicians felt it was acceptable to interfere between an employer and his workers in order to correct notorious abuses in the Poor Law system. The 1802 Act was not viewed as a 'Factory Act' as such.

But 'free labour' children outnumbered parish apprentices in some mills. At Bolton in 1819, Samuel and Thomas Ashton's Tottington mill only employed thirty-seven parish apprentices; the rest of its 250 workers were locals.

Manchester factory children were mostly free labour (although some were apprentices from distant parishes). Local pauper children were only rarely apprenticed into Manchester mills. Those joining the cotton industry were more likely to be bound to a handloom weaver in his own home or workshop.

But was the factory system a force for good or evil? And was it right that children – whether conscript apprentice labour or 'free' – spent days and nights 'chained' to the machinery? On the other hand, if children's labour was curtailed, would this threaten the nation's prosperity? Men who questioned the factory system soon found themselves in a vicious political battle with captains of industry.

As we saw earlier, economists argued that interference in the free labour market, no matter how well-meant, would cause havoc. Besides, mill-owners knew what was best for their workers. Factory owners were considered as almost saintly figures by some contemporaries. Mill-owners provided a public service by creating jobs.

Sir John Sinclair, writing in 1795, felt that cotton factories were a positive boon for impoverished families: 'In most other manufactures, a woman who has a family, and becomes a widow, is in a most helpless situation'. But if a cotton mill was situated nearby, she could look forward to a better lifestyle: 'The greater the number of children the woman has, she lives so much the more comfortably, and upon such account alone, she is often a tempting subject for a second husband. Indeed, at cotton mills, it often happens that young people support their aged parents by their industry.'[1]

The Strutt family of Derbyshire believed their mills had benefits for local families as well as providing them with work: 'Before the establishment of these works, the inhabitants were notorious for vice and immorality, and many of the children were maintained by begging; now their industry, decorous behaviour, attendance on public worship, and general good conduct, compared with the neighbouring villages, where no manufactures are established, is very conspicuous.'[2]

Critics of factories believed that employing married women adversely impacted their families. Working mums who spent long hours in the mill saw very little of their children.

Doctor Peter Gaskell (no relation to novelist Mrs Gaskell) did not think that factory work was inherently harmful, but worried about its effect on family life: 'The great curse of the Factory System…is in the breaking up of all home and social affections: the father, the mother, and the child, are alike occupied, and never meet… except during the evenings'.

Babies and young children were left in the care of grandmothers, aunts or older sisters, or put out to paid childminders. Family ties were shattered, and children learnt nothing from their parents: 'the boy knows no parental control, the girl no domestic virtues nor domestic economy: the father is but an independent member of his family, and has no command over the time and earnings of his child; the mother abandons her offspring to hireling hands'.[3]

Robert Owen argued that the government should intervene on behalf of all factory children. When Owen took over New Lanark's management in 1797, he did not have enough money for all the reforms he wanted at first. He was only a partner in the firm, and trod carefully. All the improvements he made were paid for from the mill's profits.

Traveller Louis Simond visited New Lanark Mills in 1810. He was greatly impressed by this 'prodigious establishment' with its '2,500 workmen, mostly children, who work from six o'clock in the morning till seven o'clock in the evening, having in that interval an hour and a quarter allowed for their meals; at night, from eight to ten for school. These children are taken into employment at eight years old, receiving five shillings a week; when older, they get as much as half a guinea.'

Some children lived close to the factory, but others walked about a mile to work. Simond was unhappy, though, about the children's long day: 'Eleven hours of confinement, with the schooling, thirteen hours, is undoubtedly too much for children.' He felt the government should: 'interfere between the encroachments of avarice and the claims of nature.' On the other hand, he admitted: 'the little creatures we saw did not look ill.'[4]

By 1816, Owen had reduced the children's hours from thirteen to twelve, including an hour and a quarter for meals. Children under ten were not allowed to work at the mill. He introduced dancing and music lessons for the workforce. Owen believed his child workers were healthier than in other mills like those at Carlisle.

Not all Owen's workers appreciated his paternalism. One woman left Lanark and applied for a job at Monteigh, Bogle & Co.'s mills on the Clyde at Blantyre near Glasgow, in the hope of 'bettering her situation.' She didn't like the new regime at Lanark: 'they had got a number of dancing masters, a fiddler, a band of music… there were drills and exercises… they were dancing together till they were more fatigued than when they were working.'[5]

The workers at the Monteith factories (two cotton-spinning, one weaving) worked a fourteen-hour day, much longer than at Lanark. Not many children under ten worked there; just twenty-two of the 750 hands. Two children were under nine years of age; their parents were training them as piecers.

When Owen saw how much the health of his operatives had improved, he wanted other manufacturers to follow suit. He suggested to Sir Robert Peel (first baronet) that factory children's hours should be reduced to ten per day.

Peel welcomed Owen's intervention. He knew that apprentice labour in factories was decreasing, and it was now the 'free' labour children 'for whose good treatment' there was not 'the slightest security'.[6]

In June 1815, Peel introduced a new bill to protect all children (apprentices and free labour) in cotton factories. He wanted to ban the employment of children under ten, and limit older children's hours to a ten-hour day (twelve-and-a-half with mealtimes). The bill did not rouse much interest at first. But when the penny dropped for mill-owners that working practices would have to change, they mobilised. The proposal was attacked by MPs, especially factory owners, and the House of Commons threw it out.

Peel was alarmed by the sudden opposition of his fellow mill-owners. Doom-mongers prophesied that Britain's profits would suffer. Peel vacillated, and a golden opportunity was lost. At this period, opposition to reform was still fairly low-level and disorganised. If Peel had used his authority and experience as a manufacturer to really push the case for reform, opposition might have been nipped in the bud. A ten-hour day for child workers could have been achieved early in the century. Instead, Peel contented himself with calling for another select committee to gather evidence on factory children's conditions.

The 1816 committee he presided over unearthed the story of the Backbarrow apprentices and gathered testimony from mill-owners like George Augustus Lee. Lee was part-owner of Philips & Lee's large spinning-mill at Manchester. He warned that curbing children's factory work would create: 'a superfluous population of children, without future means of employment and subsistence'. Legislation would cause 'incalculable' danger to profits, and Britain's competitiveness against foreign firms.[7]

Lee and other manufacturers vowed to resist any regulation. Workers were free agents, and should fix their own contracts with masters.

Peel tried again in 1818 after Lancashire cotton-spinners petitioned parliament to shorten the factory day to ten-and-a-half hours. He knew from past experience there was no hope parliament would agree to a ten-hour day. So Peel proposed a compromise of eleven hours (plus an hour and a half for mealtimes). This meant children would be in the factory for twelve and a half hours.

He reminded the House of Commons it was 'notorious that children of very tender years were dragged from their beds some hours before daylight, and confined in the factories not less than fifteen hours.'[8]

Peel was supported by his son Robert, the future prime minister. Slavery abolitionist William Wilberforce (1759–1833) and poet Samuel Taylor Coleridge also gave their backing. Coleridge scorned suggestions that child factory workers were 'free' agents who could pick and choose what work they performed. 'In what sense…can the labour of children, extorted from the want of their parents… be called free?'[9]

Mill-owners against reform mustered their defences and published a propaganda pamphlet: Peel's 1818 bill would lead to lower wages by shortening factory hours. Families would suffer: 'as the father is deprived of the profits of his children's industry, the gains of the whole family must be diminished'.[10] This pamphlet noted that flax and woollen factories had higher mortality rates than cotton-mills, but Peel did not include them in his 1818 bill.

Lord Stanley (1775–1851), MP for Lancashire, was a firm friend of the manufacturers. He lobbied against Peel's bill. He argued that cotton factory work was no worse than other trades. Workers endured far worse conditions in the glass-cutting trades, and in coal mines and lead mines, but no-one dreamed of passing laws to protect those people. Why was the cotton industry singled out for criticism? Opponents of factory reform returned again and again to this point.

After much grumbling by MPs, the bill passed the House of Commons but came adrift in the Lords, thanks to strong opposition from James Maitland, eighth earl of Lauderdale.

Lord Lauderdale (1759–1839) is one of the bogeymen of our story. This staunch upholder of *laissez-faire* stonewalled every effort for reform. He insisted interfering with the free labour market was 'contrary to every sound principle of political economy'.[11] He demanded another investigation into factory labour. Peel's bill was still-born.

Lauderdale's delaying tactics succeeded; an 1818 select committee gained mill-owners a breathing space. Some medical evidence published by this committee was rightly ridiculed in the press. One Manchester doctor refused to 'assign any limit' to the number of hours a child could work without suffering health-wise. A Yorkshire surgeon, asked if children should enjoy some playtime in daylight hours, said: 'I do not see it is necessary'. It is hard to avoid the conclusion that the doctors concerned were well paid for their testimony.

Lord Liverpool made a famous criticism of the 1818 report. He said: 'It was part of the common law of the land that children should not be over-worked, and that if all the medical staff of Manchester were brought…to prove that children worked more than fifteen hours a day without being injured, he would not believe them'.[12]

Robert Owen was dismayed by Peel's lack of progress, and his seeming deference to other mill-owners. Owen tried to get elected as an MP so he could 'make a difference' in parliament, but failed. He tried exploring other avenues for reform, such as writing to newspapers and giving talks, but with limited effect.

Fortunately, men like Manchester merchant Nathaniel Gould were prepared to spend thousands of pounds of their own money fighting to help factory children. They were undaunted as mill-owners dug in for a long battle and began a smear campaign to discredit reformers. The issue of a 'Ten Hours' day later grew from these small beginnings into a major movement.

Another select committee in 1819 found more evidence of ill-health in factories. John Boutflower, a Salford doctor, visited Sunday schools so he could compare factory children with those working in other trades. There was a 'striking' difference between factory children and others. The former were: 'very sickly… very much emaciated and reduced in their persons'.[13]

The Factory Act of 1819 was passed after lively debate in parliament. Children under the age of nine were banned from working in cotton factories. Youngsters below the age of sixteen were limited to a twelve-hour day. Mill-owners must allow half an hour for breakfast, plus an hour for dinner.

A backwards step was taken a few months later when the government amended the 1819 Act in favour of mill-owners. A new clause said that if a mill lost time because there hadn't been enough water to power the mill's machinery, the master could make up time by keeping the workers overnight. The dinner break could now be taken at any point between eleven in the morning and four in the afternoon. This meant children worked a very long time without a break in mills which did not stop for breakfast.

The factory system had also taken root in other industries like silk, flax, wool and worsteds.

Silk was a child-hungry industry. Manufacturers said that young children's fingers were suppler than adults and could handle the delicate yarn. Parental pressure played a large role, too. At Bruton in Somerset, John Ward's silk mills employed children as young as six years old 'to oblige their parents'.[14] These children worked an eight-hour day in the summer; older children (aged nine or ten) worked an eleven-and-a-half hour day. Manufacturers also 'put out' silk-winding to local people who worked at home. Mothers employed their children as helpers.

In the silk town of Congleton, in Cheshire, the 'greater part' of the town's 2000 mill hands were 'children from five years old upwards' in 1816. They worked a twelve-hour day. At James Pattison's mill, the 181 child workers outnumbered the 114 adults. This firm had taken three batches of pauper apprentices from St Andrew's workhouse at Holborn between 1800 and 1805, but by 1816 they had all served out their time.

Here, too, parents pushed to get their children into the mill when they were only six years old. Pattison said it kept them 'out of mischief' and had the added bonus of keeping down the poor rates.[15] At nearby Macclesfield, a seventy-six hour week was the norm in silk mills: four hours longer than Congleton and Derby.[16] Nottingham children did not enter the silk mills until they were eight years old.

Flax was another long-established industry undergoing mechanization, although processing methods remained primitive in remote areas of Ireland as late as the 1870s. Linen cloth was woven from flax and cotton, and before cotton rose to pre-eminence, linen was a thriving Lancashire industry. The first flax-spinning factory, Low Mill, was built by Darlington men John Kendrew and Thomas Porthouse on the river Skerne in 1787.

During the nineteenth century, towns like Leeds, Dundee and Aberdeen became renowned for their huge flax-spinning mills. The Marshalls were a famous Leeds manufacturing family. Children in Leeds mills worked from 6 a.m. until seven at night in 1819. Halifax children worked to 'nine or ten at night… several work all night' when trade was busy.[17]

Woollen and worsted mills were also notorious for their long hours. Woollen fabrics (broadcloths and kerseymeres) were made from wool spun from short fibres. However, in worsted and 'stuffs' manufacture, wool was combed into long fibres before spinning. Worsted yarn was woven into blankets, flannels, and merinos.

Yorkshire was blessed with lots of fast-flowing streams for power and good access to coalfields. The first woollen factory was founded at Leeds in 1793 on the banks of the River Aire. The quantity of woollen cloth produced in the West Riding more than doubled between 1788 and 1805.

Machinery successfully replaced the processes of spinning and 'scribbling' wool (untangling the fibres before they were 'carded' ready for spinning), formerly done by hand. Young children at Leeds in 1800 earned three shillings a week for tending the machines; older children earned five to six shillings. They 'were thus already a source of profit to their parents, as well as able to earn a good living for themselves.'[18] Two decades later, two-thirds of the Leeds workforce in mills was under the age of eighteen; they worked a thirteen-hour day.

The worsted industry was formerly very prosperous in the south-eastern counties of England. Norwich was famed for its beautifully dyed fabrics. The first worsted factory, however, was a Lancashire innovation, built by Thomas Edmondson at Dolphinholme, near Lancaster, in 1784.

Yorkshire clothiers then successfully turned their attention to the worsted trade. The first steam-powered worsted mill was founded by Ramsbotham, Swain & Murgatroyd at Bradford in 1790. The introduction of steam led to a rapid expansion of the Yorkshire worsted industry, and Norwich manufacturers could not compete.

Some Yorkshire woollen and worsted mills ran for twenty-four hours a day, and working conditions for child workers there led to accusations of 'slavery' in the popular press.

Cotton manufacturers had not allowed the 1819 Factory Act to cramp their style. A Lancashire cotton spinner wrote to the *Mechanics Magazine* in May 1825. Spinners and their piecers regularly worked a fourteen- or fifteen-hour day, and children began working in mills before they were six years old: 'their parents not being able to keep them at home longer, on account of wages being so low, assert that the child is above nine years of age, in order to get them employed'. The writer had had great hopes of the 1819 Act, but it was flouted 'with impunity'.[19]

When it became clear the 1819 Act was ineffective, efforts were made in parliament to amend it. John Cam Hobhouse (1786–1869), travel writer and friend of the poet Lord Byron, was a Radical politician. He introduced a bill in 1825 which proposed tightening up the 1819 Act and limiting the cotton factory working week to sixty-six hours. The shorter hours clause came to grief in the House of Lords, which changed it to a sixty-nine-hour week. The 1825 Act gave children a thirteen-and-a-half hour day. On Saturdays, their hours were reduced from twelve to nine.

Around this time, some operatives in textile towns like Manchester, Stockport, Bolton and Blackburn, formed 'Short Time Committees' dedicated to achieving a ten-hour day. They wanted adults' hours reduced in factories, but pragmatism was needed. Any such proposal put before parliament would be seen as a fabulous beast. It was difficult enough to interest legislators in children's hours.

The committee hoped that if children's hours were reduced, their own hours would follow suit, hence freeing up more jobs for men. Few workers were willing to join them, however. They were terrified of losing their jobs. If a worker lost his job, he would not get another without a 'character' from his master, who was unlikely to write one for a troublemaker. And factory hands and parents were not all in favour of shorter hours; they were worried they would have less money to live on.

Yorkshireman Richard Oastler (1789–1861) first became interested in the factory question in 1830, while staying with friend John Wood, a Bradford mill-owner.

Oastler was a Tory and slave trade abolitionist. Wood asked why Oastler, who campaigned so fiercely against the slave trade, did nothing about the 'cruelties' in mills on his own doorstep.

In Wood's own mill, children worked for thirteen hours with forty minutes for lunch. In neighbouring mills, children worked up to eighteen hours a day. They were flogged by the overlookers, cheated out of their wages by a system of fines, and 'daily sacrificed for gold'.[20]

Oastler was incredulous at first. He had lived for years in the Yorkshire textile districts. He had noticed many poorly and lame factory children in the course of his charitable work. But it never occurred to him to link children's poor health with the mills. Richard assumed that poverty and miserable living conditions were to blame. When he saw the great factories ablaze with lights all night, he viewed them as signs of prosperity.

Wood made Oastler vow to do whatever he could to stop the cruelty. Wood in his turn supplied tens of thousands of pounds for the Ten Hours movement, and made improvements in his own mills.

Once Oastler's eyes were opened, he rolled up his sleeves, seized the torch of Owen's 'ten hours' idea, and lit the flame of a massive popular movement.

The very next day, he wrote to the influential *Leeds Mercury*. His letter on 'Yorkshire Slavery' was published on 16 October 1830. Oastler began by praising the efforts of slave trade abolitionists in his home county. Then he spoke out: 'Thousands of our fellow creatures…the miserable inhabitants of a *Yorkshire town*, are at this very moment existing in a state of slavery *more horrid* than are the victims of that hellish system – "colonial slavery"'.

The streets awash with anti-slavery leaflets were 'every morning wet with the tears of innocent victims at the accursed shrine of avarice, who are compelled (not by the cart-whip of the negro [sic] slave-driver) but by the dread of the equally appalling thong or strap of the overlooker, to hasten, half-dressed, *but not half-fed*, to those magazines of British infantile slavery – *the worsted mills in the town and neighbourhood of Bradford*!…Why should not the children in them be protected by legislative enactments, as well as those who work in cotton mills?'

Oastler's bombshell caused uproar. There was a huge debate in the press. His lurid and emotive literary style was criticised, but no-one could dispute the basic facts he dragged out into the open. The public was outraged on the children's behalf.

The consciences of the more humane Yorkshire manufacturers were pricked. Over twenty Bradford mill-owners held a meeting to discuss Oastler's charges. They deprecated children's long hours, and discussed what practical steps they could take to change 'the custom of the trade' which they followed as a matter of 'self-preservation'. If one firm cut its hours, the others could take away its business by supplying their customers with cheaper goods. Legislation was the only way to ensure a fair deal for all.

Oastler's campaign fell on fertile ground throughout the textile districts. The kindlier cotton masters also favoured reform, but were caught in the same trap as the woollen manufacturers. Everyone must cut their hours at the same time. It was not just a matter of profits. If a mill-owner went bust, all the men, women and children who depended on the factory for a living suffered as well.

Mill-owners of the white and red rose counties joined forces and petitioned parliament to bring all textile factories under regulation, to ensure that unscrupulous manufacturers could not undercut them.

Accordingly, John Cam Hobhouse and Lord Morpeth brought in a more radical bill in 1831. They proposed an eleven-and-a-half hour working day, and banning children under nine from all textile factories, including silk.

What could possibly go wrong? Many mill-owners and operatives strongly supported the measure. But the mill-owners were not as united as they appeared. A large body of masters comprising Halifax worsted mill-owners, Scottish flax-spinners, and West Country woollen manufacturers lobbied against it.

The amended 1831 Act which came into force restricted all youngsters under eighteen to a twelve-hour day plus mealtimes. Night work was banned for all workers under twenty-one. The Act made it easier to convict mill-owners who evaded the law. But the most important part of Hobhouse's bill was lost: the Act only applied to cotton mills. Other textile mills were left unregulated.

The short time committees were bitterly disappointed by the bill's failure. The battle for reform did not fizzle out, however. It grew white-hot.

On 29 October 1831, the *Leeds Intelligencer* published another letter by Oastler, addressed to the working classes of the West Riding. He rallied them on the need for a Ten Hours bill. 'Can it be believed that in England, in the nineteenth century, in a "reforming" House of Commons, a bill limiting the hours of labour for children of nine years of age in ALL factories to twelve per day, should have been refused, because it was "too liberal"?'

But there was a limit to what Oastler could achieve, because he was not an MP. To have any hope of changing the law, he needed someone 'on the inside' of the houses of parliament. Hobhouse was not prepared to go any further. He felt that a ten-hour day was unachievable, and was also worried about the possible impact on industry's competitiveness.

Michael Thomas Sadler (1780–1835) was just the man for the job. Born in Snelston, Derbyshire, Sadler was a Tory evangelical keenly interested in helping the poor. He believed that Ireland should have a Poor Law so its destitute people could be cared for. Malthusian doctrines cut no ice with Sadler, who wrote an eloquent if unscientific polemic against the parson's theories. Sadler was Oastler's friend, and once he grasped the issues involved, he took the factory children's cause to heart.

Sadler and Oastler (the 'Factory King') made a great double act. These passionate challengers of the system punched above their weight, harrying the government, writing letters to the papers, tirelessly giving speeches to rallies, and so on. Oastler reduced audiences to tears with his stories from the factory floor: One little girl, frightened she would not wake up at four o'clock in the morning ready for work, repeatedly woke in the night crying, 'Father, is it time? Father, is it time?' She was often too tired to come home from the mill after work, and hid in the bags of wool to sleep. Oastler said the child 'dragged on that dreadful existence' for several years before she died.[21]

The issues involved cut across party lines. Tories favourable to reform like Oastler and Sadler were joined by Radicals like William Cobbett and 'Honest' John Fielden.

Fielden (1784–1849) was a highly principled and caring manufacturer. When he was a small boy, Fielden worked in his father Joshua's mill. He knew the cotton business inside and out. John and his brothers ran a hugely successful cotton manufacturing business at Waterside, Todmorden. Fielden Bros. prided themselves on good relations with their workforce, using a mixture of sound business sense and paternalism. John, who was brought up as a Quaker, became interested in Unitarianism, and set up Sunday schools in the Todmorden area in the early 1800s. The Fieldens also built a school for their factory children in 1827.

Their mills consistently worked shorter hours than other firms, and strikes were allegedly unheard of on their premises. The Fielden brothers were not noted for paying good wages. However, when business was poor, instead of slashing wages or laying off hands, the Fieldens switched to short-time working. They built up a stock of their goods (at some financial risk) and waited until trade recovered. Their workers knew that their jobs were secure (a major consideration at that time) and were duly grateful.

When Fielden became MP for Oldham alongside William Cobbett in the newly reformed parliament of 1832, he soon made his presence felt. Fielden worked tirelessly for the Ten Hours movement, although it made him unpopular with other Todmorden mill-owners. His book *The Curse of the Factory System* was published in 1836, the same year that Fielden Bros. adopted a ten-hour day in their own mills. John Doherty, trade unionist and short time committee member, and the Rev. George Stringer Bull, vicar of Bierley, near Bradford, were also active campaigners.

John Fielden campaigned on behalf of the handloom weavers, too. By the 1830s, they had little hope of earning a decent living.

When new mule-spinning machinery first came into vogue, cotton weavers were kept in full employment from this sudden yarn bonanza. Weavers in Paisley (near Glasgow) were so prosperous, they saved up to buy their own homes.

Cotton-weavers fell victim to new technology after Edmund Cartwright's power-loom was patented in 1785. The earliest power-looms were powered by water; steam was introduced later. Power-looms were slow to catch on at first. The cloth they wove was of poor quality, but Lancashire manufacturers worked hard to improve the technology. No handloom weaver could match the power-loom for speed and price of the finished cloth, and their earning power was eroded.

Weavers suffered great hardship all over Britain. Irish weavers earned just 7s for weaving a piece ninety-three yards long. In Lancashire, Bolton weavers were reduced to 4s 1½d per week. Manchester weavers were left with only 1½d per day to buy food and clothing after paying for rent, fuel and candles.

John Fielden spoke out on the weavers' behalf, ironic considering his power-looms were putting weavers out of work. In its early days the Fielden family 'put out' the cotton spun in its mills to hundreds of local weavers. Later, the firm installed power-looms so it did not lose ground to competitors such as the

Ashton family at Hyde. The Fieldens still employed over a thousand handloom weavers in the 1830s. But inevitably, as their powerloom capacity increased to over 800 machines, they needed fewer handloom weavers.

Fielden found it impossible to hold back the economic tide single-handed. He tried to introduce a minimum wage for weavers, but his competitors refused to co-operate.

To maximise their earnings, weavers taught their children how to work the loom as soon as they were tall enough. Fielden told a select committee in March 1835: 'The weavers are compelled by necessity to set their children to work at a time when they ought not to do it. If they can get them into a loom, and get 1s or 2s a week from their earnings, they are glad to do so…'[22]

The trade was overcrowded. There were 840,000 handloom weavers in Britain, and this pushed wages downwards. Impoverished handloom weavers sent their wives and children into the mills so they could make ends meet.

Domestic work was also completely unregulated; it was considered an infringement of personal liberty to interfere with a man's home. As noted earlier, pauper children were apprenticed out to handloom weavers as well as factory masters.

'Children of all ages' worked a fourteen- to sixteen-hour day alongside cotton weavers in Lancashire, Yorkshire, Cheshire and other counties. They worked in damp, unventilated rooms; cellars were often used as loom-shops. London children were sent north to loom-shops in Oldham, Heyside and other cotton towns where 'the utmost possible quantity of work was extracted from them'.[23] Huge numbers of children were employed in small domestic textile workshops.

Sadler did not let the grass grow under his feet. Early in 1831, he introduced a Ten Hours bill into the House of Commons. The bill proposed banning all children under nine from all textile factories. Children and young people would be limited to a ten-hour day during the week.

When Sadler's bill came before the House of Commons for its second reading on 16 March 1832, he gave a rousing speech. Sadler commended factory children to the protection of the House. One by one, he demolished his opponents' arguments against factory reform. Sadler denied that parents and children were 'free agents' who could work for as long and hard as they chose. As he spoke, Sadler showed MPs a leather whip with several thongs. He slapped it loudly on the table to demonstrate the manner in which women and children were 'flogged' by the 'tyrant overlooker.'[24]

Sadler's fiery rhetoric met instant opposition in the House of Commons, however. The chancellor of the exchequer, Lord Althorp, said the bill was 'ill-advised'.[25] Manufacturers asked for a fact-finding select committee so they could rebut Sadler's accusations. The issue was too important: fresh evidence was needed.

The Sadler Committee report of 1831–2 is a deservedly famous document. (Historian E. P. Thompson wrote 'it has an authenticity which compels belief').[26] Sadler interviewed over eighty witnesses (workers and doctors) and gathered a great deal of distressing evidence. He was determined to make out a watertight case for reform.

Many witnesses said they were crippled from excessively long hours spent in the mill. Elizabeth Bentley, a twenty-three-year old Yorkshirewoman, worked as a little doffer when she was six years old at Mr Busk's flax mill at Leeds. (She removed full bobbins and replaced them with empty ones). 'I was kept constantly on my feet…The overlooker I was under was a very severe man…I have been strapped severely'. She said children's parents were too frightened to complain when their children were beaten, in case they got the sack.

Later she worked at flax wet-spinning. Flax was spun either 'dry', or by wetting the fibres, which produced a finer thread. Elizabeth said: 'I have been wet through to my skin; and in winter-time, when myself and others have gone our clothes have been frozen, and we have nearly caught our death from cold.' Elizabeth's posture was straight until she was thirteen, but afterwards she became 'considerably deformed in person'.[27]

Medical witnesses presented a more united front this time. Doctors queued up to testify that factory work undermined people's health, and spoke in favour of a ten-hour day.

Witnesses also alleged that mills were highly immoral places. Women and girls working nights were sometimes subject to unwelcome attention from the overlookers. Sadler claimed the mills 'were little better than brothels'.[28]

The Sadler Committee report was immensely controversial. Mill-owners accused the committee of bias: the operatives were asked 'leading questions'. Mill-owner Robert Hyde Greg claimed the witness evidence was a mass of: 'gross falsehoods and calumnies'.[29] He complained that none of the witnesses gave evidence under oath. Greg rebutted Sadler's accusations of immorality in the mills. Factory girls were no more immoral than any other working-class girls. Others argued the most damning cases of cruelty referred to abuses long since corrected.

Now fate took a hand. Sadler fell foul of a political reform movement: the Great Reform Act of 1832 (which broadened the franchise). The Act stripped parliament of the 'rotten boroughs' with very few voters. Sadler's seat Aldborough was a rotten borough, so he left parliament in June 1832. He stood for Leeds in the general election that December. His opponent was Thomas Babington Macaulay. Leeds was full of mill-owners who opposed Sadler, and they had the vote. The workers, who supported Sadler, did not have the vote. The result was a foregone conclusion. Sadler lost, and the battle for factory reform lost one of its biggest champions

What would happen to Sadler's bill? Luckily, supporters of reform did not have far to look for a new leader. They put their trust in the mightiest hero of our story: Lord Ashley.

Chapter 5

Time to Sleep, and Time to Play

Anthony Ashley Cooper, eldest son of the sixth earl of Shaftesbury, was born on 28 April 1801 in Grosvenor Square, London. His childhood could not have been more different from those of millions of children growing up in the slums of the great cities, and tumbledown hovels of the countryside. Although Ashley was born 'with a silver spoon in his mouth', this earl's son spent many years of his life fighting to protect less fortunate children.

Young Ashley's early childhood was far from happy. The sixth earl was a brusque, despotic man. His mother was a socialite, uninterested in her children. Anthony's parents spared no expense on his education, but were strict, cold disciplinarians, unloving to Ashley and his siblings (he had three sisters and five brothers). The lonely little boy was befriended by a family servant, Maria Millis. Maria was a devout Evangelical, and her teaching greatly influenced Ashley. When he was seven years old, he was sent to a boarding school at Chiswick. He hated the school, and was bullied. Maria died while he was away from home, which must have increased his loneliness.

Five years later Ashley went to Harrow, where he settled down happily at last. During his schooldays there, something happened which affected him deeply. He witnessed a pauper's funeral, and was horrified by the drunkenness of the participants and total lack of respect shown to the deceased. Ashley's great sympathy with the poor and his life-long quest to help them was partly inspired by this unsavoury scene.

Ashley's career began like many other noblemen's sons. In 1819, he read Classics at Christ Church, Oxford, where he gained first class honours. Then he enjoyed a tour of Europe. In 1826, his family's influence netted him a seat in the House of Commons as member for Woodstock.

Ashley was a morbidly sensitive, anxious young man. His feelings of unworthiness were compounded by his father's attitude towards him and his sisters. The sixth earl refused to let his son live at the family home in Wimborne St Giles, Dorset, or at their Grosvenor Square house. Ashley was only allowed brief visits home.

Ashley was a Tory at a time when the party was in turmoil over issues such as Catholic emancipation, which he supported after initial doubts. His politics were informed by his religion. This deeply devout man longed to serve God but was constantly tortured by self-doubt. A strong sense of duty enabled him to put a brave face on his inner torment. Ashley worked immensely hard and doggedly for causes he believed in.

The first social issue where Ashley made a real difference was an inquiry into the way mentally ill people or 'lunatics' were housed. Doctors had little understanding of mental illness, and sufferers were treated abominably. They were locked or chained up for years at a time in private madhouses in disgraceful conditions: sleeping on straw, clothed only in rags. A person who became well again had little hope of being released into society. Pauper 'lunatics' were penned up in dank cellars, or the local jail, or just dumped in the workhouse.

Ashley served on the 1827 select committee which investigated the treatment of 'lunatics', and the following year two Acts were passed to provide better facilities for them and combat their abuse. Lord Ashley continued working to help the mentally ill until the day he died.

In 1830, Ashley married the beautiful and charming Lady Emily Cowper, or 'Minny' as she was affectionately known. (Minny was the daughter of the fifth Earl Cowper, but historians suspect she was really the natural daughter of Lord Palmerston, who married her mother Lady Cowper after the earl's death).

It proved a happy marriage, and Minny was a great comfort and support to him through the years to come. That same year, he became MP for Dorchester. Ashley survived the turmoil of the Reform Bill (which he opposed) and was returned to the House of Commons in the winter of 1832.

This was a critical juncture for the Ten Hours movement. Sadler had failed to get a seat in the newly reformed parliament 'to the disgrace of Leeds, and to the misfortune of the people of all England'.[1] The short time committees needed someone to take over the Ten Hours bill, and quickly. Sadler's bill would be lost unless an MP could be found willing to sponsor it through parliament.

Strangely enough, the factory question had barely surfaced on Ashley's mental radar, despite the heated debates in parliament. The first time he seems to have taken an interest was when he read some of the Sadler committee evidence in *The Times*. Shocked by the revelations, he wrote to Sadler to ask if there was anything he could do to help, but after receiving no reply (probably because Sadler had his hands full), forgot all about it.

No-one else wanted to take on the thankless task of factory reform, and moves were afoot by the government to bring in an Eleven Hours bill to replace Sadler's. Time was running out. Ashley's good work on the 'lunacy question' had shown he was a caring politician, so the Rev. G. S. Bull approached him. He begged Ashley to help factory children and take over the Ten Hours bill.

At first Lord Ashley was stunned by the proposal. He was an aristocrat. How could he speak on behalf of the workers? He had no common ground with them. He was staunchly Conservative, and suspicious of trade unionism. If he took over the bill, he could look forward to a world of trouble and worry, and was unlikely to get preferment from the Tories.

Party politics was not really a factor in Ashley's decision, however. He was guided by his devout religious feelings. (He had recently become involved with Evangelicalism). If he took up the factory children's cause, he could help future generations grow up with greater opportunities to get an education and worship God. He said: 'I believe it is my duty to God and to the poor, and I trust he will support me'. He had grave doubts about his ability to get the Ten Hours bill through parliament but: 'It seems no-one else will undertake it, so I will'.[2]

Once Lord Ashley had made his mind up, he carried on Sadler's fight in earnest. At a reform meeting in London in February 1833, he called the system of factory labour 'an atrocity'. He had taken up the cause as a 'matter of conscience'. All the hard work had already been done by Mr Sadler, who deserved 'the enduring gratitude of millions'. Until Sadler's committee had uncovered the 'horrid truths' of life in the mills: 'the guilt attached to the perpetrators only; but if we now permit this terrible system to be any longer continued, the guilt will descend upon the whole nation'.[3]

The House of Commons cheered Ashley when he proposed the Ten Hours bill, but it was not long before he met resistance. Government ministers, in particular Lord Althorp, still believed in laissez-faire, and worried that shorter hours would cause distress in the textile districts. Lord Althorp had caught 'cotton masters' influenza', as the *Times* wryly put it.[4]

Mill-owners against reform were spoiling for a fight. North Lancashire MP Wilson Patten spoke for them in parliament. The masters sent a petition demanding another factory commission: they had not been allowed to present evidence to Sadler's committee. They wanted to 'have a turn'. Ashley protested, but they got their way. The bill's supporters were aghast; the short time committees were bitterly disappointed. Great anger was felt in the textile districts. Workers felt that the Sadler committee evidence was so unanswerable, there was no need for any further delay to the Ten Hours Bill.

The 1833 Factory Commission was set up in April. The commissioners included Edwin Chadwick, Thomas Tooke and Dr Thomas Southwood Smith, and Leonard Horner. Tooke was an economist; Southwood Smith and Chadwick were later involved with sanitary reform. Chadwick would soon be vilified as one of the prime movers of the Poor Law 'reforms'. Horner will later play an important part in our story. He campaigned for years to help working-class children in his role as factory inspector.

For the present, however, the commission was regarded by the short time committees as the tools of the manufacturers. Oastler and his supporters were determined to show their disgust at the failure of Sadler's bill. As the factory commissioners toured the textile districts, protests erupted wherever they went, to shame them into hastening reform.

Oastler then staged a series of theatrical publicity stunts designed to tug at people's heartstrings and win them over. The factory children themselves would demand action.

The commission arrived first at Manchester. Crowds of children massed at St Peter's Field (site of the Peterloo 'massacre' in August 1819, when yeomanry cavalry charged a peaceful crowd of protesters).

The children carried banners bearing emblems including: 'A Muzzle for the Steam Giant' and 'Manufactories without Child-Slaying'. They marched through the streets of Manchester to the York Hotel, where short time committee member Philip Grant handed in a letter on their behalf: 'Tell the King the actual state in which you find us... you will be repaid by good wishes from the grateful hearts of thousands of little children like ourselves'.[5]

At Leeds on 16 May, a mass meeting of children from the flax and woollen mills gathered outside the hotel where the commissioners were taking evidence. The children had given up their lunchtime: many boys wore hats bearing the emblem 'The Ten Hours Bill'. Six youngsters were taken inside the hotel to meet the commissioners and give them a letter 'from the children'. The letter protested against the mill-owners who lived in 'plenty and pride at the expense of the sweat, the blood and the life of toil-worn childhood'.[6]

When the children had dispersed, Richard Oastler arrived as if by magic, trailing a huge crowd of supporters. He confronted the commissioners, and accused them of being 'in cahoots' with the mill-owners. They protested their whole object was simply to gather information. Oastler replied: 'Any old washerwoman could tell you that ten hours a day was too long for any child to labour'.[7]

The following month the commission visited Bradford, where they were wined and dined by flax mill-owner Mr Marshall. Ten Hours supporter John Wood refused to let the commission enter his factory. He said his operatives were so angry about the commission's appointment, he feared they would not get anything like a 'respectful' response to their enquiries. On 5 June, the commission arrived in Union Street during the mill dinner break. The moment they were spotted, they were surrounded by hordes of children and mill workers, who sang a special song composed by Oastler:

> We will have the Ten Hour Bill,
> That we will, that we will,
> Else the land shall ne'er be still,
> Never still, never still.

Parliament say what they will,
We will have the Ten Hour Bill
We shall have no commissioning,
We will have the Ten Hour Bill!'

The children's mothers heckled and scolded the august visitors, who hid in a mill yard until the factory bell rang for the end of dinner. That evening a 'deputation of factory cripples', followed by another vast crowd of factory children and adults, presented the commission with another letter: 'We are willing to work, but we will not be worked to death...We ought to have time to learn, time to eat, time to sleep, and time to play.'[8]

Reformers, workers, and mill-owners awaited the commission's report on 28 June with immense interest. As the workers had hoped, the report corroborated many aspects of Sadler's enquiry.

Critics had claimed that the cruelties described belonged to the past. But Thomas Beaumont, a Bradford surgeon, testified that in local mills (apart from Mr Wood's) there were overlookers: 'who whether from caprice or bad feelings' frequently inflicted 'cruel corporal punishments'. When Beaumont treated a factory boy for pneumonia, he discovered the child had two broken ribs 'from a severe blow in the side' from an overlooker.[9]

The manufacturers were not always to blame for children's sufferings. Children were mostly directly employed by the spinners, and it was they who beat the children if they did not work fast enough. The better mill-owners forbade any corporal punishment in their mills, but it was easy for them to be disobeyed if they did not supervise their overlookers strictly enough.

James Belshaw managed a Manchester cotton mill. Ill-treatment of children in factories was 'almost universally by the spinners who employ them' and 'contrary to the regulations of any mill that he has been acquainted with'.[10] He knew several spinners sacked for cruelty. John Dixon, a spinner in a Rochdale mill, confirmed that children were sometimes beaten by the spinners and overlookers even if the mill-owner did not allow it.

'Anne J.', an eleven-year-old doffer in a Manchester cotton-spinning mill, said the overlooker threaten to 'bag' (sack) the children if they did not work hard enough. "W.W.', a girl piecer at McConnell's mill, said she was once off work for a fortnight after being badly beaten by the spinner who employed her. (Workers were too frightened to give their full name. Several operatives were sacked for talking to Sadler's committee).

One of the witnesses was Robert Blincoe, the former apprentice we met earlier. He said: 'I think the children are still beaten by overlookers; not so much however, in Manchester, where justice is always at hand, as in country places'.

Robert refused to send his own children to work in a factory: 'I would rather have them transported...I would not have a child of mine there because there is [sic] not good morals; there is [(sic] such a lot of them together that they learn mischief'.[11]

The story of Wigan girl Ellen Hooton (age ten) caused a sensation when the 1833 report was published. William Swanton, the overlooker at Eccles' mill, fastened heavy iron weights to Ellen as a punishment for running away. Ellen was not badly hurt, but the episode inevitably strengthened the connection between factory work and slavery in the minds of the general public.

On the other hand, some Scottish mill-owners were singled out for praise. Dr Barry said he had not come across any cases of 'cruelty, gross oppression, nor punishment attended with corporeal injury'. He believed that many masters showed 'almost parental kindness' to their workers.[12]

The 1833 commission went to great lengths to establish if factory work was inherently unhealthy. A child worker in a modern, clean, well-ventilated mill was more likely to be healthier than one in a ramshackle old building with a low roof.

But was ill-health a product of factory work, or living conditions at home? Dr Hawkins said: 'Most travellers are struck by the lowness of stature, the leanness, and the paleness which present themselves so commonly to the eye at Manchester, and above all among the factory classes'.[13]

Doctors at nearby Bolton begged to differ. George Wolstenholme said he rarely saw any poorly cotton-spinners, but was often called out to treat their wives and young children at home. Richard Johnson said Bolton children were just as healthy as those anywhere else, and better grown than 'domestic drudges, miners' children, weavers, winders, dressmakers' and so on.[14]

In the West Country factories where 'fine cloth' was made, factory children were 'strikingly healthy', with the exception of Chard in Somerset.[15] West Country children were often seen playing in the fields after their work.

William Chadwick, a Rochdale woollen manufacturer, said the atmosphere in woollen factories was less polluted than in cotton mills. However, children in woollen factories were more likely to become 'crooked', because of the awkward angle at which they held their bodies while piecing together the carded yarn. Chadwick admitted he stopped children working as piecers in his own mill when they were twelve years old, so they would not grow up deformed.

Factory hand George Braid gave evidence on the flax and tow mills of Dundee. The flax-spinning industry was an important employer in Scotland, Leeds and Ireland. The flax plant had many different uses. Long fibres from the plant stems were used to manufacture linen cloth and towelling. The shorter, inferior fibres or 'tow' were used to make ropes and cord. Processing flax created a great deal of dust, and many mills were very poorly ventilated. They were extremely hazardous places in which to work.

When Braid visited the Old Tay Street and New Tay Street mills, he was appalled by the number of operatives suffering from lung disease, or who had lost fingers and limbs. In the New Tay Street tow preparation room, he found nine operatives with breathing difficulties from the all-pervasive flax dust. Two of those affected were youngsters Mary Baird (twelve) and James Dawson (sixteen). All the operatives enjoyed good health before working at the mill. John Mackay (sixty-seven), was very poorly indeed; Braid said Mackay had the appearance of a ninety-year-old.

Machinery was not boxed off properly at Chalmers & Hackney's flax mill on Old Tay Street where: 'no less than four individuals… have lost their limbs… from the present nefarious system'. A few years previously, nineteen-year-old William Brown lost his hand and part of his arm when he got caught up in the carding engine: 'the machinery is still in as dangerous a condition.'[16]

David Yule, a fireman (engine minder) at the same mill, previously had two sons working there. When his twelve-year-old son lost his left arm in the same carding engine, he instantly removed his other boy from the factory: 'for fear of accidents… and has not allowed any other child of his to be so employed'.[17]

Braid was most disturbed by the case of James Hume, a 'poor young boy' who could neither read nor write. James (twelve) lost a whole arm in the machinery at Chalmers & Hackney's mill. After two months' convalescence in the infirmary, he was forced to return to work 'from dire necessity…having no other means of supporting his miserable existence'. His master paid him just 3s 3d per week.

Braid did not mince his words: 'This case will show you…the despicable plea which the opponents of Sadler's bill bring forward, when they say that the glory of this mighty nation will henceforth decrease if the legislature interfere betwixt master and servant'. He believed that hard facts should 'awaken the minds of all those who are not the paid agents of tyranny and oppression'.[18]

Conditions were better at Craig's flax dry-spinning mill at Preston Holme (Edinburgh). The mill employed 181 workers, including eighty-one girls and twenty-two boys aged nine to thirteen. They worked from six in the morning until eight at night, including ninety minutes for meals.

All the workers at Craig's mill spent forty minutes of their breakfast hour in the compulsory (but free) school. They could all read and write. The youngsters looked healthy but were 'very much fatigued at night'.[19] Both parents and children said they would much rather work from six until six at night, even if it meant a reduction in wages.

There were several flax-spinning mills at Dunfermline, then a fast-growing town. The working conditions at wet-spinning mills were far more unpleasant than dry-spinning. Children at James Kirkland's mill endured 'wet and filthy' conditions in 70ºF (21 Celsius) heat. The atmosphere was 'hot, moist, steamy and disagreeable'. The children, some of whom worked barefoot, were 'wet through' from the spray kicked off by the spindles. They looked 'filthy, bedraggled, and miserable, but robust for age, and healthy looking'.[20] Several workers were off work owing to influenza.

At Wilson & Malcolm's mill, also in Dunfermline, the children wore pinafores, and 'splash-boards' prevented the children from getting soaked. The flax-spinners had to stand all day (except at meal-times). Janet Nelson (fourteen) and Janet Salmon (thirteen) worked in a Kirkcaldy wet-spinning mill (near Dundee). Both were pale and thin, and looked 'over-worked… and under size'.[21] Their hands were chapped from getting constantly wetted by the spray.

Despite meeting girls like these two Kirkcaldy teenagers, the 1833 commissioners felt that young people's hours did not need restricting. They believed that children were less likely to be harmed by factory work when they reached puberty. (Ashley's bill wanted a ten-hour working day for all workers under eighteen).

The commissioners found plenty of evidence that younger children needed protection, however. In the north-east, especially Bradford, where Oastler claimed some of the worst conditions prevailed, the commission found 'undoubted' proof that five-year-olds worked a thirteen-hour day, and children from nine years old who worked a fourteen or fifteen-hour shift.

The commission spoke to witnesses from Sadler's much-maligned committee the year before. Dr Charles Loudon examined John Dawson, a twenty-eight-year-old Leeds tailor, who began working in a mill when he was six or seven years old. When he was nine years old, his limbs began to 'bend'. Loudon had 'no doubt the direct cause of the crooked state of his limbs was the long hours'.[22]

Loudon was shocked to see the painfully twisted limbs of 'unfortunate' William Hebden, who began in the mills when he was only five. Long hours almost certainly caused his illness. The doctor also spoke to Elizabeth Bentley, the 'little doffer', now twenty-four. He felt her 'deformed' state was owing to poor food and disease as well as long working hours.[23]

Loudon concluded: 'I think it has been clearly proved that children have been worked a most unreasonable and cruel length of time daily, and that even adults have been expected to do a certain quantity of labour which scarcely any human being is able to endure'.[24] (This 1833 commission was supposedly biased *towards* the manufacturers, remember). No child should work more than eight hours a day, and no-one 'under any circumstances' should work more than twelve hours daily in any industry, not just factories.

Robert Baker, a member of the Royal College of Surgeons and a Leeds doctor for eight years, did not think Leeds factory workers looked unhealthier than others. Nevertheless, he was emphatically in favour of children being protected by law. Baker wanted night work banned: it was 'contrary to nature and unhealthy'.[25] Children younger than eleven years old should be kept out of the mills altogether. Robert Baker, in his later role as a factory inspector, spent many years fighting to improve factory children's schooling and education.

It was perfectly possible for mill-owners to shorten hours without ruining their business. The commission interviewed William Sharp junior, a Bradford surgeon, on conditions in the mill belonging to John Wood. (The same Mr Wood who launched Oastler on his crusade for factory reform). Wood had put his own house (or rather factory) in order. His mill now worked a ten-hour day, and: 'the health of the children' had much improved.[26] Wood had taken on sixty more operatives to achieve this reduction in hours, and also built a school for his factory children, which they attended for two hours a day.

The 1833 commission was satisfied that changes must be made. Children who worked the same hours as adults suffered permanent damage to their health. They had no opportunity to go to school, and 'they are not free agents, but are let out to hire, the wages they earn' going straight to their parents or guardians.[27]

So, much to everyone's surprise – both pro- and anti-reformers – the commission recommended shorter hours for factory children.

However, the commission criticised Ashley's Ten Hours bill, which did not give enough protection to young children, and went too far in protecting older ones. Younger children were most at risk from long hours; even a ten-hour day was too long for them. The commission adopted Loudon's suggestion of an eight-hour day for nine- to thirteen-year-olds. To minimise inconvenience to mill-owners, the commission suggested children work in teams of relays and keep the wheels of industry turning that way. However, youngsters over thirteen were old enough to make their own contracts for work with employers. There was no need to legislate for them.

Lord Althorp brought in a new factory bill in line with the commission's suggestions, with the blessing of the House of Commons. Althorp said that Ashley's bill would take bread from the mouths of the very families he was trying to help. He was prepared to give factory children some protection in law, but did not want to interfere with working families' 'domestic arrangements' more than necessary. Althorp was convinced that mill-owners faced 'extreme danger' from foreign competitors if working hours were reduced too far.

William Cobbett, Radical MP for Oldham, commented sarcastically on the House of Commons' 'wonderful discovery': 'Hitherto we had boasted that the shipping interest, the maritime commerce, and the agriculture of the country, etc., were the principal means of her support, but the House had that night discovered that it was 300,000 little girls in Lancashire. For they had found that, by taking off two hours a day from the labour of these little children, the manufacture of the country would be totally ruined, and grievous competition all over the globe would effect the destruction of the empire'.[28]

The Ten Hours supporters were unhappy about the eight hours clause. An eight-hour shift was much better for small children, but they knew that unless all factory workers started and finished work at the same time, mill-owners would find it easy to overwork them.

Therefore, Ashley protested against the government's new measure. (He felt because he was the workers' spokesman, he should go along with their desire for ten hours for all.). He wanted teenagers to have some protection, and pointed to the 1833 committee's medical evidence, but to no avail. His Ten Hours bill was defeated in July. The government's new factory bill, 'Althorp's Act', successfully went through parliament on 29 August 1833.

The Factory Act of 1833 applied to children working in cotton, woollen, worsted, hemp, flax, tow, linen and silk mills (lace-making was excluded). The inclusion of other textile mills was a major step forward for reformers.

To give manufacturers time to adjust, the Act's provisions did not come into effect immediately. After 1 January 1834, children and young persons under eighteen were banned from working more than twelve hours per day (a sixty-nine-hour week). Young workers between the ages of nine and thirteen were classed as 'children'. When they became thirteen years old, they were classed as 'young persons' until they became an 'adult' at eighteen. No child under the age of nine was allowed to work in a textile factory, except silk mills, which had no minimum age.

During the first year of the 1833 Act, children under eleven were limited to a forty-eight-hour week (so if they worked six days, they only worked eight hours a day). No child in this age group was permitted to work more than nine hours in one day, except in silk mills, where a ten-hour day was allowed. The forty-eight-hour week was extended to children under twelve in the Act's second year, and children under thirteen in the third year.

Night work (from eight-thirty at night until five-thirty in the morning) was banned for all persons under eighteen. Christmas Day and Good Friday were set aside as holidays. The children were also entitled to a minimum of eight half-days off per year.

However, if a mill had problems with its steam engine, or insufficient water for its water-wheel, depending on its motive power, the mill-owner was permitted to make children and young persons work longer hours than specified in the Act to make up for lost time. There was obvious scope for abuse here by unscrupulous employers.

The 1833 Factory Act set one ground-breaking precedent: administrative machinery was put in place to enforce the law. Four inspectors were appointed with powers to enter any factory by day or night to check on child workers and 'make enquiry respecting their condition, employment and education'. The inspectors were Leonard Horner (for Scotland), Robert Rickards (north-west England), R. J. Saunders (England), and T. J. Howell (Wales).

The inspectors must ensure that factory children went to school. Every child must have a school attendance certificate signed by a teacher. Children working up to forty-eight hours per week must attend school at least two hours every day, six days per week. If no school was available, inspectors were authorised to establish one, but they were not given funds to build any, so this clause was initially a non-starter.

In order to 'prove' that underage children were not illegally employed, a doctor must provide a certificate for every child under thirteen in each mill. At that time there was no compulsory registration of births (it was introduced in 1837), so it was extremely difficult to prove a child's true age. This piece of paper certified the child 'had the ordinary strength and appearance' of the correct age for factory work.[29] Young people (teenagers) were also required to have an age certificate.

The 1833 Factory Act had one astonishing omission. There was no provision to prevent children being hurt by mechanical hazards in mills. As we saw earlier, children's lives and limbs were in great danger from unfenced moving machinery in factories. Horrible injuries were caused by some manufacturers' refusal to spend a few extra shillings to box off shafting, straps or machinery rotating at high speed. Girls and women were most at risk because of their long hair and skirts, which easily got caught up.

Francis Sharp, a surgeon at Leeds infirmary, treated eighty-nine injuries (including two fatalities) caused by machinery in the space of just three months. The sister of one little boy who died broke both her arms trying to extricate him from the machinery.

Robert Blincoe lost part of a finger while working as an apprentice at Lowdham mill near Nottingham. He told the 1833 Factory Commission that mills were not safe places for children: 'They are so liable to have their fingers catched [sic] and to suffer other accidents from the machinery; then the hours are so long, that I have seen them tumble down asleep among the straps and the machinery, and so get cruelly hurt'.[30]

Few people had any concept of 'health and safety' at work. Mill-owners argued that workers should take care whilst on their premises. If children like

John Hume in the Dundee flax mill were injured or killed, it was their own fault. They probably didn't look where they were going, or were playing about. Factory inspectors had an uphill fight on their hands when they tried to change this attitude, which was deeply entrenched.

Yet the opening skirmish had been won. Factory children's hours had been reduced, and they had a chance to go to school. But for social reformers, and the newly appointed factory inspectors, the battle was only just beginning…

Chapter 6

Fight the Good Fight

As the 1833 Factory Act came into effect, the inspectors began the difficult task of ensuring compliance with the new regulations. Nowadays the 'nanny state' is a by-word for an over-officious government, poking and prying into people's everyday lives. But we have already seen what conditions were like when manufacturers were left to their own devices. It is difficult to imagine how revolutionary it was to have a government official or 'spy' appear on a mill-owner's doorstep and check on the way he carried out his business.

The Factory Act pleased no-one except the government. The inspectors faced open hostility from all sides: manufacturers, workers, parents, and the magistrates who dispensed the law. All interested parties in the textile districts were on the alert to see how the new Act would work.

Lord Ashley, still smarting over the loss of his 'Ten Hours' clause, felt he should 'give the act a fair trial', whilst reserving the right to criticise the government if necessary.[1] He was keen to ensure that inspectors had sufficient powers to do their job.

Factory inspectors faced huge logistical problems. They were few in number at first and had a vast territory to cover. They relied heavily on manufacturers' good will, and faced all kinds of obstructions while trying to do their job. Inspectors had the power to enter any factory, but their assistants or 'superintendents' could not enter without the mill-owner's permission. Some managers simply refused to let them in, saying it was inconvenient. Or they turned out all the lights when an inspector arrived, which gave underage child workers time to run away. One mill-owner waited until the inspector was inside the factory, locked him in and turned off the lights – no laughing matter if any machinery was still running.

Workers at Healy New Mill, Ossett (Yorkshire), tried to fool superintendent Robert Baker by hiding underage children in bags of wool. But Baker spotted a pair of tiny feet sticking out of the top of a bag. If there was illegal working in mills where the master co-operated and let government officers in, what were conditions like in the others? Inspectors wanted their superintendents to have the right to enter any mill.

It was not an easy job. The noise inside the mills was deafening: 'The din of the machinery, which, if there be any power-looms at work, beats the Falls of Niagara all to nothing; the rapid motions of the several wheels and shafts…

distract the mind, and at first produce a sense of weariness which it is not easy for a visitor to overcome'.[2]

And there were hazards all around them. Mill-owners had a terrifying disregard for safety. Inspector Leonard Horner discovered one room 'where thirty young people were employed, and in the very passage where they must walk to and from their work, there was a hole eighteen inches square, immediately beneath which I saw three large iron cogged-wheels rapidly revolving; and anyone falling through this hole would inevitably be crushed to death, or fearfully mutilated. A shilling expended on some boards and nails would have removed all danger, without in the least interfering with the machinery below'.

The mill owner said: 'We have never met with any accident!'[3] He admitted the hole could easily be mended, however. Horner wanted safety measures included in the Factory Act, even if it would be difficult to frame legislation to cover every eventuality.

Mill-owners soon realised the Act had more loopholes than a fishing-net, and openly disregarded the law. Time and again, the factory inspectors' efforts to enforce the law were frustrated by JPs who were factory owners, or friends or relatives of them. Magistrates refused to convict, or inflicted a derisory fine.

If a factory inspector prosecuted a mill-owner, a child might be too frightened to give evidence of overwork before a magistrate. One little girl at Stockport answered 'I do not know' to every question at a court hearing in 1840, even though she previously told the factory inspector she worked illegally long hours.[4] Cases like these caused rumblings of discontent amongst the factory hands.

The inspectors reported regularly to the government on how well the law was working, and the state of trade in the manufacturing districts. The new administrative machinery worked well on two levels: the government had its own eyes and ears in the factories, and the inspectors had a 'hot-line' to the secretary of state. This enabled men like Leonard Horner to press for changes to the law.

Now, the Act's aim was to stop children being over-worked. But factory inspectors were worried when they discovered that in other respects, the new law disadvantaged the very children it was trying to help.

When the new Act came into force in January 1834, large numbers of child workers under the age of eleven were kicked out of the mills. Mill-owners did not want the bother of all the form-filling required by the Act, or to pay for a school for their factory children, which they viewed as a 'tax' on their businesses.

Factory inspector Robert Rickards said the children suffered 'great distress' and needed parish relief. Mill-owner Robert Hyde Greg claimed the children were left to wander the streets 'in idleness and misery'.

Rickards warned that more children would be thrown out of work as each age group's hours were restricted. He advised (presumably he had been chatting to mill-owners) that when hours were limited for eleven- and twelve-year-olds, it could 'prove fatal to manufacturing prosperity'.[5] He wanted that section of the Factory Act repealed.

And some families did suffer real hardship when children lost their jobs in the factories. So parents sent their children down the mines, or found work elsewhere. They still needed their children's wages.

Lord Ashley was very concerned about the factory commission's proposed system of 'relays' of child workers to keep mills running, and his misgivings were soon justified. This section of the Factory Act allowed mill-owners to use two sets of child workers in one day, up to a maximum of eight hours per set.

Factory inspectors found it almost impossible to enforce the eight hours limit for nine- to thirteen-year-olds. Children's hours could be worked at any time during the factory day, and could be done in instalments. Mill-owners sent children in and out of the factory at odd times, or the spinners kept them longer than they should. Inspectors could not tell how many hours a child had actually worked unless they stayed all day, which was impractical when they had so many mills to visit.

The operatives were very unhappy with the relay system, too. Canny manufacturers using two shifts of children, for up to eight hours, worked the adults for up to sixteen hours a day. The factory hands still wanted a ten-hour day for all. They believed the best way of achieving this was to fix a ten-hour day for each factory's 'motive power': the mill-engine. That way adults and children would start and finish work together.

The 1833 Act did not compel mill-owners to provide adequate ventilation for workers; it only required factories to be whitewashed inside to keep them clean. Sir George Head, who toured around Britain during the mid-1830s, was favourably disposed to the factory system. He felt the 'portraits of misery and over-fatigue' in mills were exaggerated: 'With respect to the general state of the workmen, and especially the children in the factories, I certainly gained, from personal inspection, a happy release from opinions previously entertained…' Head claimed whenever he visited a factory he found a 'crowd of apparently happy beings working in lofty, well-ventilated buildings'.[6]

Head was shocked, though, when he visited a rag-grinding factory at Batley Carr near Dewsbury, Yorkshire. In these factories immensely powerful machines 'ground' or shredded old rags into waste fibres or 'shoddy'. The shoddy was mixed with wool, processed and woven into 'new' cloth. Each rag-grinding machine was attended by three or four boys and girls. This was a revoltingly smelly job, because the filthy rags were not cleaned before processing. Head said 'a single whiff of air' from the shop floor was 'almost more than could be endured.'

The machinery generated huge quantities of dust in confined, unventilated rooms. The workers could hardly see each other. The children, covered from top to toe with 'downy particles', looked like 'brown moths.'[7] Workers wore handkerchiefs over their mouths to try to stop the dust getting into their lungs.

These mills were covered by the Factory Acts, and in 1836 inspector Robert Baker prosecuted Taylor, Ibbotson & Co., a shoddy firm in Batley Carr, for overworking children. (There were several shoddy firms in the district. It's possible this was the same factory Head had visited). This case caused a stir in the newspapers because of the leniency shown by local magistrates.

Baker discovered four young lads (twelve to fifteen years old) had worked from six o'clock on the morning of Friday 27 May until four o'clock on Saturday afternoon, only stopping for meal breaks. They rested for one hour at midnight. Baker told the master he would be severely punished, as he felt it was a case of real cruelty.

The inspector charged the firm with four separate violations of the Factory Act. In theory the owners, if found guilty, faced a fine of £80 (£20 for each offence). In their defence, the factory owners said it was the first time the boys worked all night. A boiler burst, and there was not enough power to work the rag-grinding machines and other machinery together, so the shoddy machines had to run all night. Magistrates only fined the firm five pounds for each offence despite evidence that the mill-owner falsified time-keeping records.

Was this really the first time children were overworked by this firm? Night work was commonplace in Batley. During the same sessions, several more firms were fined for working children at night, and illegally overworking children under ten.

The more humane mill-owners were anxious for the scope of factory legislation to be widened so the more aggressive masters could not undercut them. They resented all being tarred with the same brush.

One factory owner who carried on working in the same old ways was John Douglas of Holywell. Mr Brotherton (MP for Salford), a seasoned campaigner for reform, called Douglas 'a determined and active opponent of factory legislation'.

In 1837, inspector T. J. Howell prosecuted Douglas for overworking young people at Holywell. They worked from seven o'clock on Saturday evening until five o'clock on Sunday morning without a break. The day shift worked from half past five in the morning until eleven o'clock at night, with rest breaks totalling an hour and forty minutes: just under sixteen hours' labour. Howell said he had never seen any workers as 'wan and haggard' as those at the Greenfield cotton mills. The magistrates fined Douglas £19.

It was very difficult for inspectors to prove to a magistrate that a child was too young to work. Parents showed their family Bible to 'prove' little Johnny's age. The entry of a child's birth might be crossed out or altered. Some families bought a brand new Bible and rewrote all the dates when their children were born.

The inspectors also had problems with the 'surgical certificates' (signed by a doctor) to 'prove' children's ages. The system was useless in practice. Doctors disagreed on what the 'ordinary strength and appearance' of a nine-year-old should be. Parents could easily hoodwink a doctor and get a certificate showing Johnny was thirteen, so he could work for twelve hours, even though he was only ten or eleven. They sent an older child to see the doctor in Johnny's place. Mr Brotherton said that 'a system of fraud and deception' was widely practised.[8] There was a thriving black market in lost and stolen certificates.

In the early days of the inspectorate, any doctor could sign certificates to say children seemed the correct age. If a mill-owner felt a local doctor was unnecessarily strict, he found another who did the work 'better'. Some doctors were surprisingly ready to sign certificates for tiny children. Parents soon got wind of this. If one doctor refused their child a certificate, they took him round the mills until they found a doctor who would.

At Healy New Mill, the owner fell out with the doctor who issued certificates, and brought in another one, Dr Smith, who was more amenable. In 1838, inspector Robert Saunders prosecuted the mill-owner for employing underage children, and the firm was fined ten pounds. A short time later, inspector Bates found children in the mill so tiny they could not possibly be working legally. Dr Smith had certified the children as thirteen years old even though the children themselves had told him they were under twelve. Bates summonsed Dr Smith and the owners of Healy New Mill for knowingly using false certificates, but Wakefield magistrates threw out the case on a technicality.

Following cases like this, inspector Robert Rickards put in place a system whereby he appointed doctors in his district (the north-west) with the sole power to sign age certificates. He did not technically have the legal authority to do this, but it was such a good idea, the home secretary allowed him to continue, and all the other factory inspectors followed suit in their areas.

None of the disasters prophesied by opponents of the Factory Act happened. Leonard Horner said: 'Not a single mill throughout the United Kingdom stopped a day for want of hands'.[9] The battle over hours did not disappear, however.

Early in 1836, the Factory Act was about to come into operation for twelve-year-olds (a nine-hour day). Poulett Thomson (vice-president of the Board of Trade) introduced another bill into parliament. Following the inspectors' reports of children being sacked, Thomson wanted to repeal part of the 1833 Act to enable twelve-year-olds to work full time (twelve hours). This stirred up the short time committees like a nest of hornets. They sent many petitions against the proposal.

Lord Ashley stepped in again. The government's own commission in 1833 had said twelve-year-olds should not work as long as adults. Why had it now gone against its own advice? The motion passed, but with such a tiny majority the government felt unable to implement it.

Ashley was becoming disenchanted with the short time committees' continuing agitation for a ten-hour factory day for all. He did not want young children's hours increased. E.C. Tufnell, one of the 1833 factory commissioners, was amazed by the contrasting motives of philanthropists and those of the factory hands. The former wanted to stamp out cruelty to working children, and long hours. None of the factory hands Tufnell interviewed cited those reasons for supporting a Ten Hours bill: 'I am perfectly satisfied that motives of humanity have not the smallest weight' with them. Tufnell believed their sole view 'was to get the wages of twelve hours with the work of ten'.[10] Considerations like these led Ashley to drop a Ten Hours bill he proposed in 1837.

The factory hours question became overshadowed by other important social issues which rocked the 1830s and 1840s: the new Poor Law of 1834, Chartism, and the Anti-Corn Law League.

The short time committee members became embroiled in protests against the new Poor Law, which was violently opposed by Oastler and tub-thumping cleric Joseph Rayner Stephens (later editor of the Radical *Ashton Chronicle*).

Meanwhile, the Ten Hours movement suffered several setbacks. Michael Thomas Sadler died in 1835; he was only fifty-five. People said his excessive labour on behalf of factory children wore him out. Three years later, Oastler was sent to the Fleet prison for debt. He was not one to sit on his laurels, however. He continued lobbying on behalf of 'the much-injured and helpless factory slaves' and harangued 'the oppressors of the poor' with new journal *The Fleet Papers*.[11] Stephens was also locked up the following year for making a seditious speech.

Oastler and the operatives were also furious about a labour migration scheme. Mill-owners could not get enough children of the correct age to work in 'relays', and were short of hands generally, so they asked Poor Law Commissioners to help. Destitute agricultural families in southern England were told that jobs were available for them in the textile districts. If they refused to go, they were threatened with the workhouse.

Over 300 families migrated in 1836 (1,200 people went to Lancashire alone), but the scheme was not very successful. Families who had grown up in the countryside found it difficult to settle in towns. Mill-owners hired the families at fixed low-wage contracts, and when a trade slump hit the following year, they suffered terribly.

The factory hands resented the migrants because they brought down wages. Families composed of widows with four or more children were preferred by mill-owners, although 'a father would not be objected to' providing he had 'numerous' children who could earn a wage.

The system of apprenticing pauper children to faraway mills, condemned nearly four decades earlier, made a comeback as parish overseers tried to save money.

The firm of McConnell & Co., Manchester, now owned Cressbrook Mill in Derbyshire. Parish overseers at Milton workhouse in Kent agreed to send twenty young people to Cressbrook for three years. When the news leaked out, their relatives moved heaven and earth to get them out of the workhouse: 'the guardians were deprived of the opportunity of sending a single child, as proposed'.

Richard Muggeridge was in charge of the scheme to aid labour migration from south to north. He admitted that in factories where apprentices still worked, the youngsters were 'a dispirited and discontented class, infinitely worse clad, and less respectable in their appearance than the children of the same ages who are their fellow work-people'.[12]

This did not stop him placing pauper children with 'respectable' factory masters. William and R. Turner, owners of Helmshore mill in Lancashire, offered places to eleven girls and six boys from Bishop's Stortford workhouse. The youngest children, who included Lydia and Charlotte Sharp, were twelve years old. They were to stay at Helmshore until they were twenty-one. The children received a weekly wage rising from 2s 6d in their first year to 6s 6d in their final year.

Some Bloomsbury children were not as lucky as those from Milton and Bishop's Stortford. The parishes of St Giles in the Fields, and St. George, Bloomsbury, sent eighteen girls to work for Mr Christie, owner of a cotton-doubling mill at Edale, Derbyshire. The youngest was only nine years old. The girls were not formally apprenticed, so they were not covered by the apprenticeship Acts.

Inspector Robert Saunders found the girls 'in a most unhealthy condition', and contacted their home parish (via the Poor Law Commissioners) to say they should go back home. They would be better cared for in the workhouse. But the St Giles guardians did not think there were 'sufficient grounds' to interfere with their arrangement with Mr Christie. Before the children were sent out, they checked they would be under 'the moral superintendence' of Christie and his wife.

Saunders quizzed Christie on the exact nature of his agreement with the parish. Christie who said there was no legal contract, just a promise 'the children should not be chargeable until they were twenty-one'.[13]

The Christies had moved away from the town on account of its damp, cold and unhealthy climate, so the girls did not have any 'moral superintendence' at all. The vestry clerk at St. Giles wrote to a local clergyman to check up on them. He replied that the climate was too cold for the children and they looked poorly. But nothing was done to help them. By 1840 three girls had died; another was very ill, and expected to die at any moment. Saunders was deeply frustrated; he had no legal powers to interfere.

Meanwhile, the short time committees were also occupied with upsurges in trade union activity, in which Robert Owen played a leading role, and the dawning of the Chartism movement.

Chartism, founded in 1837, was fuelled by industrial unrest, mass unemployment and high food prices. This vast working-class movement comprised several different factions: some peaceful, some highly militant. The aims of the 'People's Charter' included universal male suffrage, vote by ballot, and parliamentary reform. Chartist activism convulsed society, and the middle classes feared that revolution was nigh.

The Chartists held mass meetings in the textile districts and the Midlands. The Bull Ring at Birmingham witnessed violent scenes when local magistrates and police broke up their gatherings.

However, the Chartists, led by Feargus O'Connor, Francis Place and others, could not agree on the best tactics to achieve their objectives. Should they petition parliament, organise a general strike, or start an armed uprising, as some hot-heads wanted? When parliament spurned the Chartists' first monster petition (with over a million signatures) in the summer of 1839, workers were extremely bitter.

South Wales was a Chartist flashpoint. Activists simmered with resentment when local Chartist hero Henry Vincent was jailed and badly treated. On the night of Sunday 3 November 1839, several thousand armed rebels launched a daring three-pronged attack on the town of Newport.

The men, led by John Frost, planned to take over the town and then rescue Vincent from Monmouth jail. The mayor of Newport, John Phillips, aided by soldiers and special constables, swiftly quelled the insurrection. The soldiers launched a volley of deadly fire on the mob. Bullet-holes were still visible on the local pub years later. Fourteen rioters paid the ultimate price for their fight for freedom. Eighteen-year-old George Shell from Pontypool was one of those who died. Over fifty people were injured. The rest of the rebels fled, but the ringleaders were captured, tried and transported to Botany Bay.

Although the Chartist movement was not directly concerned with improving children's working conditions, incidents like the Newport uprising raised an important question: would workers be less likely to rebel if they were better educated?

Two-thirds of the 11,300 children in the South Wales mining districts did not go to school. Boys as young as seven years old earned three shillings a week, so their parents thought there was little point in them going to classes. A boy learnt to be a 'good miner' from an early age, and once down the pit 'he learns nothing else'.[14]

Factory children were very poorly catered for in the matter of schools, too. As we shall see later, the educational clauses of the 1833 Act proved of limited value.

Leonard Horner made out a strong case for reform on political, economic and humanitarian grounds in his book *On the Employment of Children* (1840). If workers were properly educated, crime would decrease, and social and industrial unrest disappear. Horner believed that Chartist rioters had been seduced into lawlessness and violence. Because their childhoods were spent working. they had grown up deplorably neglected and ignorant.

The Factory Act was 'productive of much good' but could have achieved much more. Horner complained of 'the inhumanity, injustice, and impolicy of extorting labour from children unsuitable to their age and strength; of subjecting them, in truth, to the hardships of slavery'.

Children were used as cheap labour for ruinously long hours 'in almost all branches of industry... It is in vain that we build schools, if the children have no time to attend them; if the children of our working classes are to be raised from their present degraded condition, by means of education, it is obvious that it can only be done by securing to them, in the first instance, the time necessary for it'.[15]

Critics of reform declared that more state interference in industry was unreasonable and an assault on parental rights: 'humanity running riot'. Horner argued they were mistaken: the government should introduce more, not less, protective legislation to help thousands of 'neglected, oppressed and helpless children'.

New legislation was the only way to check the 'growing, unnatural, and vicious practice of parents making their children work to enable themselves to live in idleness and profligacy'.[16]

Children under the age of eight should be banned from industry, with the exception of those working at home, under a parent's eye. (Even Horner did not dare advocate interfering with the 'sanctity' of the Englishman's home). The nation would be more prosperous if it invested in its workers by educating them.

Horner wanted a 'half-time' system for factory children under thirteen, with the dinner break as the dividing line. (Robert Owen suggested something similar for older children over two decades earlier).

Children should only work half a day, either before or after dinner. No child under thirteen should begin work before 5 a.m. or finish after 8 p.m. Every parent, or master profiting by the child's labour, should set aside part of the child's wages every week to pay for its education.

Horner had an ally in Lord Ashley, who had not given up on a ten-hour day for teenagers. Ashley had dissociated himself from Richard Oastler, however. Blackburn magistrates had refused to hear a complaint against a manufacturer under the Factory Act because it was 'Oastler's law'.[17] The choleric Yorkshireman retaliated by suggesting factory children should spike the machinery with their grandmothers' knitting-needles if JPs did not enforce the law. Ashley could not countenance any suggestion of sabotage, and did not write to him again.

Lord Ashley was very anxious for more industries to be controlled by the factory inspectorate. He visited the manufacturing districts in 1841. It was a time of great hardship: the 'hungry forties'. Trade was shockingly bad, and Ashley wanted to see for himself how the factory hands and their children lived. He was struck by the pitiful state of the child silk-workers in Macclesfield, and kept up pressure on the government.

By now the short time committees had changed tack. Instead of demanding a limit to a factory's 'motive power', they pressed for women workers to be restricted to ten hours, hoping this would effectively give men a ten-hour day, too. The inspectors also wanted protection for women factory workers. During their factory visits, they had been greatly struck by the long hours they endured.

In 1843, the Home Secretary, Sir James Graham, introduced a new bill to regulate factory children's labour. The bill included a clause for a comprehensive, mandatory system of education supervised by the church. This idea aroused a whirlwind of opposition from religious groups, for reasons to be discussed later. The bill was hastily dropped, and a great opportunity was lost.

Graham re-introduced the bill the following year without the offending educational clauses. At this point Lord Ashley pounced. He spotted a chance to introduce a ten-hour day for teenagers, and proposed an amendment to Graham's bill.

Mill-owner John Bright (1811–1889) now enters our story. The reformers' party did not have a monopoly on men of high principles. The anti-factory reform brigade included men like Bright, who were against factory legislation from personal conviction as well as economic considerations.

Like Fielden, John grew up in the cotton industry. His father Jacob owned mills at Rochdale. Bright came from a devout Quaker family, and the Brights took a paternal interest in their factory hands. No child was ever 'strapped' at a Bright mill. After John left school, he helped run his father's business.

Bright spent years agitating for a more democratic voting franchise. He was a slave trade abolitionist and anti-Corn Law campaigner. The Anti-Corn Law League, led by Bright and mill owner Richard Cobden, spearheaded a middle-class revolt against the Corn Laws. The Corn Laws kept foreign corn out of Britain until the home price reached a certain level. In effect, the price of bread was kept artificially high, causing great suffering in the textile towns and agricultural villages. John was elected to parliament on an anti-Corn Law ticket.

Bright was convinced that free trade would lower corn prices and increase exports of British goods, helping the mill-owners. The poor would have more bread to eat. He burned to break the stranglehold of the rich landowners and farmers in parliament who clung to the Corn Laws. Labourers in Dorsetshire, home of Lord Ashley's ancestral seat, were starving in tumbledown hovels. Bright was furious about the relentless spotlight shone on factory conditions. He believed that factory workers enjoyed far better conditions than agricultural labourers. Bright was not against a ten-hour working day in principle; what he objected to was government interference between master and man.

When Ashley proposed a Ten Hours bill in March 1844, he reviewed the findings of the 1833 Factory Commission, and reports of the factory inspectors. He denied that he was singling out mill-owners for criticism. 'We are called upon to give relief', he said, not because factory labour was the 'worst' in Britain, but because 'it is oppressive, and yet capable of alleviation'.[18]

John Bright challenged him angrily. He said the charges against mill-owners were 'all calumny', and reminded Ashley of the miserable state of the Dorsetshire peasantry.

Ashley could not defend himself. He had not yet succeeded to the family estates, and did not have the power to interfere with his father's management. He felt it was disrespectful to blame his father in public.

Bright said that when Ashley was: 'surveying the manufacturing districts, he looked through a telescope which magnified all their miseries close to his eye, while when he turned his attention to his own districts he reversed the telescope so as to remove the evils that existed there to the greatest distance, and reduce them to the smallest dimensions'.[19]

Bright also clashed with Ashley over a 'factory cripple' named William Dodd, who had written a lurid book against the factory system. He claimed that Ashley had been given a false idea of mill-owners by Dodd's tales of woe. Ashley defended himself. He had been kind to Dodd, and believed his story, but never made use of any of his statements in his campaigns.

While the Ten Hours debate was ongoing, respected economist Nassau Senior (1790–1864) published his 'Letters on the Factory Acts'. He used a series of calculations to 'prove' that over the course of a working day, it took eleven hours for a mill-owner to cover the cost of his investment, overheads and running costs. Senior believed all the profit was made in the twelfth and final hour of production. Therefore, if the factory day was shortened by an hour, the mill owner's profit would be wiped out. If two hours were knocked off the factory day, he would in effect run at a loss.

This theory caused much heated debate, and was quoted in parliament as an argument against the Ten Hours legislation. But Senior's calculations were disputed by several writers in the newspapers.

In spite of all these arguments, the House of Commons passed the Ten Hours clause. Ashley was jubilant, and all seemed set fair for it to become law. But the government was very unhappy, and dug its heels in. There was absolute bedlam in the House of Commons. The whole debate was reopened, and settled by the intervention of Sir Robert Peel (1788–1850). Peel (the second baronet) was the eldest son of the Sir Robert who pioneered the Health and Morals of Apprentices Act in 1802.

Peel junior formerly supported his father's proposals to limit factory hours, but now the leopard changed its spots. He was convinced that free trade, not legislation, would ultimately lead to better conditions for the working classes.

He pointed out that Ashley's bill effectively limited men's shifts to ten hours, as well as women and children. (Which was precisely what the short time committees were hoping for). Peel calculated that reducing the working week as proposed would wipe out seven weeks' manufacturing time, which would hit Britain's exports.

Peel believed the government knew what was best for workers' welfare, even if it meant going against their wishes. He threatened to bring down the whole administration unless MPs reversed their vote on the ten hours section of the Act. The House of Commons supinely rolled over and 'played dead'. The Ten Hours clause was lost.

The Factory Act which became law on 6 June 1844 was a compromise. The previous Factory Act of 1833 banned children under nine years old from textile factories except silk mills, which had no minimum age limit. To pacify mill-owners, the 1844 Act lowered the age when children could begin work in textile factories from nine to eight years old. This was a retrograde step, but otherwise the Act incorporated several of Leonard Horner's ideas.

The 'superintendents' or sub-inspectors now had powers to enter factories and factory schools. A minimum age of eight was introduced for silk mills at last. (Horner said 'There never were any sound reasons' for treating silk mills as a special case).[20] Women workers were given protection for the first time. Females under twenty-one were now classed as 'young persons' and subject to a maximum twelve-hour day. Teenage boys worked a twelve-hour day until they reached eighteen, when they were classed as adults.

One of the most important innovations of the 1844 Act was Horner's 'half-time' system for children under thirteen. This had a great impact on factory children's lives. They now went to school in the morning or afternoon. The working day for eight- to twelve-year-olds (eight to eleven years in silk mills) was reduced to six and a half hours.

Ashley was disheartened yet undaunted at the loss of his Ten Hours bill for teenagers. He introduced another bill into parliament two years later but was forced to abandon it. He was undergoing a massive crisis of conscience.

Lord Ashley's position as MP for Dorset (an agricultural county) had become increasingly untenable. He was haunted by the great distress amongst workers owing to the high price of bread. He was in a real quandary, because his election by Dorset's farmer voters was on the understanding he would support protectionism. Finally, Ashley decided he could no longer support the Corn Laws. He resigned from parliament in 1846, even though this meant abandoning his Ten Hours bill after years of self-sacrifice to the cause.

Ashley asked John Fielden to baby-sit the bill. It was defeated by just ten votes. The Ten Hours reformers did not have much longer to wait to achieve their objective, however. Their victory was aided by a political earthquake.

In 1846, Cobden and Bright's heroic campaign against the Corn Laws bore fruit and breached the government's defences at last. Sir Robert Peel, a free trader, had secretly wanted to repeal the Corn Laws for some time, but knew his party would never allow it. His hand was forced by the Irish potato famine of the mid-1840s. The rising death toll and horrendous suffering in Ireland meant that Peel could no longer morally justify restricting corn imports. He repealed the hated Corn Laws.

Peel's far-sighted act caused uproar amongst the Tories (many of whom were landowners and farmers) and he resigned, forcing a general election.

When parliament returned, the Ten Hours movement had far more support in the House of Commons. The mighty Peel was safely out of the way. Fielden seized his chance and proposed a Ten Hours bill once more. This time he was successful.

Ironically, Fielden's victory was partially owing to a deep trade slump. Business was very bad. Mills had closed, or switched to short-time working, and were only running for seven hours a day. Opponents of the bill could not argue that reducing shifts to ten hours would adversely affect trade; mill-owners could not afford to keep their mills open that long anyway.

The Ten Hours Act became law in the spring of 1847. Women and all persons under the age of eighteen were limited to a maximum ten-hour day: a fifty-eight hour working week. (Mills closed early on Saturdays). The new Act came into full operation for women and children on 1 May 1848. The short-time committees were overjoyed. They were victorious at last – or so it seemed.

We need to retrace our steps a little in our story. In 1840, Lord Ashley felt that success was imminent for the Ten Hours movement (mistakenly, as we have seen). He felt the cause of the factory children was 'safe in harbour', and was keen to tackle another project very dear to his heart.[21]

Leonard Horner had commented: 'it would not be difficult to draw up a tolerably long list' of occupations in which children were overworked, and where the processes involved were 'extremely prejudicial to health'. Child workers in Nottingham lace-mills worked twenty-hour shifts, and people complained of 'atrocities in coal pits'.

Horner had spoken to an eleven-year-old Lancashire pit boy whose work was to 'drag a basket of coal to which he was yoked, in a place where he could not stand upright, and walking in water above his ankles'.[22] Why weren't these children protected by law?

Ashley wanted to help children like these, too, but first he must win over parliament. The best way forward was to collect such irrefutable evidence that the government would feel morally obliged to act.

In a keynote speech to the House of Commons on 4 August 1840, Ashley asked parliament to investigate the plight of children working in mines and manufactures not covered by the Factory Acts. 'Few persons', he said, had any idea of 'the number and variety of the employments which demand and exhaust the physical energy of young children... the country should know at what a cost its pre-eminence is purchased'.

Ashley cited the factory inspectors' reports as ammunition for his campaign. Children as young as seven worked in tobacco factories for twelve hours per day. In the Potteries, plate-makers' boys worked in 120 degrees (F) of heat. Carpet weavers' assistants at Kidderminster worked for up to eighteen hours at a stretch. Pin-makers' labour was sold by their parents to pay off their own debts: in this 'system of slavery... parents sell the services of their children, even of the tenderest years, for periods of long and most afflicting duration'. Children were deprived 'of all means of education, while their health is undermined, and utterly destroyed'.

Ashley's persistence led to the appointment of the landmark Children's Employment Commission. Its first report into the mines two years later revealed such tales of 'suffering, ignorance and shame' that society demanded action...[23]

Chapter 7

Over-burdened: Life Down The Pit

'Our knees tremble sorely in the stooping –
We fall upon our faces trying to go;
And under our heavy eyelids drooping,
The reddest flower would look as pale as snow.
For all day, we drag our burden tiring,
Through the coal-dark underground...'

(*The Cry of the Children*,
Elizabeth Barrett Browning, 1842).

Down in the darkest depths of the earth, far from the light of the sun, child miners endured long days and nights in desperate toil. Until Lord Ashley hauled the coal industry into the daylight for public inspection, few cared how Britain's miners lived and died.

The rapid changes in technology sweeping through the cotton and iron industries were not mirrored in the smaller coal mines. Working conditions in some areas were almost medieval in their primitiveness. A few improvements had been made: for example, the introduction of the Newcomen engine for pumping water out of the shafts. Railed roads were laid in some mines to make it easier to move coal from the pit shaft to the surface. But the coal had to be pushed, pulled or dragged from the coal face where the miners worked, which was often a considerable distance from the main 'roads' underground.

The height of the coal seams varied according to the area's geology. 'Thin seams' in the West Riding, Lancashire and Shropshire were as narrow as twenty inches high. 'Thick seams' in Durham, Northumberland, Derbyshire, Cumberland, and South Staffordshire ranged from four to six feet high. Mining districts like the West Riding had both thick and thin seams.

The mines of north-east England had the most technologically advanced and efficient haulage methods. These pits had very thick seams and ponies were used to move loaded waggons along tramways.

But in the thin seams of the West Riding of Yorkshire, Lancashire, and the Forest of Dean, haulage methods were simple and brutal. Children were beasts of burden, harnessed by a belt and chain to a heavy wooden tub of coal, which they dragged along on all fours.

Worst of all were the mines in the east of Scotland, where the old-fashioned, oppressive 'bearing system' was still used. Here the miners cut the coal, and their wife and daughters carried it up to the surface on their backs. This grossly inefficient practice (desperately hard work for females) continued long after windlasses and ropes were introduced in other parts of Britain to haul baskets of coal out of the pit.

For centuries, too, Scots miners and their families were owned body and soul by the colliery owners, owing to an archaic law dating back to 1606. If people did any work at all for the coal-master, they became chattels: part and parcel of the coal mine. If the mine was sold, the miners and their bearers (wives and children) were included in the deal. If they tried to escape, they were sent back to the pits.

Strange to relate, this dreadful serfdom did not act an incentive to recruitment, and when demand for coal rose steeply during the Industrial Revolution, Scottish mines did not have enough workers to cope with orders. An Act of 1775 graciously allowed new mine workers in Scotland to be employed as free labourers. However, another quarter of a century passed before all Scots miners and their families were freed from this age-old tyranny.

One of the earliest writers who tried to raise public awareness of the miner's lot was Richard Ayton, who visited a Whitehaven mine in 1813. The William Pitt colliery was a 'showcase' enterprise noted for its modernity.

Six hundred people and more than one hundred ponies worked in the pit, which produced over 486,700 tons of coal per annum. The intrepid explorer, nerves jangling after a perilous descent in a basket hauled by rope into the gloom of the mine, was greatly shocked by colliers' working conditions. The sight of young girls, half naked, covered with dirt, and swearing as they drove pit ponies past him, excited his pity and horror. They were: 'ragged and beastly in their appearance, and with a shameless indecency in their behaviour'.

Ayton was greatly upset by the servitude of the little trappers who opened trap-doors for the ponies to pass through. They were 'compelled to linger through their lives, in silence, solitude, and darkness, for sixpence a day.' When young children first went into the mine, they screamed and struggled with terror from the darkness, but gradually became inured to their 'cruel slavery'.

He claimed sexual goings-on (even incest) were commonplace underground. Children grew up without morals or shame. Ayton made a heartfelt plea to government, not only to ban women and children from the mines, but also to protect children from their parents' avarice. 'These dismal dungeons are certainly not fit places for women and children…' It was against the law to for a man to starve his child or flog it to death, but perfectly legal for him to condemn it to 'loathsome and unhealthy work.'[1]

The general public's ignorance about miners was as dark and deep as a mine-shaft. Colliers were thought of as lawless, vicious, uncivilised wretches. 'Respectable' folk did not venture near mining communities. Some people seriously believed miners and their families lived out their lives permanently underground and only rarely visited the surface. Miners were out of sight and out of mind.

The dangers of pit work were well known to the colliers, but scarcely heard of outside the mining villages. Accidents were so commonplace, the local press rarely bothered to report them. Deaths were just part of everyday life.

Explosive gases were amongst the biggest killers in the mining industry. 'Fire-damp', common in many pits, was a volatile mixture of methane and other gases. It was highly combustible. 'Choke-damp', composed of nitrogen, carbon dioxide and other gases, often appeared in the aftermath of an underground explosion. It was heavier than air, and smothered the miners. 'Black-damp' or carbon monoxide was another toxic gas: once the miners were overpowered by its effects, they were unlikely ever to wake again.

Gas was a particular scourge of the north-east pits. A spate of horrific accidents occurred in the Durham and Northumberland mining districts between 1794 and 1815. Thirty-three men and boys perished at Hepburn in 1805. In May 1812, a terrific explosion at the Brandling Main pit at Felling killed ninety-seven of the 127 miners employed there; three of those rescued died shortly afterwards from their injuries. Another explosion in October the same year killed twenty boys and four men at Harrington Mill pit, near Sunderland. Felling was the scene of another tragedy on Christmas Eve, 1813, when twenty-three men and boys, and twelve pit-ponies died.

Water was another underground foe. An immense flood in the mine workings at Heaton Main colliery, Newcastle, on 3 May 1815 ended the lives of seventy-five men and boys, and all the pit-ponies. When water from some old workings burst through into the pit, the men near the entrance ran for their lives, and sounded the alarm. The mine's lower workings were flooded to a depth of thirty-three fathoms (just over sixty metres). The miners were trapped in a higher part of the seam, unable to reach the main shaft. One of the families involved lived at nearby Byker. It lost three members in the disaster: John Thew and his sons George (twenty) and William (seventeen). Another son, John, escaped when the alarm was first raised.

The doomed men and lads survived for a short while after the deluge. They had plenty of water, but little food, and were forced to kill and eat one of the ponies. Local miners on the surface made frantic efforts to dig fresh shafts, and pump out the water in the flooded shaft, but they were too late to rescue the men. The miners' air gradually ran out…

Several months passed before the bodies were recovered. Elizabeth Thew, wife of John senior, instantly recognised her son William by his red hair. He was a great favourite with his mother, and would say to her: 'Mother, when I am a man I'll work hard for you, and keep you like a lady.' William and John junior were regular scholars at Byker Sunday School; the older boy learned to write in evening class. When William's body was recovered, a precious relic was discovered in one of his pockets: a tin candle-box.

William had painstakingly engraved a message on the box using a nail: 'Fret not, dear mother, for we were singing while we had time, and praising God. Mother, follow God more than ever I did.' On the other side of the tin, William carved a letter from his father (who was illiterate): 'If Johnny [William's brother] is saved, be a good lad to God, and thy mother. John Thew.'[2]

William's wish to look after his mother came true in an eerie kind of way. The story of William and his little tin box was used by well-wishers to raise much-needed funds for Mrs Thew and her remaining children. But it was not enough for the family to live on, and three years after the Heaton Main accident, Mrs Thew lost another son down the pit.

The dreadful loss of life in gas explosions, which were often ignited by miners' candles, inspired engineers Sir Humphry Davy and George Stephenson to help the workers. Both men independently invented a safety lamp in 1815.

Unfortunately, safety lamps were not always reliable. They required very careful handling by the miners. The lamps were fragile, and if damaged, were as lethal as a candle if gas was present. Many miners preferred the clear glow of candle-light, because safety lamps gave only a gloomy illumination.

A great disaster was caused at Row Pit, Harraton Colliery on 30 June 1817 by the reckless stupidity of one John Moody. He refused to use a Davy lamp, and insisted on using a candle. His workmates twice snuffed out his candle, but Moody obstinately unscrewed a Davy lamp to re-light his wick. The immensely violent explosion which followed blew miners right up the main shaft (146 metres deep) and out onto the surface. The Hills family lost ten members in this accident: a grandfather, his two sons, and seven grandsons.

One of the bodies recovered from Row Pit was a young boy on his first visit to the mine. His father was holding his hand so he could become accustomed to the strange, dark world underground, when the explosion occurred. The boy's father survived; a niche in the rock somehow protected him from the blast.

The 1819 select committee report on children's factory labour mentioned colliery children. Boys at the Dunkirk colliery in Lancashire worked from six or seven in the morning until five in the afternoon. At Worsley and St Helens,

'Girls work in the same way as boys, having only a thin covering and a small petticoat, the boys only with their trowsers [sic]'.[3] Boys aged eight and older toiled underground for eleven hours a day alongside the men at Dukinfield; the surface workers did shifts of up to thirteen hours. Staffordshire and Warwickshire pit boys were roughly the same age as Lancashire lads. But no-one in government took much interest in child miners for over a decade.

Tyne and Wear pitmen tried to improve the terrible conditions they endured with their sons. They petitioned parliament in 1825 and 1831. They told of their dangerous, harsh working lives, with no security of employment. The long hours that pit boys spent underground led: 'to the destruction of health, and of almost every chance of education and moral improvement.'[4] The boys' contracts were for a fourteen-hour day, but it took a long time to travel to and from the coal face. They were away from home for up to seventeen hours.

When the north-east miners' contracts with the owners expired, they refused to accept new ones unless the masters agreed to shorter hours for the boys. The miners wanted a fairer wage, and a more accurate way of assessing the coal they wrought. (Canny masters used lots of different tricks to under-estimate the amount of coal the men dug out, to reduce their wages). The colliers wanted an end to the truck system, in which they were forced to spend their wages in the master's own 'truck' store or 'tommy-shop'.

The masters agreed to limit the boys' labour to twelve hours a day, but relations were still strained; the men went on strike in 1831 and 1832. Parliament was unmoved by the men's petition. The issue of children's labour underground slumbered once more until the 1833 Factory Commission, when E.C. Tufnell boldly ventured into a Lancashire pit.

Tufnell interviewed Thomas Gibson and George Bryan, who had worked in the Worsley coal mines since they were little boys. Gibson and Bryan said when they first entered the mine there were 100 girls and boys at work. The children earned just three or four pence per day for working up to thirteen hours. They had little to eat during their shift, perhaps a bit of bread and cheese.

The mother of one of the witnesses was a poor widow, and 'over-burdened… she had nothing to give me'. The lad sometimes went hungry all day. If there was 'foul air' in the pit, and he tried to eat something, he was sick. One of the coal seams was only two feet high; the children's backs were cut and bruised from rubbing against the ceiling. Both witnesses hinted at the colliers' lack of morals condemned by Richard Ayton a decade earlier. They said the boys and girls were sometimes 'very loving with one another…there are many bastards'.

Another miner, William Bradshaw (seventeen), said he began work at the New Engine pit, Walkden Moor, when he was eight years old. He dragged tubs of coal on his hands and knees using a belt and chain. The belt, fastened around his waist, was linked to the basket with a chain. Each load weighed four hundredweight. This was called 'hurrying' or 'putting'. Smaller children worked two to a tub, pulling and 'thrutching' (pushing) the load along. They became almost bald from pushing against the tub with their heads. The children worked half-naked; both boys and girls wore trousers. Some children worked barefoot, and others wore clogs.

Beatings and 'purring' (being kicked) were common. If the children didn't do their work properly, the collier they worked for hit them or beat them with a pick-handle.

After talking to the lads, Mr Tufnell decided to see the Worsley pit for himself. In order to reach the coal face, he was first lowered down by bucket. After a journey by boat along the 'navigable level' (canal) which ran through the workings, Tufnell landed safely. He clambered through a small tunnel into a seam only three or four feet high, where he found it 'impossible' to stand upright.

After another boat trip, he arrived at the 'best and largest' seam in the district where coal was being hewn out. This hole was about eighteen feet square, but Tufnell could only stand tall in the centre of the excavation. The miners worked bent double; water dripped constantly from the ceiling. A shocked Tufnell declared: 'the hardest labour in the worst room in the worst-conducted factory is less hard, less cruel, and less demoralising than the labour in the best of coal mines'.[5]

At this time, however, reformers focussed on limiting children's hours in the mills. The colliery children's plight was left in the shadows until 1840, when Leonard Horner re-ignited the issue in his book *On the Employment of Children*. Horner's book included a reprint of Tufnell's report. And when Lord Ashley asked for a Children's Employment Commission into other trades and industries, he repeated some of Tufnell's evidence in his speech to MPs, hoping they would sit up and take notice.

The 1840 commission explored children's work in mines first. The four main commissioners were Dr Thomas Southwood Smith, Thomas Tooke, and factory inspectors Leonard Horner and Robert John Saunders. A dauntingly large area of Britain required investigation, so over twenty sub-commissioners were appointed and sent to the mining districts with orders to report on 'infant labour' there. In 1841, the enquiry was extended to young persons (age thirteen to eighteen).

While the commission's report was being prepared for publication, Southwood Smith suggested it should be illustrated. He felt that life underground was far removed from common experience, and the report included a fair amount of technical information. MPs might just give a cursory glance, if they read it at all.

Illustrations would help MPs grasp the report's main features in an instant. This was the first time that drawings like these were used in an official document.

The *Report on Mines* was published in 1842. The plain, brutal facts uncovered by the commission still make shocking reading today. As Harriet Martineau commented, the 'suffering and brutalization' of young mine workers 'exceeded all that had ever been known, or could be believed'.[6]

We do not know precisely how many children worked underground. Not all colliery owners co-operated with the investigation. The commission only established the proportion of children and young people to adults, which varied according to the district. Over one-third of the workforce was under eighteen in the Durham, Northumberland, Glamorgan and Derbyshire mines. Fewer than one-third of the workers were under eighteen in west Scotland and Midlothian.

The age when children first entered the pit depended on the thickness of the coal seams, family poverty, and local custom. Children as young as four were recorded, but on average, girls and boys went underground when they were eight or nine years old.

Now the pit owners, when asked the ages of children in their mines, uniformly over-estimated them. If investigators had relied purely on the owners' evidence, they would never have discovered the truth, because the coal masters 'seldom or never' entered the pits. In the West Riding of Yorkshire, masters stoutly declared they had no child workers younger than ten or eleven, but the commission found 'overwhelming' evidence they regularly worked 'at the ages of five, six or seven'.[7]

As in Richard Ayton's day, children started out as 'trappers', for which they earned a few pence. These small workers went underground when the pit opened in the morning and stayed until work finished for the day. Their job was very important. They opened and closed the 'trap-doors' which regulated the air flow through the pit.

The mine needed good through ventilation to give the miners air to breathe and prevent the build-up of deadly gases. If a trap-door was propped open, for example, when it was supposed to be closed, the current of air circulating through the pit was interrupted.

The trappers sat alone for hours in the dark, unless they had a candle, or another miner passed by with a waggon. Six-year-old Susan Reece, a trapper in a South Wales pit, said she 'didn't much like the work'.[8] In the South Durham pits, 135 of the 235 trappers were under ten years old.

John Saville (seven) worked at the Soap Pit, Sheffield: 'I stand and open and shut the door; I'm generally in the dark, and sit me down against the door; I stop twelve hours in the pit; I never see daylight, except on Sundays. I fell asleep one day, and a corve [coal-tub] ran over my leg and made it smart'.[9]

When children were a little older they began moving the coal for the 'getter' or 'hewer' from the coal face to the bottom of the shaft. In places where the seams or 'roads' were over four feet high, coal-waggons were hauled by ponies or donkeys led by boys. This was much easier work for the children than dragging along tubs or baskets of coal by muscle power as in the thin seams.

Children normally worked for a family member (typically their father or maybe an uncle), unless they were apprentices. In the poorest districts some children were hired by workers and paid by them. Others worked directly for the pit-owners, or contractors in the mine.

The youngest children of all were found in the South Wales pits. The valleys were the heart of a great coal-mining and iron-working district, with miners' and iron-workers' homes huddled together near the pits. The sub-commissioners for Wales took the trouble to learn Welsh so that they could speak directly to the miners and children without an interpreter.

South Wales miners carried tiny children down into the pit on their backs, even if they were still 'in petticoats'. The pit owner gave them an extra cart (a 'tram' or 'dram') of coal for their own use for every helper they took underground.

William Richards (age seven and a half) began working at Buttery Hatch colliery in Monmouth when he was four years old. He said: 'I been [sic] down about three years. When I first went down I couldn't keep my eyes open. I don't fall asleep now; I smokes [sic] my pipe'. This 'intelligent and good-humoured… little fellow' wore a cap 'furnished with the usual collier candlestick', and a tobacco pipe stuck inside his buttonhole.[10]

Thin seams could only be worked by children. Like the Lancashire boys Mr Tufnell interviewed a decade before, they dragged or pushed tubs of coal using a girdle or belt and chain. The children paid for the harness out of their wages. (Miners paid for all the tools, candles, gunpowder etc that they used). The belt and chain was used in the West Riding, Lancashire, and Derbyshire and North Wales. The belt blistered and cut the children's skin, and their bodies became stunted from prolonged stooping.

Children started work in North Wales pits when they were about seven years old; it was rare for five- or six-year-olds to go down. Several boys admitted they were very frightened when they first went underground, but they soon got used to it. They were encouraged by their parents, who wanted their wages: 'no sooner is a collier's son able to exert a little muscular force than he becomes an underground machine, destitute of the slightest mental cultivation'. Investigator H. H. Jones, who interviewed the children, found their condition 'pitiable' and 'grievous': 'The air they breathe is full of dust and noxious gases, and dangers surround them on all sides'.[11]

Was it really necessary to use young children? In Ireland, it was extremely rare for tiny children to work underground, although a few young boys worked as trappers. Most youngsters in the Irish pits were teenagers. They loaded waggons with coal and pushed them along rails to the foot of the shaft.

Why didn't the mine-owners dig out the thin seams so there was enough space for ponies to be used, or for the children to stand upright? The sad truth was there was no profit in making the seam higher: 'the expense would be more than twice over what the coal was worth… if the coals could only be got in that way, they would never be got at all…'.[12]

In the Forest of Dean, where young workers were called 'hod-boys', one master admitted there was no necessity for them to crawl along in two-foot six-inch seams. There was 'soft stuff' above the coal, which could be easily excavated to give the boys more head room. But the owners did not want to reduce their profits. The commission concluded thin seams could never be worked: 'without inflicting great and irreparable injury to the health of the children'.[13] However, despite this finding, pit-owners were allowed to use boys in thin seams for many years after the 1842 report.

Accidents were inevitable when very young children were given responsible jobs such as 'trapping'. An explosion at the Jarrow pit in January 1826 was allegedly caused by eight-year-old Norman, a trapper who left a ventilation door open. At Bigge Pit, Willington in 1841, nine-year-old Richard Cooper left his trap-door unmanned to play with two other children. The explosion which followed killed over thirty people, including four little boys. The following year, another trapper who left his post caused an accident at Thornley pit.

Young boys were employed as 'engineers' or 'enginemen' in Derbyshire, Lancashire and some Yorkshire pits. Boys earned about 7s per week from the age of twelve for this vital job. The engineers controlled the engine which wound parties of workers up and down the mineshaft. A moment's inattention was fatal. If they did not stop the basket or tub carrying passengers at exactly the right moment, the tub continued up and over the overhead pulley, injuring the workers or dashing them into the mineshaft below.

Children loomed large in the accident statistics. Of the 349 people who died in English collieries in 1838, fifty-eight were below the age of thirteen, and sixty-two were aged thirteen to eighteen. Over one-third of the fatalities were under eighteen.[14] (No reliable statistics are available for fatalities in Scotland and Wales during this period).

Parish apprentices were also sent down the mines. An investigator called the practice: 'a slavery… as reprehensible as ever was the slavery of the West Indies, which justice and humanity alike demand should not longer be endured'.

Apprentices were found in south Staffordshire, Lancashire and Yorkshire, and west Scotland pits. As was the custom, they received no wages, just their food and clothing, and were bound until they were twenty-one. The apprentices worked for years 'solely for the benefit' of their masters. They toiled away next to the 'free' children in the mine, who were well paid: a fourteen-year-old at Bilston earned 14s per week. The apprentices learnt no useful skills, just 'a little dexterity'.

At Bilston in Staffordshire, over 200 apprentices were used as cheap labour. One miner had more than forty apprentices over a twenty-five-year period. The apprentices were made to hew coal in unsafe parts of the mines 'where other men will not let their own children go'.

When Thomas Rayner, a surgeon at Birstall (in the West Riding) began serving as a Poor Law Guardian at the Dewsbury Union workhouse, he was amazed to find that local colliers could pick and choose child apprentices. They took them from the workhouse regardless of age or size. If a child was younger than nine, the guardians did not ask for formal indentures, since they were not supposed to bind them at such an early age. Rayner kicked up a fuss, but the other guardians did not like 'to be interfered with'.

One five-year-old child, Thomas Townsend, was taken by a collier to work as a hurrier. He was rescued and returned to the workhouse when his grandfather and other relatives complained, and threatened to tell the Poor Law Board he was under age.

Halifax apprentice boy Thomas Moorhouse was badly beaten with a miner's pick by his master. He was half-starved, and resorted to eating old candle ends left in the workings. Thomas ran away and found a new master, who looked after him kindly and kept him in 'victuals and drink'.[15]

Free labour children were ill-treated, too. In a Halifax mine, one of the sub-commissioners found eleven-year-old Harriet Craven 'crying very bitterly' because the 'getter' (collier) had beaten her.[16] She wanted to go home, but she had not 'hurried' enough coal for her master. Beatings were by no means universal, however. Some pit owners and overlookers refused to allow any corporal punishment.

Child colliers did not have any regular holidays except Christmas Day, Good Friday, and perhaps Whit Monday. Depending on the pit, they had one day off a week or once a fortnight, usually the day after payday. Yorkshire children played football and cricket on waste ground near the pits on their day off. If they were very tired, they spent the day in bed.

Workers' health was dependent on the state of the mine. Heart and lung diseases were common from overwork and bad air. Some pits were warm and dry; others were wringing wet, and the children got soaked. Many miners were too old and worn out for underground work by the time they were forty.

The back-breaking work in backward and badly-run mines made adults and children complain of incessant, painful fatigue. In the most modern and best-regulated mines, however, where older and bigger children were employed, they were not excessively over-tired at the end of the day.

The commissioners were surprised by the 'strong' and 'robust' appearance of some children such as the hod-boys of the Forest of Dean, even though they worked in thin seams. They looked healthier than children in other occupations. This was because there were some advantages to being a collier child. They earned a good wage, so their parents could afford to give them a good diet and keep them well clothed.

As always, this depended on the family home. John Harvey (thirteen), a carter boy at the Crown Pit in south Gloucestershire, was never given enough to eat by his parents. He was dressed in rags, and 'never had a pair of shoes or stockings in his life'. John had a 'drunken father and improvident mother' who spent all his wages of three shillings a week.[17]

Women and children worked above ground at the pit brow as well as underground. They emptied coal out of tubs, and sorted the coal. Surface work was dangerous, too. Children were frequently killed or injured. They were run over by heavy coal waggons, or fell down the pit shaft, which was rarely fenced off securely.

Older children also helped out as surface workers at lead and copper mines. They washed, broke up and sorted the ore. It was rare for small children to work underground in metal mines, as it was so difficult to extract the metal from the rock. In the Cornish tin mines, most child workers were over the age of ten, but young children were found working below ground in the ironstone mines of the Forest of Dean and Glamorganshire.

The Victorian public was greatly shocked by the number of women and girls working underground, although they were only found in particular districts. In the Durham and Northumberland pits, females had not worked below ground since about 1780. Colliers in Oldham were dead against female labour, even though other Lancashire pits used it. No women or girls worked underground in south Staffordshire, the Potteries, Derbyshire, North Wales, or Ireland.

Females worked below ground in the West Riding, Lancashire, South Wales and east Scotland. As noted earlier, the women of east Scotland endured: 'barbarous and cruel slavery'.[18] Women and girls of all ages carried the coal on their backs to the surface via a succession of steep, rickety ladders or spiral stairways. Boys only rarely did the heavy labour of shifting coal from the face to the shaft, then up to the surface. Some fathers ruptured themselves as they strained to lift a load onto their daughter's back.

These pits had an exceptionally high proportion of children and teenagers (mostly girls) to adults. Jane Peacock was five years old when she started work at the Preston Links colliery near Tranent. Coal-putters David Neil and William Kerr began work when they were just six years old. Janet Cummings (eleven) had: 'no liking for the work. Father makes me like it'.

Margaret Leveston (six) carried loads of coal of fifty-six pounds in weight in a basket on her back. The basket or 'creel' was supported by a strap across the forehead. If this broke under the weight of coal, the girls below might be knocked off their ladders and hurt. Margaret, 'a most interesting child, and perfectly beautiful', made ten to fourteen 'rakes' [journeys] every day. 'The work is na guid; it is so very sair [sore]', she said. A 'rake' for one little girl was a distance greater than the height of St Paul's Cathedral in London, and she made this slow, laborious journey several times a day.

In east Scotland, children learned to hew coal when they were only nine or ten years old, whereas in Lancashire pits, few boys under eighteen hewed coal, as it was considered extremely skilled work. James Neil (ten) said that he first began hewing 'eighteen months' ago. His labour was 'gai [very] sore. Place of work is not very dry. I work from four and five in the morning till six or seven at night, and it fatigues me much'.[19]

In the west of Scotland, very few women and girls worked in the pits, but restrictive practices by the miners encouraged the use of child labour. These miners were limited to a 'darg' (day's work) of up to four shillings' worth of coal. If they took their sons down with them as helpers, they finished their 'darg' more quickly.

When a child reached the age of ten, he was considered a 'quarter man' and his father was allowed to mine an extra shillings' worth of coal. When he was about sixteen, the lad counted as a 'three-quarter man' and was allowed to hew coal for himself.[20] As in Lancashire and Cheshire, the children pushed and pulled loaded waggons (one child in front, one behind) too, but railed roads made their work easier. The waggons carried from 2½ cwt. to 11 cwt of coal, depending on the mine.(1 cwt = 112lb or 50.8kg).

The biggest sensation was caused by the report's damning allegations of the 'demoralizing' (immoral) influence of pit life on girls and women. The West Riding mines were supposedly a hotbed of vice. Witnesses claimed that sexual intercourse was commonplace underground. John Simpkin, a Drighlington collier, said: 'I have had children by them myself, and frequently had connexion' with girls in the pits'. Thomas Bedford, who worked in the same area of Leeds, said: 'lasses... are exposed to bad things in the pit.'[21]

Girls did not grow up with the skills to be good wives and mothers. Barnsley collier Matthew Lindley thought women and children should be banned from the pits: 'the girls are worse than the men in point of morals, and use far more indecent language… there is not one in ten of them that knows how to cut out a shirt and make one, and they learn neither to knit nor sew.'[22]

Following the report's publication, Lord Ashley demanded sweeping reforms. He had read the report with a mixture of 'shame, terror, and indignation'.[23] Ashley's task was made easier than in the case of factory children because the publicity surrounding the report generated a terrific head of moral steam.

Paradoxically, the successful passage of the first Mines Act through parliament was probably more owing to the report's suggestions of great promiscuity underground, than women and children's terrible working conditions.

The report's graphic illustrations of children on all fours hauling heavy weights in narrow tunnels certainly aroused great pity. However, the pictures of colliers working naked or semi-naked, and partially-clad boys and girls caused a media frenzy and were reproduced many times. As Harriet Martineau dramatically put it, child miners lived: 'in an atmosphere of filth and profligacy which could hardly leave a thought or feeling untainted by vice'.[24]

A careful reading of the report suggests that complete nudity was not that common. It was more prevalent amongst adults toiling away in the hottest part of the mine. It was far safer for workers to wear some kind of clothing: boots were essential kit.

On 7 June 1842, Ashley introduced his mines reform bill. He wanted all females, all boys under thirteen years old, and parish apprentices banned from the pits. A minimum age of twenty-one was set for enginemen. The bill passed the House of Commons successfully, and in the committee stages, a clause was added allowing statutory inspection of the mines. Ashley admitted it might be difficult or even dangerous for an inspector to poke his nose underground: 'I for one should be very loth [sic] to go down the shafts to do something which might be distasteful to the colliers below'.[25]

When the bill reached the House of Lords, Ashley's idealistic plans hit bedrock. It was the bill that nobody wanted. The House of Lords was packed with coal-owners. These aristocrats had no need to defer to public opinion. Ashley had real trouble finding anyone who would sponsor the bill. Eventually, Lord Devon took it on.

The bill's biggest opponent was major colliery owner Lord Londonderry. He mobilised other colliery masters and flooded parliament with petitions condemning Ashley's bill.

Londonderry sank his teeth into the commission's evidence like a pit bull terrier and tore it to shreds. He dismissed the graphic illustrations in the report as 'disgusting pictorial woodcuts' and deplored the bill's 'supposed necessity'. If boys under thirteen were banned underground there would be no 'nursery for pitmen'. Coal production could be halted in some areas. Females did not work in Durham and Northumberland pits, where Londonderry's mining interests were situated, but he saw no reason why they should not work in other mines. He objected to the idea of inspection underground. An inspector would be a 'perfect pest' and play havoc with discipline.

Londonderry made a threatening speech: 'As a coal-owner, I should say to any inspector, "You may go down the pit how you can, and when you are down you can remain there, or get up as you can"'.[26]

This snide comment raised hackles amongst the Lords, and they made sure an inspector had the requisite powers to enter a mine. But the inspection clause was amended so it became almost useless. An inspector could only monitor the condition of workers, not mine safety. Furthermore, just one inspector of mines was appointed for the whole of the UK.

When the Mines Reform Act finally passed the House of Lords in July 1842, it was greatly battered by its opponents. Women and girls were banned from the pits, but the minimum age for pit boys was lowered to ten. Lads could work as enginemen as young as fifteen. Working hours were left untouched, even though children toiled far longer than in cotton factories. Parish boys could be apprenticed to coal-miners from age ten, but their indentures must terminate at eighteen, not twenty-one.

The Act did some good in the ensuing months. Now that very young children were no longer allowed to work as trappers, accidents owing to problems with ventilation fell sharply in pits in north-east England.

However, the new law was difficult to enforce. Some women could not afford to lose their jobs in the pit and went down anyway. Boys under ten were found below ground over ten years after the Mines Act. The most persistent offenders were mine-owners in South Wales, Staffordshire, and Yorkshire. Managers refused to stop the practice when challenged because other pits allowed it. After a couple of prosecutions for under-age working failed in the courts, pit managers knew they could flout the law with impunity.

Mines inspection was somewhat improved by an Act of 1850 which permitted inspectors to report accidents and 'make inquiry into' the state of mine workings, equipment and ventilation.

By the mid-1850s, the number of mining inspectors was increased to six, but they encountered huge logistical problems. It was virtually impossible for such a small number of men to visit every pit. Many miners never saw an inspector. And the miners were greatly unimpressed by the inspectors' habit of letting the pit-owners know of their visits in advance, so the masters had time to 'tidy up' potential problems before inspection.

Major accidents from gas explosions continued to reap a fearful harvest. The tragedy at the Victoria Colliery at Nithshill, near Paisley was just one of several mining disasters during the year of the Great Exhibition.

Sixty-three men and boys were in the Free-Trade pit in March 1851 when a massive fire-damp explosion erupted: 'The scene in the vicinity of the pit ...was most distressing. A large crowd of female relatives of those burned alive in the pit were crying bitterly, and waiting with anxious solicitude to learn something of the fate of those who were near and dear to them. One woman had four sons as well as her husband in the pit. The shock of the blast was felt by the colliers connected with some neighbouring pits, and they were so much alarmed that they refused to go to their workings.'[27]

All but two of the miners died. The funeral procession was so large that the wall of the parish church was partly demolished to allow all the hearses into the churchyard.

Economies by pit-owners played a part in some tragedies. Many pits had two shafts down to the seam, which made it easier to ventilate the mine. It was cheaper, however, to excavate only one entrance to the mine workings. If the shaft became blocked for some reason, the miners had no way out. This deadly peril was well-known to pitmen.

The dangers of a single shaft became a matter of public notoriety following a catastrophe in the New Hartley pit, Northumberland. On 16 January 1862, a large section of the pit's beam engine fractured in two. Over twenty tons of cast iron fell into the pit shaft and blocked the only route in or out of the mine. Two hundred and four miners, including fifty boys, were trapped at the bottom of the pit.

For days, the local pitmen dug like furies in treacherous conditions to rescue the entombed miners. When they finally reached the trapped men, it was too late. The miners were overcome by gas about thirty-six hours after the accident. Fathers, brothers, and sons were found huddled together in little groups; one man was discovered: 'with his little boy's arms clasped about his neck'.[28] One poor woman lost six sons and her husband.

Over twenty other mines in north-east England had single-shaft entrances at the time of this disaster. Three years later, an Act of Parliament required mines employing twenty persons or more to have two entry shafts so a similar accident could not happen again.

Safety improved as technological advances were made, but industry's demand for coal was insatiable, and deeper and deeper shafts were sunk. During the last few decades of the nineteenth century and the beginning of the twentieth century, on average 1,000 miners died in mine accidents annually.[29] According to one estimate, a miner was killed every six hours underground.

So long as young lads were allowed to work in the pits, they faced the same dangers as men. The age when they were allowed underground was raised to twelve in 1861. Boys aged ten to twelve could work if they produced a school certificate showing they could read and write. Boys under twelve were not banned until 1872, but even then, pits with thin seams were exempted. Pit owners insisted boys were indispensable: it cost too much money to excavate a bigger seam.

Early in the twentieth century, over six decades after Ashley's 'Report on Mines', boys wearing harnesses could still be found dragging sledges of coal like pit-ponies in the thin seams of the Forest of Dean. It was as if time had stood still underground.

Chapter 8

The Devil's Nursery

The 1842 Mines Report was followed by another vast survey into the 'great fields of infant labour'.[1] The Children's Employment Commission discovered that the child workers of Britain's potteries worked shifts up to sixteen hours long.

The Staffordshire potteries were world famous. Its artisans transformed different coloured clays into beautiful china, porcelain, bricks, and drainpipes.

In the early eighteenth century, only very coarse earthenware was made in England. Cheap crockery was imported from Delft in Holland, and fine porcelain from China.

Earthenware manufacture in Staffordshire was confined to a few scattered hamlets. Burslem was renowned for its coarse porous pots called 'butter-ware', which helped keep butter cool and fresh. The pots were glazed with salt. In 1700, the town had twenty-two glazing ovens.

Josiah Wedgwood (1730–95) brought fame to the Staffordshire potteries. He was the son of a poor Burslem potter, who barely scraped a living. Wedgwood's father died when Josiah was just eleven years old. He began his working life 'throwing' pots for his brother. Wedgwood was forced to give up working a potter's wheel when a childhood illness affected his left leg so badly that he had to have it amputated. After some unsuccessful partnerships, he went into business on his own.

Josiah experimented with different glazes, and revolutionised the manufacture of earthenware. In 1763 Wedgwood introduced a hard-wearing, beautiful 'cream-ware' which made him famous. Queen Charlotte was so impressed by its beauty, she commanded it to be called 'Queen's Ware', and made Wedgwood 'Her Majesty's Potter'.[2]

A contemporary of Wedgwood, Mr Cooksworthy of Plymouth, discovered (circa 1777) that Cornish clay could be used as an ingredient to make high quality porcelain equal to the fine wares of Sèvres and Dresden. As a result, porcelain factories grew up in Staffordshire, Derby, Worcester, and near Rotherham.

Wedgwood's works at Burslem, and later at Etruria (1769) were among the wonders of the age. However, the Etruria works relied heavily on child labour, and Wedgwood's second son, another Josiah, gave evidence to Sir Robert Peel's 1816 select committee. Most child workers at Etruria were over ten years old:

103 children were aged ten to eighteen, and just thirteen were under the age of ten. More boys were employed than girls.

Wedgwood said his works were generally a 'very healthy' place, although he admitted one part of the process was 'unwholesome': dipping the pots in white lead glaze.

The children worked up to thirteen hours in one stretch when the men worked overtime. Wedgwood said the men decided how long they worked: 'I have nothing to do with that'. So, the children's long hours were down to the workmen's avarice? 'I should be loth [sic] to apply the term avarice… it is the desire of the workman to get more wages, that induces him to work extraordinary hours'.[3] In many cases, children worked for their fathers.

Journeymen potters learnt the trade by serving a seven years' apprenticeship from the age of thirteen or fourteen. Younger children helped carry moulds and do other odd jobs for the potters. The men were paid by piecework, and they paid the children out of their own wages. The children gave their money to their parents.

The nearby Methodist chapel had a Sunday school with 200 scholars. Most children could read, but fewer knew how to write. Wedgwood built a day school with enough room for fifty children, who paid a small fee to attend.

Wedgwood did not believe that the government should interfere with children's working hours. The factory would not be able to complete rush orders quickly if a time limit was set, and workers would object to losing money, so 'we had better be let alone.'[4]

By the 1830s, the population of the Potteries had grown to around 60,000 people. This formerly 'bleak and barren' district had been transformed into towns with 'spacious and well-built streets' with 'elegant villas'. The Potteries now held an 'enviable rank…in the commercial world of two Continents'. Canals went right past the doors of its 'numerous and extensive manufactories' so boats could convey their wonderful wares across Britain.[5]

In Staffordshire, pottery-making was concentrated in the 'six towns' of Stoke, Hanley, Burslem, Felton, Longton and Tunstall (Stoke-on-Trent) and other nearby towns. There were also potteries in Derbyshire (such as the Denby works), the West Riding of Yorkshire, Tyneside, Bristol, and Scotland. These only employed a few hundred children and young people in total. The 1840s commission felt that the porcelain factory at Worcester looked after its child workers well.

Samuel Swain Scriven investigated the Staffordshire potteries. The seventy-nine firms which sent returns to the Commission employed 12,407 people, of whom 1500 were under thirteen, and 3,715 aged between thirteen and twenty-one.[6] (The 1841 census gave a larger and hopefully more accurate picture. More than 15,000 people worked in the Staffordshire potteries; over 5,600 were under the age of twenty).[7]

The most recently built workplaces were 'on a scale of great magnitude… some possess considerable beauty'. They were well-ventilated, light, and 'airy'. Older buildings were far more numerous and varied greatly in size: some housed 800 people, others about fifty. Scriven said: 'they are, with very exceptions, low, damp, close, small, dark, hot, dirty, ill-ventilated and unwholesome.'[8] The workshops where Egyptian ware was made were the dirtiest. The privies were revoltingly filthy and there was a total lack of privacy.

Several thousand young people (aged thirteen to twenty-one) were apprentices. Very few young people were legally bound; their parents could not afford to pay the £1 premium for indentures. Scriven felt both master and servant were losers on this account. Boys knew they did not have to serve out their time. They left when they had only half-learnt the trade, and took work at reduced rates. This increased competition for jobs, and depressed wages.

Manufacturer George Philips employed over four hundred workers. He thought that if the children were properly apprenticed: 'they would look up to their masters, and be more disposed to follow good examples'. The masters in their turn would take more interest in the children, and make them better members of society.

Philips believed that the boys' wages should not be given to them directly: 'Lads of fourteen and upwards… get from 7s to 8s per week, and being masters of such amounts before they know the real value of money, often squander it away at the ale-houses'.[9] Many youngsters left home early, moved into lodging-houses, and mixed with very bad company.

Children did many different jobs in the potteries. They worked as 'jiggers', 'mould-runners', oven-boys, 'dipper's boys', apprentice painters and figure-makers. On average they earned about 2s per week. Adults earned good wages: from 9s to £3 per week. A family with two or more children who worked together had the potential to earn £3 to £4 per week. Working in the potteries 'saved' children from going down the mines at an early age; it was rare for boys to go underground until they were at least thirteen.

The jiggers and mould-runners helped the dish, plate and saucer-makers, and they worked extremely hard in ferociously high temperatures. The jigger turned the potter's wheel. The mould-runners carried pots to and from the stoves, in and out, on their feet all day. Sometimes boys did both jobs. They worked in temperatures of 100–130°F. Each day, the boys carried up to 3,840 lbs of pots and walked over seven miles.

Children regularly worked for fifteen hours a day or more because potters clung to the old ways of time management. They drank from noon on Saturday until Tuesday or Wednesday morning (they must have had strong stomachs). After their drinking session, they needed to earn enough for the next week. For the remaining weekdays they kept the children at work from half past five in the morning until nine or ten at night. The boys, in particular the mould-runners, wilted under these oppressive hours. 'Without almost a single exception' they were 'pale, thin, stunted in growth, weak and unhealthy...great numbers of them die from atrophy and consumption'.[10]

Twelve-year-old Sampson Beard worked at Thomas Godwin's earthenware factory at Burslem. He was a mould-runner for William Machin: 'I first came to work at five years old'.[11] It was rare for children to begin work as young as Sampson; age seven or eight was more common. In the Scottish, Bristol, and Derbyshire potteries, ten was the usual age for starting work.

The youngest children worked in the 'dipping' and 'scouring' departments and helped the plate, saucer, and dish-makers. The men and boy helpers in the dipping and scouring rooms faced an insidious danger. The boys cleaned and brushed the pots, then took them to the men, who dipped them in a glaze and gave them back to the boys for shelving and drying. After the glaze had dried, the children moved the pots to another part of the factory.

This highly poisonous glaze contained lead, and sometimes arsenic. The men's and boys' hands were always wet, and their clothes saturated with this liquid. Constantly handling the rough pots made the skin of the boys' fingers very smooth and delicate, and they often bled, which speeded up absorption of the lead into their bodies. The workers ate in the dipping-rooms, and rarely bothered to wash their hands first.

Any doctor who saw the 'dull' and 'cadaverous' faces of the workers knew they did not have long to live. A 'blue line' along the workers' gums was a warning that the lead was doing its deadly work. The men and children suffered from paralysis, 'painter's colic' and epilepsy. Children endured terrible stomach pains. Dipper John Cooper said he would never allow his son to work for him as a helper: 'I love my child, and would rather that he should live'.[12]

The young women who worked in the scouring-rooms suffered from lung diseases. When the china was fired in the kiln, it became covered in lots of tiny flint particles from the 'saggars' or containers it was fired in. These workers scoured off the particles with sandpaper and brushes. The air they breathed was full of these fine particles, which settled on their lungs and shortened their lives.

On the positive side, it is cheering to note that apart from the long hours, many potteries children were kindly treated and appeared 'happy and comfortable'. A few firms allowed corporal punishment, but it was 'rarely severe', and others banned it altogether.[13]

Children learning the 'elegant art' of decorating the pots (painting, gilding, flower and figure-making) worked in warm, dry, comfortable rooms.[14] If the girls in the painting departments were well-behaved, the master gave them a little tea-party once a year. The girls played games and were 'merry as crickets'.[15]

To their credit, the masters in the Potteries spared no efforts to ensure children had access to moral and religious education. The problem was the children's parents. They earned good money, but could not resist the temptation of the bit extra their children brought in. They took their children away from school at an early age, and the children were far too tired after work to go to evening classes. Unsurprisingly, the commission found: 'the ignorance of the Young People throughout the district is absolute'.[16]

If relatively well-off working-class parents were keen for their children to work, imagine how much pressure was put on children by impoverished parents. The pin-masters of Warrington, Birmingham and Wolverhampton openly exploited parents' poverty and ignorance by lending them money. The only way parents could repay the loan was by selling their children's labour. Lord Ashley denounced this 'legalised slavery' of infants.[17]

Master pin-makers offered hard-up parents a loan on condition they signed a bond promising their children would work to pay off the debt. The bond might be for a few months or up to three years. The bond was enforced by the local magistrates. (One master was said to employ four or five hundred children under this system). If the parents' debt was not repaid when the bond terminated, the master kept the child until it was. Some parents were always in debt.

When Mr Tufnell visited a Warrington pin-heading workshop for the 1833 Factory Commission, it reminded him 'more of an infant school than of anything else'. In a typical establishment: 'A large room is filled with small tables, at each of which sit four children; about thirty or forty altogether in a room, and certainly of ages lower than I should suppose it possible could be employed in any other gainful occupation. The majority of those I saw did not appear to be above seven or eight'.[18]

Each child, working a treadle with its foot, fastened pin heads onto pin shafts by repeatedly hammering them into place by means of a heavy weight suspended in a wooden frame. Their bodies were bent in a 'C' shape as they worked. The children were regularly beaten to keep their minds on their work. They earned about eightpence per week, sometimes more.

A decade later, the 1843 commission found Warrington pin-making children as young as six working from seven in the morning until nine at night (with two hours for meals). The children were only paid for each full ounce of pins they made, and were often cheated by the overlooker.

Birmingham child pin-makers were 'in every respect ill-used'. They worked up to thirteen hours a day, and passers-by often heard them crying. The children were always hungry, and were dressed in rags. Their parents only cared about 'getting their wages to spend in drink'.[19] One of the pin-masters felt sorry for the children's raggedness, and gave them aprons and cotton dresses to wear. These clothes were instantly pawned by their parents, and the children found another employer.

If an item was made of metal, a child's hands almost certainly made or finished it in some way. The largest concentrations of infant labour in metal manufactures were in the Birmingham and Sheffield areas.

Birmingham was dominated by the sheer immensity of its industrial landscape, which greatly impressed travellers. 'The cupolas and the spires of churches appear intermingled with the conic and square-formed chimnies [sic] of rolling-mills, glass-houses, and other manufactories, which also seem to rival them in height'.

The city hummed with activity. Visitors were deafened by the clatter of engines, hammering of the presses, and whirling of wheels. The 'deep sounds of ponderous machinery' were punctuated by the 'roar of guns, in their occasional discharges from the proof-house'.[20]

Robert Southey, who visited Birmingham early in the nineteenth century, said his heart ached 'at the sight of some many human beings employed in infernal occupations', and the miserable state of the workers. 'Our earth was designed to be a seminary for young angels, but the devil has certainly fixed upon this spot for his own nursery garden and hot-house'.

The city was renowned for its wonders: 'in no other age was there such so astonishing a display of human ingenuity', but the workers paid for it with their health and strength. The filth all around was 'sickening'.[21] Dirt and dust from the workshops filled people's lungs with every breath and sank into the pores of their skin.

Vast numbers of children and young persons worked in the Birmingham's metal trades: in brass and iron foundries, rolling-mills, and steel pen-making. There were very few large factories. Child workers made buttons, screws, nails, and pins in small workshops, and in tin-plate and japanning shops. Ironmongery was the chief industry in the outlying districts; mostly boys and men were employed here.

Children generally began in the metal trades when they were eight or nine. (It was only in pin or nail-making that tiny children were employed). Girls were just as skilled as boys. They made tin toys, punched out washers and did japanning work. Children made nails, screws and chains at places like Dudley, Sedgley and Stourbridge. 'The girls can make the nails well; some of them as well as a man; some of them have a great gift this way.' Workman Thomas Billingham said when he was a boy, he hardly ever saw any girls making chains and chains, but now 'ten times as many girls as boys' did the work.[22]

At Willenhall near Wolverhampton, 1,000 boys worked in the town's staple manufactures: locks, keys, bolts, files, currycombs and so on. Children were 'put to the vice' as young as seven or 'from any age at which they are able to hold a file, until the age of twenty-one.'[23]

The children worked as 'out-door' apprentices, that is, they lived at home with their parents. They spent all day in the workshops, and went home at night. They were usually apprenticed for seven years when they were fourteen years old. Their parents did not pay a premium. Instead, their child was given a wage at a reduced rate, so the master was still in profit. As in the potteries, parents did not bother to formally apprentice their children. They hoped their boy would learn enough to earn a wage before he was twenty-one. Their parents agreed a wage with the craftsman. When the child became skilled enough, he was usually paid by the piece.

Parish apprentices were indentured as 'in-door' apprentices; many were bound illegally, without going through the proper formalities. Some masters had several apprentices, even though they did not have a home of their own. Their apprentices slept on the floor of their lodgings.

Sadly, having power over a small human being brought out the worst in some brutal masters. The Black Country masters were downright savage. Robert Jones at Willenhall half-starved and shamefully beat his boy apprentices. A kindly journeyman, shocked at the way the boys were beaten, tried to persuade the boys to come with him to a constable to complain, and promised he would speak up for them. But they were too frightened to go.

The small masters (the locksmiths, key and bolt-makers) were the most vicious. They hit their apprentices with tools, straps, sticks, even horsewhips. Boys at Sedgeley (Wolverhampton) were hit with a red-hot iron, or had a 'flash of lightning' thrown at them. When a piece of iron was taken red-hot from the forge, fiery particles streamed from it. The metal worker normally just threw them on the ground in a shower. But if he was in a bad mood, he directed the hot particles (the 'flash') towards his apprentice. The child might be hit in the face by the particles. If they fell on his clothes or inside his shirt, he had to shake them out quickly before they burned.

When a boy at Darlaston was beaten 'with a red-hot iron', the magistrates threatened to cancel his indentures, but the boy's master 'promised to behave better in future', so the child stayed with him. Boys were treated more kindly at nearby Wednesbury.[24]

Sheffield was famous for its cutlery trade, which employed 3,255 children and young people. Boys outnumbered girls by three to one. Children ground knives, forks, files, and did the 'hafting' on cutlery (joining the parts together, polishing and finishing them). They worked as file-cutters, made saws, forged blades, and so on. Sheffield children were fairly well looked-after, on the whole. Only the 'small cutlers' were said to ill-treat their child workers.

The most dangerous work was edge-tool grinding; mortality amongst the workers was 'appalling'.[25] The boy sat on a bench (a 'horsing'), and pressed the knife he was grinding against a rapidly rotating stone wheel. Workers were killed or injured if the grindstone broke without warning.

As the knife or fork ground against the stone, particles of stone and metal filled the air the child breathed. These workshops were badly ventilated, which made the problem worse. Particles settled in the workers' lungs.

There was no cure for 'grinders' asthma'. As the disease progressed, they became too ill to work, before dying at a very early age. Children began working as grinders when they were fourteen, but cases of eight- and nine-year-olds were recorded. Fork-grinders died by the time they were thirty-two. If water was used in the grinding process, the men lived a little longer: about forty years old.

When a needle-making manufacturer, Henry Cocker, perfected a special type of flue to carry away the dust, the men kicked it down and broke it. They were worried that if their working conditions were improved, more people would join the trade and wages would go down. They knew they were doomed to a short life, but did not care so long as they had a 'merry one' and earned good wages. The local doctor warned the grinders they would be ill so long as they stayed in the same trade, but nothing deterred them from working, or 'from apprenticing their children into the same fatal trade'. The 1843 commission was convinced that this 'prodigal waste of human life' demanded action from the government.[26]

Glass-making was a highly skilled occupation where boys earned high wages once they learned the craft. This ancient art gained its first real stronghold in Britain in the early seventeenth century, after James I banned the use of wood as fuel for glass furnaces (to preserve England's forests). North-east England became the centre of a successful glass-making industry, owing to the vast Durham and Northumberland coalfields' virtually inexhaustible fuel supply for the furnaces. Tyneside glass dominated the industry in Britain for over two centuries. Glass was also made in Lancashire, London, the West Country, Yorkshire, Scotland and northern Ireland.

Glass was manufactured in 'houses': huge brick cones eighty to 100 feet high, and fifty to sixty feet in diameter at the bottom. The cones were major landmarks in the glass-making areas. Later in the century, glass-house design changed. A large shed was constructed around a central chimney, which took away the furnace smoke, and these were cooler, more pleasant places to work in.

Glass is made by heating sand, limestone and soda ash (or potash) in a furnace until it reaches an extremely high temperature, when it turns into a molten fluid or 'metal'. The glass 'metal' was incredibly versatile. The master craftsman used a blowpipe to blow the metal into a hollow ball or globular mass. He used a variety of techniques to create items like bottles, cheap window glass, or more complex pieces like cruets. Boys helped the glass-blowers by 'gathering' the molten metal in the furnace onto the end of the blowpipe. They assisted the blower as he worked the metal into the correct shape.

Boys started out as apprentices. Formerly, glass-blowers limited the numbers entering the trade to keep wages high. Fathers taught sons their skills, and newcomers were discouraged. But in the 1840s, demand for workers soared after the excise duty on glass was lifted, and skilled hands were in short supply. Glass-making firms recruited local lads as apprentices to fill the gap.

Glass-houses were extremely busy places. The heart of the cone was the furnace. It was dark and gloomy inside, with little fresh air, and fiercely hot. Men and boys worked by the light of the furnace's red maw. Boys busily trotted back and forth to the furnace to 'gather' glass. Or they ran to and from a small furnace to re-warm the glass while it was being shaped.

Very young boys did not normally work at the searingly hot furnace mouth. They were 'takers-in,' taking finished glass items into an annealing oven (lehr) to undergo a long, slow cooling process (so it didn't crack). They helped clean the blowpipe, which needed cleaning every time the glass-blower used it.

Large sheets of window glass were made by 'casting'. Molten glass was tipped from a huge ladle onto a massive casting table. The metal was spread out by an immensely heavy roller until it formed a uniform sheet of 'plate' glass. After cooling, the glass was polished until it was beautifully clear and lustrous. The Ravenhead works at St Helens first began casting glass in 1776. They competed against Tyneside firms like Messrs Isaac Cookson & Co., whose glass rivalled 'every similar establishment in Europe in the size, fineness, and brilliancy of the plates produced'.[27]

When the Children's Employment Commissioners visited in 1843, Newcastle and South Shields were still major manufacturing centres. Few children were found in the north-east, London and Birmingham glass-works. Most children and young people were employed in the Stourbridge and Lancashire works. In general, girls were not employed in the furnace areas. They helped wash the finished glass, or worked in the polishing rooms at plate-glass firms like Cookson's in Newcastle.

Boys started work when they were eight or nine, although some masters would not take them until they were twelve years old. In Ireland, they started rather younger: age seven and up. As in the metal trades, children were 'out-door' apprentices, hired and paid by the owners of the glass-houses.

Glass-blowers earned good money: Birmingham men earned 25s to 45s per week. Children under thirteen earned from 3s to 5s, depending on the area, and 9s to 10s when older. At Newcastle Broad and Crown Glass Works, apprentices were allowed half their earnings as spending money. The other half was saved for them until the end of their apprenticeship, when they were given a lump sum of £25 or more. Wages were lower in Ireland; children earned 4s per week, plus another 4d for extra pieces of work done.

Workers' shift times depended on their firm's speciality. Crown, flint and bottle glass required different heating cycles. In plate, sheet and crown glass-making, the complete manufacturing cycle from melting the 'charge' of glass in the furnace, using up all the glass metal, then cooling down the furnace, was called a 'journey'.

The furnace ruled the glass-workers' lives. Night work was common. Twelve-hour shifts were needed to make crown glass. Flint glass-men began in the small hours on Monday morning, then worked six-hour 'journeys' until the metal was used up. The men and boys ate their meals when they got a breathing space in the furnace cycle.

The glass bottle-house men worked the boys hardest. Bottle-makers did five journeys a week of ten- or twelve-hour shifts. The boys were exhausted when they finished their shift: 'It would never be allowed if it were known... what a boy at a bottle-work goes through'.[28]

The glass-blowers and their boy helpers were exposed to great heat during the manufacturing process. At Mr Rice Harris's Birmingham glass-works, the temperature was 200F near the furnace mouth where the boys stood to gather the molten 'metal'. At the Nailsea Crown Glass works, temperatures reached a blistering 330F. The men's and boys' clothing got scorched as they worked.

Poor health was the downside of furnace work. Workers suffered from sore eyes, rheumatism, stomach and lung complaints. Investigator Mr Leifchild felt that boys in the north-east were promoted to glass-blowing when they were far too young; some were only twelve years old. One young man he interviewed complained he felt giddy with exhaustion after blowing glass for hours.

Boys also worked in the glass-cutting, grinding and polishing rooms. The health of the glass-cutting boys gave great cause for concern. At Stourbridge, boys helped the glass-cutters by 'feeding' the cutting wheel with dry putty powder, which contained large amounts of lead. These boys constantly breathed in lead dust. If the boys didn't wash their hands, then ate their dinner, they ingested lead that way, too. In Lancashire works, where twenty to thirty people cut glass in one room at a time, the air filled with dust, and lung disease was common.

However, the 1843 Commission found few instances of severe corporal punishment; the owners would not allow it. Glass-blowers' helpers were sometimes given a 'cuff', however.[29] At Birmingham, the masters gave the boys treats to encourage them to work hard. They received a Christmas box, and money to spend at the fair. Stourbridge glass-blowers gave the boys small presents of money if they behaved themselves.

The glass-house boys worked extremely hard, and had little sleep, but at least they were well paid. The furnace boys were much better off than many other working children in one respect: they didn't work weekends. If apprentices mastered the skills involved in glass-making, they could look forward to a relatively prosperous future.

Having a new frock or piece of lace should not be a matter of life and death, but countless children and young people fell victim to the demands of fashion.

Youngsters queued up in droves to enter the millinery and dress-making trades. If you were an impoverished young lady from a middle- or upper working-class background who had to earn a living, a job as a seamstress or dressmaker seemed ideal; it was considered a genteel and clean occupation. There was no dealing with nasty dirty machinery, or hob-nobbing with the lower orders. Jane Austen's aunt, Philadelphia Austen (1730–1792), was apprenticed for five years to a London milliner when she was fifteen years old.

Girls entered the millinery trade as an apprentice at the age of fourteen, but unlike other industries, they served just two years (three in Lancashire). The girls did not earn a wage while indentured, even if they worked overtime. When they had served out their time, they entered the trade as 'improvers'.

Hundreds of sixteen-year-old 'improvers' flocked to the big fashion houses in London every year. At least 15,000 young women were employed in London alone. This figure did not include the 'great numbers' of 'journeywomen' working in their own homes. In Liverpool, there were 1,000 milliners, dress-makers and bonnet-makers under the age of eighteen. The girls paid a premium to join the best firms.

Incredibly long working hours were endemic in the trade. Investigator R.D. Grainger said that millinery hours were: 'quite unparalleled in the history of manufacturing processes… there is no class of persons in this country, living by their labour, whose happiness, health and lives are so unscrupulously sacrificed as those of the young dress-makers'.[30]

Starting and finishing times depended on the season and the establishment. In Liverpool, Warrington and Nottingham, a twelve-hour day was supposedly the norm, with an hour and a half for meals.

The excessive workload in the busy summer season took its toll on the girls. At Nottingham, a 5 a.m. start and 11 p.m. finish time was common, but some girls worked on into the small hours of the morning. Bath dressmakers regularly worked from eight in the morning until ten at night, or eleven in summer. At Belfast, the working day was slightly shorter. Girls at Miss Williams' dress-making establishments in Armagh worked from seven in the morning until nine at night. Two of the girls there were only twelve years old; the others were in their teens.

The worst conditions of all were in the metropolis. Girls worked all night if the firm had an emergency order. One girl worked seventeen-hour shifts for three months in a row. Many mistresses allowed no more than ten to fifteen minutes for mealtimes.

They lost their appetite and grew 'thin and emaciated' from exhaustion. The better firms treated their girls as part of the family, and gave them 'the best meat' and 'the nicest food'.[31] Others provided coarse, unpalatable fare such as salt beef or cold mutton and the girls could not stomach it.

Some mistresses saved money on their live-in apprentices by refusing to give them any dinner on a Sunday, unless they were needed for work. Many of these girls were far from home and without any friends, so they wandered the streets all day until they were allowed back into their mistress's establishment.

Doctors roundly condemned the 'slavery' of the young milliners and dress-makers. Frederick Tyrell, a London surgeon, told the commission the sad story of a 'fair and delicate girl, about seventeen years of age', who came for treatment after she went totally blind. Tyrell said there was no hope of her recovery. The girl was apprenticed to a dress-maker in the West End. Before her eyesight deteriorated, 'her general health had been materially deranged from too close confinement and excessive work.' The final straw was a rush order for mourning dresses: 'She stated that she had been compelled to remain without changing her dress for nine days and nights consecutively'.

During this time her kindly employer allowed her a little rest on a mattress on the floor for an hour or two. 'Her meals were placed at her side, cut up, so that as little time as possible' was spent eating them. Tyrell regretted he had not encouraged this girl and other cases 'as flagrant and distressing' to try and seek compensation from their mistresses.

A 'beautiful' orphan girl who came to the Royal London Ophthalmic Hospital for treatment was more fortunate. She, too, was apprenticed to a milliner, and was in the final year of her indentures. She worked eighteen hours a day, 'sometimes even more; and her meals snatched with scarcely intervals of a few minutes from work'. Her eyesight was failing, and she was in the early stages of 'consumption'.

One of the hospital staff, assistant surgeon John Dalrymple, made the girl appeal to her mistress for a break. The mistress told her that 'in this last year of her apprenticeship her labours had become valuable'. She was entitled to make her work, 'as a reward for teaching' her the trade. The girl threatened to take her case to the Lord Mayor, and the doctor warned the mistress the girl would be 'incapable of labour' if she continued work. The mistress grudgingly cancelled her indentures, and the girl's eyesight was saved.[32]

When these girls grew up, they were too ill to work after their apprenticeship finished. One doctor thought that dress-making was as bad as needle-grinding in its dire effects. The girls' health was permanently affected; they were 'always ailing.' Just one bout of sustained overwork in the high season was enough to give girl's constitution 'a shock from which it never recovers'. Even if she rested a few days, she never regained her health. The dressmakers themselves admitted: 'no men could sustain the labour which is imposed on these young and delicate women'.[33]

Mr Grainger was convinced he had not got to the bottom of everything that was going on. Some girls he interviewed were clearly too frightened to give evidence. He was especially disgusted by some hard-hearted employers who refused to let their girls see a doctor when they became ill.

The dressmakers were directly responsible for the girls' ill-treatment, but the demand for gowns to be run up as quickly as possible came from well-to-do society ladies. The mistresses did not dare say 'no' to them. If employers had insisted on being given more time to complete work, then the girls could have worked shorter hours. The milliners paid a terrible price for society's callousness.

Shirt-makers and trouser-makers also endured long hours for a tiny pittance. 'A vast number of women and children' were employed in slop-work in and out of the capital. (Cheap ready-made clothes such as shirts and trousers were called 'slops', and were sold in 'slop-shops'. The workers who made them were 'slop-workers'). Wages had shrunk, and were still falling.

Elizabeth East was a widow with three children living in London. The family earned six or seven shillings weekly if her two older girls (aged nine and twelve) helped, and they all worked hard, sitting up 'half the night' a couple of times a week.[34] If they worked fewer hours, they earned just four shillings a week. The family could not survive on these wages and relied on the parish for aid.

Another needlewoman, Elizabeth Harding (nineteen) was charged with stealing a shirt in November 1843. She contracted with a 'middlewoman,' Mrs Davies, to make fine shirts for sixpence a day. She had to complete each shirt within twenty-four hours. In order to finish each garment on time, Elizabeth worked an eighteen- or nineteen-hour day, for which she earned a grand total of three shillings per week.[35]

Poverty forced needlewomen to pawn the materials given to them by their employers (in fact, it was expected of them) so they could afford something to eat while at work. Later, they redeemed the goods so they could finish their work. They were effectively working at a loss.

Thomas Hood (1798–1845) was appalled by a court case. A starving widow, Mrs Biddle, who had just had a baby, was prosecuted by her employer after getting into debt. She pawned the goods entrusted to her so she could buy food for her small children, and was unable to finish her work in time. Her employer accused her of slacking; a hard worker could earn seven shillings per week. Mrs Biddle defended herself. She could only earn that sum if she worked day and night, seven days a week. When the court heard of Mrs Biddle's miserable living conditions, she was spared a prison sentence, but she and her infants were sent to the workhouse.

Hood wrote his famous 'Song of the Shirt' (first published in *Punch*'s Christmas issue for 1843) to draw attention to the needlewomen's plight:

Work – work – work
Till the brain begins to swim!
Work – work – work
Till the eyes are heavy and dim!
Seam, and gusset, and band,
Band, and gusset, and seam,
Till over the buttons I fall asleep,
And sew them on in a dream!

O, men, with sisters dear!
O, men, with mothers and wives!
It is not linen you're wearing out,
But human creatures' lives!
Stitch – stitch – stitch,
In poverty, hunger and dirt,
Sewing at once, with a double thread,
A shroud as well as a shirt.

Hood's poem was talked about everywhere, and reprinted many times. When the Children's Employment Commission's searing report on the millinery and needlework trades was published, the *Times* suggested that 'leaders of fashion' shop at the places which did not overwork their girls to ensure 'many young blossoms' would no longer 'perish prematurely on their stem'.[36]

A society to help needlewomen was formed early in 1844. Subscribers paid a sum of money for which they received clothes made by the needlewomen at a fair price. They were not allowed to work more than twelve hours a day (!). The subscribers distributed the clothes among the 'deserving poor'. The society did not last long, however, and stories of 'white slaves' in the millinery and related trades continued to appear in newspapers.

Boys and girls were employed in the tailoring trade, and Dickensian stories of overwork were commonplace here, too. In October 1850, a coroner's inquest was held at Guy's Hospital in London on Robert Minton, a tailor's apprentice who died from neglect. He worked from six in the morning until ten or eleven at night, and even later on Saturdays. He had had no clean bedding for three years. A few days before he died, he went home and begged his mother to take him away from there. His mother went to confront Robert's mistress. She asked her to give Robert some gruel, as he was so ill. She replied: 'Gruel indeed; what next?' The jury at the inquest found that Robert had died from typhus fever, but added they felt he had been very unkindly treated.[37]

Young children in the lace-making industries paid a high price for the exigencies of fashion, too. Machinery was slowly driving out hand-made lace, and the machines were tended by children. Nottingham was the most important centre (with over 2,750 machines in the 1840s), but the industry extended into Leicestershire and Derbyshire. Machine lace was also manufactured in the West Country and Isle of Wight.

Some lace-making machines were steam-powered, but others were powered by a large, heavy wheel turned by hand. Young children found this extremely hard work. Boys and girls worked as 'threaders' and 'winders', who 'wound' or filled the bobbins with thread. The 'threaders', as their name suggests, threaded the machine with yarn ready to make a piece of lace. This process took three and a half hours. The children watched the lace's progress as it was being manufactured, and stopped the machine if there was a problem. This was very tiring on their eyes. They tended two or three machines at the same time, replacing the bobbins as each piece of lace was completed.

If the children were only needed for a few hours at one factory, they went to another to thread the machines there. Some children worked for two or even three masters at once in factories a couple of miles apart. The machines ran from sixteen to twenty hours per day, and sometimes for twenty-four hours. The operatives who employed the children beat them if they were not there on time to re-thread the machine as soon as it had finished.

The children had little time to eat or sleep, and often dozed on the floor or on a table. George Stinson (thirteen) got 'very tired and sleepy' when he worked as a threader. His father stopped him working at the factory 'as the work was so hard'. William Hinde, a twenty-nine-year old operative, said: 'Hundreds have been sent to the grave by this work.'[38]

Sarah Pymm said her children went out at all hours of the day or night, winter and summer, to start work. She always sat up waiting for her children to come home, and often went into the street, hoping to see them return.

Most child workers in the machine-lace districts were employed in mending, embroidering, drawing, hemming or otherwise 'dressing' the lace. 'Great numbers of children' began work at 'an early age… as soon as they can hold a needle'.

Lace 'drawing' was a finishing process for machine lace which was done in people's homes. The lace came off the machines in sections joined together by threads. The 'drawers' pulled out these joining threads with a needle. Mr Grainger found many cases of 'mere infants' at work. Children worked for their parents, who were hard taskmasters.

One of the most shocking, though thankfully rare, cases was in Walker St, New Sneinton, in Nottinghamshire. The mother of this family of 'lace-drawers', Mrs Houghton, had four daughters. The eldest, Harriet, was eight years old. In the summer months, when there was most daylight, the mother and two older girls worked from six in the morning until darkness fell; in winter from seven in the morning until ten at night.

Four-year-old Mary began work at the same time as her older sisters, but her mother let her finish a little earlier, at six in the evening. The children never got the chance to go out and play. They took meals when they could. Their mother only allowed them fifteen minutes for each break. Eliza, barely two years old, 'has tried and drawn a few threads out'.

Grainger was aghast: 'Unless I had obtained personal knowledge of the fact… I should have hesitated to have reported that, in this country, a child was placed at work by its parent before it was two years old.'

While Grainger talked to the children, Mrs Houghton constantly interrupted with: 'Mind your work', 'Make haste,' 'Take care,' and 'Now mind your work'. The children told Grainger that the work tired their eyes. Working with black thread was particularly miserable, 'dree [dreary] work.' The long hours of confinement had not yet affected these young children's health. 'The children are very fine and pretty girls, and appear healthy; the two younger sit perched on chairs, their legs being too short to reach the ground'.[39]

Lace-drawers and lace-runners (who embroidered patterns on machine lace) were 'very sickly and delicate looking'. The lace-runners sat for 'many hours' as they sewed, and became prone to a peculiar distortion of the spine as they grew older.[40] They became unfit to do any other work, and were doomed to stay as lace-runners for as long as their sight held out.

One could continue almost ad infinitum with stories of the children who worked in 'fearful conditions', as Lord Ashley said, in over 'one hundred and fifty trades'.[41] The 1843 Commission also reported on calico-printing, hosiery, printing, paper-making, tobacco and many other trades.

How well a child was treated was largely a matter of luck. On balance, parish apprentices were probably worst treated, whether they worked down the mines or in a workshop. Even here there were exceptions. Some parish apprentices at Willenhall (where there were instances of terrifying cruelty) were 'well-fed, well-clothed, and have even a few pence occasionally for pocket-money'.[42]

One investigator was struck by children's 'uncomplaining' testimony despite long hours and meagre pay. He ascribed this to their complete spiritual poverty. They did not expect anything better. If they were punished by their master, they must have 'deserved it'.

Children's health was a major concern. They were 'delicate, pale and sickly'. Some were exposed to noxious chemicals and polluted atmospheres, and much more could have been done to stop workers suffering. This was partly a question of educating employers and workers. The better masters provided washing facilities for the 'dippers' who used lead glaze in the Potteries, but workers did not bother to wash their hands.

The Commission found instances of 'robust, active and healthy' children, but even they were under-sized for their age. Children did not get enough to eat and were dressed in rags. They complained they could not go to Sunday school or church because they did not own any decent clothes or shoes.

Parents' attitudes were condemned by the Commission. They rarely evinced any desire to limit their children's hours. On the contrary, they were horrified by any suggestion the government might interfere and restrict their children's hours, and reduce their earnings. 'The order of nature' was 'reversed' – children supported their parents, instead of being supported by them.

Midlands children were said to have little affection for their parents or any 'sense of moral duty' towards them. 'The child instinctively feels that it is used as a mere bit of machinery'. Any affection they had for their parents was soon worn out, because their only value to their parents was their ability to bring in a wage as early as possible. Family ties were broken up when children worked so young: 'Brothers and sisters are separated at an early age… and soon lose all mutual affection or interest, if any had existed'.[43]

All too often children grew up like their parents: ignorant, foul-mouthed, and with immoral habits. Children were influenced by the older workers they

1. England and Wales. Map by E. Weller for Walter McLeod's *Hand-Atlas*, Royal Military Asylum, 1854. Nigel Wilkes collection.

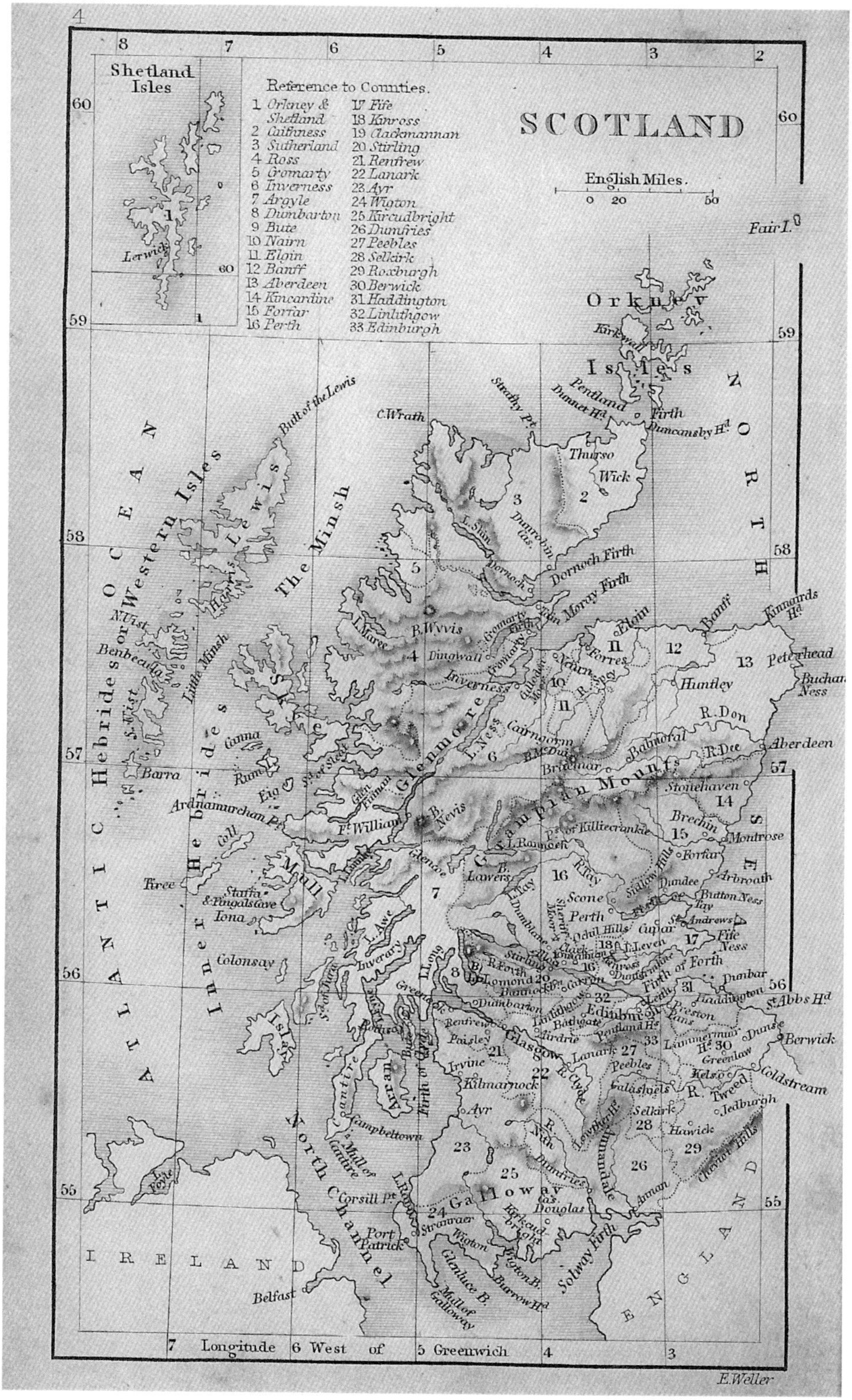

2. Scotland. Map by E. Weller for Walter McLeod's *Hand-Atlas*, Royal Military Asylum, 1854. Nigel Wilkes collection.

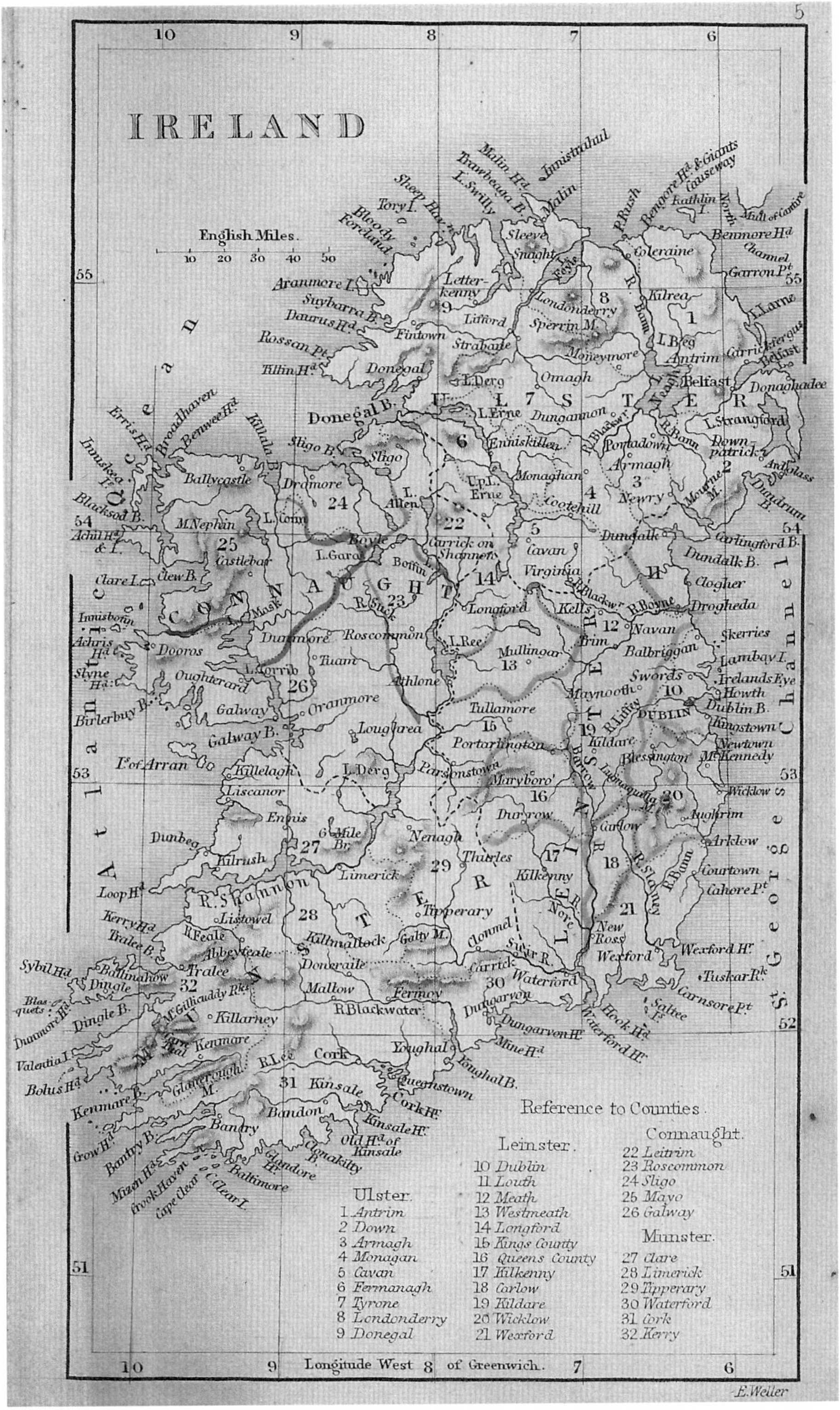

3. Ireland. Map by E. Weller for Walter McLeod's *Hand-Atlas*, Royal Military Asylum, 1854. Nigel Wilkes collection.

4. *Industry and Idleness*, Plate I. Fellow apprentices Francis Goodchild and Thomas Idle at their looms. *Hogarth's Works, 3rd Series*, Chatto & Windus, c.1880.

5. Ashton-under-Lyne, 1794. Published by J. Stockdale. In 1794, there were ten small cotton spinning mills in Ashton-under-Lyne. By the late 1830s, over eighty cotton firms in the town employed over 4,300 children under eighteen.

6. Mule Spinning Room, 1860s. Child piecers and scavengers at work in a cotton spinning mill, supervised by the overlooker. Charles Knight's *Pictorial Gallery of Arts Vol. I*, (c.1862)

7. Silk doublers at work. Charles Knight's *Pictorial Gallery of Arts Vol. I*, (c.1862).

8A, 8B, 8C. These illustrations for a children's story set in the 1820s graphically illustrate conditions in a Welsh pit. Men and boys descended the pit in a basket. Conditions in the pit were often wet, and there was always the danger of a firedamp explosion. *Sunday at Home*, 21 July 1877.

9. Anthony Ashley Cooper, seventh Earl of Shaftesbury. Engraving by unknown artist, Rev. Edward Lightwood's *The Good Earl*, (London, 1886).

10. Lord Ashley visiting the coal mines of the Black Country, circa 1842-3. (Lord Ashley succeeded to the earldom in 1851). Engraving by unknown artist, Rev. Edward Lightwood's *The Good Earl*, (London, 1886).

LORD SHAFTESBURY VISITING THE COAL MINES OF THE BLACK COUNTRY, 1842-43.

11. Block printer and tierer or 'tear girl'. Children as young as six worked for twelve hours or more helping block printers. Charles Knight's *Pictorial Gallery of Arts Vol. I*, (c.1862).

12. Llewenni (Lleweni) Bleachworks, Denbighshire, designed by Thomas Sandby for Thomas Fitzmaurice. Engraving by Thomas Sandby, 1792. A very grand bleachworks. Children were employed in many branches of the bleaching and finishing trades.

13. Rolling the steel for pens at Hinks, Wells & Co., Birmingham. Some boy helpers were only nine years old. *Illustrated London News*, 22 February 1851.

14. Flint Glass Furnace. Charles Knight's *Pictorial Gallery of Arts Vol. I*, (c. 1862).

15. Feeding the Chickens. Unknown artist, c.1860. An idealized view of rural life.

16. Oxen pulling haycart. Unknown artist, c.1790. Young lads living in the countryside sometimes found work as carter's boys.

17. Child chimney sweeps were a familiar sight in the 1860s. John Leech, '*Pictures of Life and Character'*, *Punch*, (Bradbury & Evans, 1863).

A DREADFUL SHOCK TO THE NERVES.

"PLEASE, MEM, LET'S COME UNDER YOUR RUMBERELLER!"

550.—Nottingham Lace-running or Embroidering.

VOL. I. S

18. Lace-running workers, Nottingham. Charles Knight's *Pictorial Gallery of Arts Vol. I*, (c. 1862). Long hours spent stitching affected the girls' eyesight and caused spinal distortions.

Price's Patent Candle Company's Works—Pressing Room.

Fig 534.

Price's Patent Candle Company's Works—Steaming and Boiling House.

19. Price's Patent Candle factory. *Record of the 1862 Exhibition*, (William Mackenzie, c.1863). Manager James Wilson's paternalism towards his child workers inspired other manufacturers to emulate him.

THE BRICKYARDS OF ENGLAND—CHILDREN CARRYING THE CLAY

20. 'Children Carrying the Clay'. Children working in a brickyard in the Potteries, Staffordshire. Engraving by Herbert Johnson, *The Graphic*, 27 May 1871.

PUNCHING OUT THE HOLES

21. 'Punching Out the Holes'. Punching out the 'fire-holes' so the kiln could cool down ready for emptying. Engraving by Herbert Johnson, *The Graphic*, 10 June 1871.

SIFTING THE DUST

22. 'Sifting the Dust.' The children sieved coal or ashes; the dust was mixed with clay to make bricks. Engraving by Herbert Johnson, *The Graphic*, 10 June 1871.

23. 'Paying the Children at the Inn'. Children might be tempted to spend their wages on beer when they were paid at the inn. Engraving by Herbert Johnson, *The Graphic*, 3 June 1871.

24. A government inspector visiting a factory. Engraving by Alfred E. Emslie, *Illustrated London News*. Vol. LXXVIII, 26 February 1881.

MR. BRIGGS HAS GONE TO THE EXHIBITION.—A BOY HOLDS HIS HORSE IN THE MEANTIME.

25. Road crossing sweepers earned a few extra pennies by holding gentlemen's horses for them. Middle class reformers worried street children like these were a menace to society. John Leech cartoon for *Punch* (Bradbury & Evans, 1863).

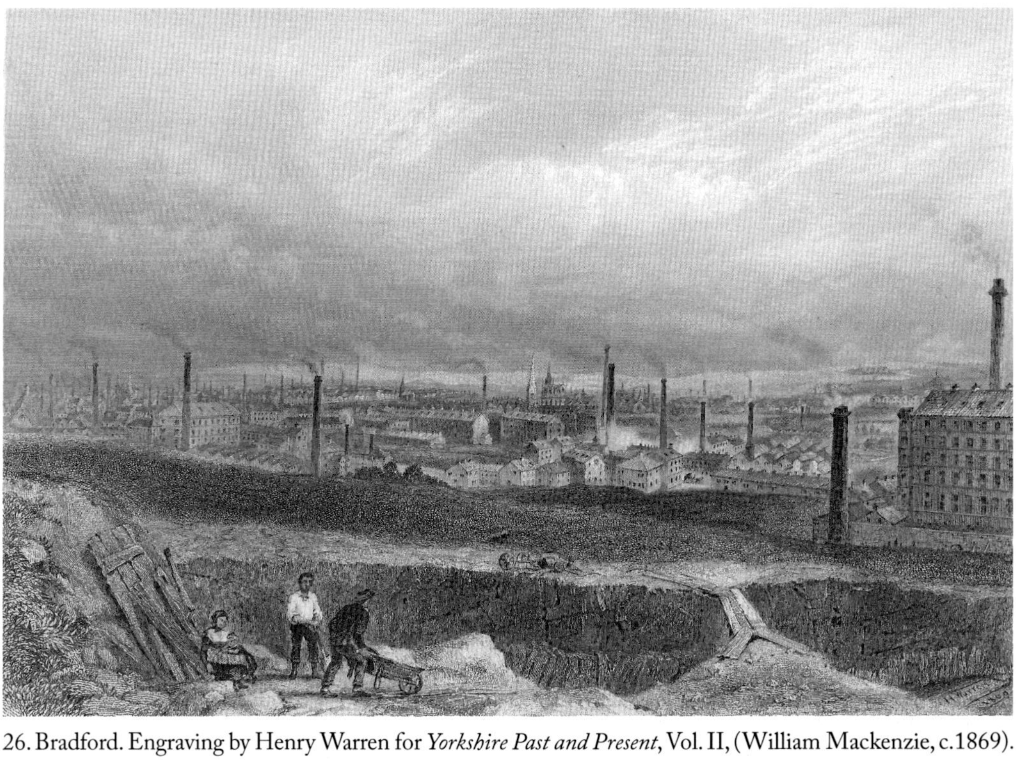

26. Bradford. Engraving by Henry Warren for *Yorkshire Past and Present*, Vol. II, (William Mackenzie, c.1869).

27. Bundle-wood workers, 1879. Engraving by F. Dadd. *Good Words*, (London, 1879).

28. Cookery demonstration lesson to School Board children at the Agricultural Hall. Engraving by unknown artist, *Sunshine*, 1891.

29. The Great Exhibition. Main Avenue looking East. Engraved by H.Bibby from a daguerrotype by Mayall. Charles Knight's *Pictorial Gallery of Arts Vol. I*, (c. 1862).

30. Queen Victoria at the age of eighteen. Engraving by J. Cochran after the painting by George Hayter. *Gallery of Engravings*, Vol. II, (Fisher, Son & Co., c.1845).

mixed with, too. Inevitably when they started work at such an impressionable age, their manners and language aped those of their fellow workers.

Now, earlier royal commissions into factories were asked to report on children's working conditions and check if previous legislation was effective. They made recommendations for tightening up the law where necessary. This was because over the years, parliament had built up a broad working knowledge of factory conditions, so these commissions felt they could comment fairly on the need for future legislation.

But politicians had little hard evidence on other manufactures, even though it was well-known that in some trades 'great numbers of children are employed at a very early age'.[44]

The government deemed it impossible to answer the question whether it was necessary (or even practical) for legislation to protect children until it amassed as much evidence as possible. Therefore, it was not part of the commission's remit to 'suggest remedies for any grievances or evils which we might find'.

So the commission was a purely fact-finding exercise from the outset. The case for potential legislation was deliberately left in abeyance.

The 1843 Commission concluded rather lamely: 'the physical and moral condition of a large portion of the working classes' required 'serious consideration' by the government. No adequate means were available 'to effect any material and general improvement' in children's lives. Successive generations would grow up in ignorance unless they had access to proper schools and religious instruction.

The Commission did suggest a possible way forward. The most humane employers believed that 'a general system of education' would have 'benefits of the highest order' for workers and the country as a whole'.[45]

The Mines Report the previous year had sparked a clamour of popular demand for change, followed by swift action in parliament. But the 1843 report was met with resounding indifference (with the exception of calico-printing children, as we shall see later).

Lord Ashley was greatly disturbed by the report's findings; so many evils cried out for remedy. There was a limit, however, to what one man could do in the face of public apathy. To have any hope of getting legislation through parliament, Ashley needed to carry the general public with him. And as he noted grimly, 'public opinion was not sufficiently ripe' to make sweeping changes.[46]

Thousands of young people and children – the tiny pin-makers, potters' boys, milliners, lace-drawers – were left without any kind of legislation to protect them at work. These children were a forgotten generation.

Chapter 9
Rural Bliss

Children in rural areas made a vital contribution to the British economy. Agricultural counties were the bread-basket for the growing industrial towns.

Agriculture was the biggest employer, as it had been for long ages past. J.R. McCulloch calculated in 1839 that there were over 960,000 families 'chiefly employed in agriculture' in England, Wales and Scotland, plus another 884,000 families in Ireland.[1]

By the time of the 1851 census, over 73,000 boys aged ten to fourteen worked on the land; more than any other occupation. In the same age group, another 25,000 boys and 10,000 girls worked as live-in farm servants.[2] (These statistics are probably too low, for reasons discussed in the first chapter).

Only a tiny proportion of children under ten were listed in the census returns as full-time agricultural labourers. The age when children could do 'useful' work on the land varied according to their strength and health, and the type of farming in the district. They did all kinds of odd jobs from a surprisingly early age. Children helped their parents on the family allotment or potato-patch, weeded crops, and gleaned after the harvest.

If the only work available was seasonal, even adults struggled to find a steady job. Some farmers preferred to give work to a man who had a family to support; others took on the cheapest labour irrespective of local hardship.

When they were about seven years old, boys looked after hens, scared birds away from newly-seeded fields (as on the Tatton estate in Cheshire), or tended cattle. The boys employed at bird-scaring sheltered under a hurdle, with a small fire to keep them warm.

By the time they reached the age of ten, boys were considered big and strong enough to lead the horses when ploughing, and help with the harvest. Teenage boys drove the horses at plough, drove carts, and did heavier work like hedging and ditching.

Boys worked the same seasonal hours as adults: 8 a.m. until 4 p.m. in winter, and 6 a.m. until 6 p.m. in summer. Their hours were longer if vital work like ploughing needed finishing. At harvest-time, they worked until late evening, depending on the weather.

Yorkshire children did not usually begin full-time work until they were thirteen. They earned about sixpence per day for weeding, tending potato crops, clearing the land of stones and so on.

Children earned more as their labour grew more valuable to the farmer. In Wiltshire, younger boys earned 1s 6d per week, and their pay increased proportionally as they grew older and hardier. A twelve-year-old could earn 2s 6d per week. The slower or less able lads might still be on 3s 6d at the age of eighteen, even though their friends might be earning a shilling a week more.[3]

In cider-making counties like Somersetshire and Devonshire, workers received cider as part of their wages. George Small, a 39-year-old farm labourer in Othery on the Somerset Levels, said when he was nine years old, he earned 1s a week and three cups of cider per day. He said: 'It is a bad thing for the young boys to learn to drink as they do'.[4] A few farmers gave adult workers land for a potato patch instead of a cider ration.

Farm work was considered a 'healthy' occupation. Blandford surgeon Dr Spooner believed that farm boys were generally 'strong and hearty',[5] but thought they should not begin field work until they were at least twelve. Boys got rheumatism and inflamed joints from exposure to cold, wet conditions. Some boys were over-worked for their age and strength. (The poet Robert Burns blamed his ill-health on his hard life as a young ploughman).

Girls were less likely to do full-time field work before age fifteen because they were not physically strong enough. They did odd jobs like the boys, or helped mind younger children while their mother worked.

Children often worked as 'live-in' servants on a farm. They were unlikely to get a place right on their doorstep. They went to stay with a farmer and his wife a few miles away, leaving home between the ages of ten and fourteen. Some got a place when their parents heard there was a situation vacant. Others were parish apprentices, expected to turn their hands to all kinds of work.

Jane Bowden was born at Ideford (Devonshire) in about 1813. She went to work on a farm when she was seven years old. Jane was apprenticed to a farmer at Cheyford after first working there 'on liking' for two years. The farm was: 'the best in the neighbourhood.' Right from the start of her apprenticeship, she was put to good use: 'leading horses to farm, dropping potatoes, digging potatoes, hay-making, harvesting, pulling turnips, feeding cattle, feeding pigs, etc. When I was about sixteen, I was kept entirely to the house, except at harvest time. House-work includes attending to the dairy, and feeding pigs, and all in-door work.'[6]

Dr Spooner felt it was unwise for girls to go out in the fields before they reached puberty, as they were more liable to become ill from the cold and damp. But everyone, even girls, mucked in and helped with the harvest: in 1843, girls earned 6d to 8d a day.[7]

How well a child was treated in its new home depended entirely on their master or mistress. The Reverend James Woodforde (1740–1803) kept a meticulous diary for many years which is a mine of information on his benevolent regime as parson and farmer.

The farm attached to Woodforde's parsonage at Weston Longeville in Norfolk provided him with an important part of his income. Servants were hired by the year, and given their food and lodging. Woodforde needed several servants to keep house and farm running smoothly: a farming man, footman, a kitchen maid responsible for the cooking, a maid of all work, and a 'yard-boy' or 'skip-jack'.

James took great care of all his servants. He treated them kindly, and regarded them as part of his family. Woodforde inoculated them against smallpox, and gave them medicine when poorly. James paid a teacher to educate his upper men servants; they were more useful if they could read and write.

The parsonage maids like Nanny Golding and Molly Dade were in their late teens when hired. Maids did not always stay very long at the parsonage. It was considered a good place to work, but they left for various reasons including serious illness. The girls also left service to get married when they found a nice young man. Sometimes they became pregnant after flirting with their young swains, which was inconvenient for the kindly but upright parson.

Over the years Woodforde employed several lads as 'yard-boys' or 'skip-jacks' to help with odd jobs in the farmyard or kitchen, or lend a hand with the harvest.

Jack Warton joined the Woodforde household in 1776, when he was about ten years old. Woodforde took him on 'out of Charity'.[8] The parson did not let Jack stay at the parsonage overnight at first, because he had not been inoculated against smallpox, so he returned home every night. Jack's 'wages' were initially in kind; just his 'victuals' and clothes. After he was inoculated against smallpox, he stayed at the parsonage full-time.

Woodforde was pleased with Jack's hard work and gave him a sixpence now and then. Later he paid Jack a yearly wage of 10s 6d, and in 1783 increased it to a guinea.

In October 1784, Jack Warton left Weston as he was 'too old for a Skip-Jack any longer'. He was now over eighteen and wanted to be 'a Plow Boy to some farmer to learn the farming business'. Woodforde was very sad to see him go: 'He has been a very good lad'.[9]

A succession of boy servants followed. Jack's place was taken by thirteen-year-old Jack Secker, a local farmer's son. Woodforde gave Jack a shilling 'earnest mony [sic]' (the traditional hiring-shilling) when he took him into his service. The new boy was paid one guinea per year, given a new hat, coat and waistcoat when required, plus an allowance for washing and mending his clothes. His family kept him in shoes and stockings.

Some of Woodforde's servants caused great upset because of bad behaviour or restlessness. Young John Dalliday got 'beastly drunk' at Woodforde's 'Tithe Frolic' (the yearly party he gave each December when the locals paid their tithes).[10]

Tim Tooley was twelve years old when he was hired by Woodforde in January 1793. Tim had only been in Woodforde's service three years when one morning he disappeared. The parson was shocked to hear that Tim's bed was empty, and all his clothes gone. (Just five days earlier, Woodforde gave Tim two pairs of worsted stockings and five shillings to buy new clothes. He would have been upset about the clothes, but Tim's disappearance was his prime concern).

A few days later, the parson discovered Tim had run away to enlist: 'his head has long run on a Soldier's life'. A jaunty Tim reappeared at the parsonage to collect his wages, with: 'a Cockade in his Hat... he has entered himself in the thirty-third Regiment of Foot. Poor Fellow, he looked happy and well'. Woodforde gave Tim the wages he owed him, plus half a crown (2s 6d) as a present.

Tim was replaced by a 'new lad', his brother Tom. Tom was not a success and was soon dismissed for idleness: 'He would do nothing at all', Woodforde noted on 10 June 1796.

Woodforde next hired John Brand 'on trial' as Tom's replacement. John was dismissed after four months. On 10 October 1796, the parson wrote anxiously in his diary that John was: 'the most saucy swearing Lad that ever we had, and am afraid if he does not soon do better, he will bring his poor Mother with sorrow to her Grave. He can do his Work well if he pleases, but cannot be trusted out of Sight, but the worst is, he is profligate'.

The parson inspired great loyalty amongst his older man-servants. Briton (Bretingham) Scurl, the parson's footman, was devoted to him for many years. He blotted his copybook on a few occasions, though. Woodforde was greatly displeased when Briton got 'tipsy' and was rather rude to him: 'He has been with me nine Years the 26. of April last, which I find is much too long for any Norfolk farm servant for they will then get pert, saucy & do as they please' (24 July 1794). The parson's 'farming man', Ben Leggatt, stayed with Woodforde until the day he died.[11]

During the 1800s, farmers in the southern and eastern counties became less keen on taking live-in servants, whether children or adults. It was much cheaper to hire workers when a particular job needed doing, as William Cobbett pointed out: 'Why do not farmers now feed and lodge their work-people, as they did formerly? Because they cannot keep them upon so little as they give them in wages'.[12]

Another consideration for farmers was that a servant hired by the year gained a settlement in the parish, which entitled them to relief in hard times. Farmers switched to shorter hiring periods or dismissed their servants just before the year was up. Live-in servants were still in demand in dairying counties, however.

The practice of taking parish apprentices as farm servants was dying out in some counties, but still ongoing in Devon in the early 1840s. When several children needed apprenticing at the same time, their names were put into a hat containing the names of all the farmers whose turn it was to take a child.

Alfred Austin was Poor Law commissioner for Devon. He believed that pauper apprentices were treated more kindly than in the past. Bad cases of abuse were fortunately much rarer. Magistrates had become more active on children's behalf. Apprentices, too, seem to have become more aware of their rights, and less shy of taking their case before a magistrate if they felt aggrieved.

Austin was astounded there was so little public debate on the merits on parish apprenticeship, even though it involved a 'practical evil of great magnitude.'

He was appalled that children as young as nine could be taken away from their parents by officialdom. 'Neither parents nor children are consulted; they are separated by an act of law, against which there is no appeal.'

It was entirely up to the master to say if a parent could see its child again. The bond between parent and child was completely severed. 'They have no control over it; they cannot object to the way in which it is brought up, nor can they interfere' unless they felt brave enough to step in when their child was ill-treated.

Austin could only assume the system continued because all classes had grown inured to it from age-old custom, but this was: 'no argument in favour' of it.[13]

Devonshire vicar Peter Benson was against the system, too. Parents lost 'all natural feeling towards their children'. Children apprenticed until they were twenty-one never learned how to manage money, or to do anything for themselves, so that even when grown-up: 'they are perfectly ignorant of managing their own concerns'.[14]

Some masters gave boy apprentices a potato patch to teach them independence. The master provided seed and manure, and the boys tended their potato patch after finishing their work for the day. When the potatoes were harvested, the master bought the crop from the apprentice.

Farmers like Edward Troode at Exminster thought it was a bad system: 'I am tired of apprentices…it answers better to pay regular wages; you have no control over apprentices; you can't dismiss them; they are a mere plague; but you can dismiss a paid boy or girl if you like, if they don't do their work properly.'[15] This grumble was probably because Troode had had a run-in with the magistrates over the way he treated his servants; he was fined £1 for horse-whipping a girl apprentice.

Jane Bowden (who we met previously) had a kind master and mistress while a child apprentice. Jane and her fellow apprentices were fed and clothed well;

she had a set of clothes good enough to wear to church on Sunday. Family and servants all ate together at the same table; they had boiled pork for dinner, and fried potatoes for supper.

Apprentices had few opportunities for education, whether at Sunday school, or a day school. Jane did not go to school, but her mistress made sure she read to her every night. Jane thought: 'Apprenticeship is a good thing when the apprentice is treated well, as I was; but that is not often.' After she served out her time, Jane was a maid-of-all-work to a chemist at Exeter until her marriage.

Mary Rendalls, a mason's daughter, did not have as good a place as Jane. Mary was apprenticed at the age of eight to a farmer at Lower Woodrow. This was a small farm. She was fed well: 'better than if I had been at home; I always had a bellyful.' Mary did similar jobs on the farm to Jane, but also heavy work such as driving the plough, in fact: 'everything that boys did. Master made me do everything. I took a pride to it, when I used to reap, to keep up with the men.'

But Mary's mistress, unlike Jane's, was bad-tempered and violent: 'she beat me very much; she would throw me on the ground, hold me by the ears, and use me very ill; I used to scream. This has happened several times a week… I still have marks on me from kicks.'[16] When the farmer beat Mary, she ran away home to her father, but he was too frightened to let her stay there. She could be sent to the local house of correction for breaking her indentures. Her brother took her to a village sixteen miles away, where she found another place to work. Austin recommended the end of pauper apprenticeship in his report.

Seven years later, the horrific murder of a parish apprentice shocked the nation. Devon farmer Robert Courtice Bird and his wife Sarah Bird were tried in 1850 for the brutal killing of fourteen-year-old Mary Ann Parson.

Mary was originally in the care of Bideford Union workhouse along with her mother Grace. The Birds weren't Mary's first master and mistress. The overseers apprenticed Mary to another farmer at first, but he did not treat her very well. He sent her back to the workhouse when she became ill and was no longer strong enough to work. When she had fully recovered, Mary was bound to Bird and his wife and went to live in their isolated farmhouse at Gawland.

At first all went well; Sarah Bird said Mary was one of the best girls she had ever had. She was a 'good, industrious girl'.[17] But in 1849 on Christmas Eve, Sarah claimed Mary began stealing and telling lies, and after that, the child was regularly beaten and starved. One day in early January 1850, Mary felt too poorly to come downstairs. She begged her mistress to give her some water, but Sarah told her to come and get it herself, or else keep her own servant.

Mary struggled downstairs, but collapsed. 'I don't know what's the matter with me,' she complained. Her mistress sent her back up to bed. By now the Birds were becoming anxious about her (or were frightened by what they had done), and Mrs Bird made a hot water bottle for Mary to warm her up. In the morning they found Mary lying stiff and cold, 'with a smile on her face'.[18]

Three days passed before the Birds found the courage to admit what had happened. Mary's mother Grace was called to the farmhouse, and Mrs Bird offered her a cup of tea. She told Grace that Mary had 'very dirty habits.' Grace's feelings can be imagined when she went upstairs, and found her child dead, covered in wounds. 'What a state my child is in!' she said to Robert Bird.[19] Mrs Bird asked her not to demand an inquest, but Grace was not so easily fobbed off, and insisted on her rights.

When the local surgeon examined Mary, she was totally emaciated and covered in abscesses, cuts and bruises. Mrs Bird went down on her knees and begged Grace not to demand an inquest, and to forgive her, for the sake of the Birds' own children.

The outraged local community asked the magistrates to intervene, and the Birds were arrested. Several farm workers testified that Mrs Bird often beat the girl with a cane, or a strong stick with long leather thongs attached to it. But none of them interfered and helped Mary.

While the Birds were in prison, Robert's uncle came to see them. The gaol-keeper's wife heard him say it was the kick that Bird gave Mary on Christmas Day which killed her.

One might assume it was an open and shut case. However, the trial became a cause célèbre because of the legal issues involved. At the original hearing, the judge ordered the jury to acquit the Birds of murder. It was impossible to prove which of them gave the blow which led to Mary's death. The Birds were then tried for assault, and found guilty. But the case went to appeal because their solicitor argued the Birds were effectively being tried for the same offence twice (which was not allowed under English law). After much legal wrangling, the Birds' conviction was upheld, and they were sentenced to sixteen months in prison with hard labour.

The newspapers were disgusted by Mary's story. It was an indictment of the whole parish apprentice system, which was almost as much to blame as the Birds. (The master of the workhouse had told Mrs Bird to chastise Mary if she did not do her work properly). The inhuman treatment meted out by the Birds caused much soul-searching, as did the baffling legal complexities which precluded the common-sense verdict of 'murder'.

The *Times* was angered by the seeming lack of compassion of one of the learned judges involved. Mr. Justice Talfourd had commented 'he did not approve' of the Birds' 'system of punishment'. The editor was disgusted: 'What shall we say to the humanity of the man who had not a single word of indignation for the surpassing cruelty of the two wretches at the bar, who had tortured to death a young and defenceless girl?'[20]

When parents had several hungry mouths to feed, a child's death might almost be seen as a blessing. Writer Alexander Somerville talked with a labourer near Salisbury. John Baillie earned one shilling and eightpence for a twelve-hour day, breaking flints for road-mending. He had a wife and two children to support: 'We had another boy, but he died two weeks aback; as fine a boy as you could wish to see he wur [sic] and as much thought on by his mother and I; but we ben't sorry he be gone. I hopes he be happy in heaven. He ate a smart deal; and many a time, like all on us, went with a hungry belly. Ah! We may love our children never so much, but they be better gone; one hungry belly makes a difference when there ben't enough to eat.'

Savage game laws meant that a labourer who took a hare 'for the pot' risked prison or transportation. Hunger drove away all respect for the law, and families often resorted to poaching, in spite of the risks. As Baillie hinted, starvation: 'makes one think on doing what one would never do.'[21] John had been transported to Bermuda for seven years for poaching while unemployed. When he and his brother were caught by gamekeepers, his brother was killed. John was hit on the head and sustained a serious injury, but he was still transported abroad. The Baillies' father died soon afterwards, heartbroken by the death of one son and the loss of his other one.

The well-tilled cornfields and neatly-clipped hedges of the great landowners' estates looked idyllic, but workers in the southern counties were suffering desperate hardship. This was the culmination of a long process which reduced their independence to mere subsistence. The humble labourer had been deprived of every little means of eking out his wages.

During 1760–70 and throughout the Napoleonic wars more and more land was 'enclosed' to increase the amount of land under cultivation, to feed Britain's growing population more efficiently. The controversial enclosure acts swallowed up the meadows, common land, and open fields where cottagers once kept a cow or pig, picked fruit, and gathered firewood.

At the same time that common land was disappearing under enclosure, rural workers lost another means of earning a bit extra. The crafts of spinning and weaving disappeared into the factories. As G.M. Trevelyan wrote, the villager became 'the landless hireling of the tenant-farmer and landlord'.[22]

The advent of factories meant there was less children's work available. Squire Henry W. Wilson told an 1836 committee on agriculture that forty years earlier, local women and children spun wool or flax at home. An eight-year-old earned fourpence per day, and a twelve year old earned eightpence. Now spinning had moved into the factories, they earned 'little or nothing.'[23]

The cost of paying for the Napoleonic wars led to higher taxes, rising prices and growing unemployment. A combination of the Corn Laws and poor harvests put the cost of bread beyond the reach of the poor, who subsisted on potatoes and turnips. Rural labourers' standard of living was pushed relentlessly downwards.

There was a distinct north-south divide, however. Wages were not uniformly low. Farmers in the northern counties and South Wales paid higher wages than their counterparts in southern England, because they faced competition from the mills or mines. In 1836, agricultural wages were 10s per week in Glamorganshire (home of coal and iron mines), a middling 9s per week in Norfolk and a low 7s per week in Somersetshire.[24]

The 1843 report found that many children did not get enough to eat. It all depended on the state of the harvest, the number of dependent children in a family, and if work was available. In some areas families lived on bread and potatoes, with a little cheese and sometimes bacon, if the family was lucky enough to keep a pig. Poorer families used the proceeds from the pig's demise to pay bills or buy shoes for the children. One doctor said: 'I know many families who do not taste butcher's meat from one year's end to another.'[25]

Increasing mechanization played a part in rising unemployment. New threshing machinery took away the work which once employed whole families. Labourers in the southern counties were worst off, and vowed to make a stand. In the summer of 1830, the mysterious 'Captain Swing' terrified farmers and landowners.

Letters signed 'Captain Swing' were sent to farmers. They threatened them with arson unless they stopped using threshing machines, or promised to raise wages. Riots and demonstrations swept through the countryside: barns and hayricks blazed, and threshing machines were smashed. The campaign spread like wildfire through southern, central and western England. Two workhouses (one at Selborne) were knocked down by men with clubs. Windows were broken, the roof dismantled and the furniture burnt on a bonfire.

The 'Last Labourers' Revolt' did not win higher wages for the starving workers, however. The rebellion was ruthlessly put down. Nineteen men were hanged; nearly 500 men and boys were transported, and over 600 imprisoned.

These draconian sentences for starving men were followed by the case of the 'Tolpuddle Martyrs' in 1831. Wages in Dorsetshire had plummeted to starvation level of 6s per week. The labourers banded together to form trade unions, as they knew they could not survive on such low wages. Six men from Tolpuddle in Dorsetshire who had joined a trade union were transported for taking an 'unlawful oath'.[26] It was not illegal to join a trade union, but the authorities were determined to make an example of them.

The labouring classes had no hope the governing classes would better their lot. All that direct action had achieved was a wholesale sweep of hundreds of breadwinners into the convict ships. Their wives and children were left behind. A sullen despair gripped the countryside, and the Reform Bill agitation the following year was left to the middle classes and industrial workers.

With such widespread poverty gripping the land, people needed their children's earnings in order to survive. The problem was exacerbated by the Poor Law reforms of 1834.

It had not gone unnoticed by the government that the arson and rioting during the 1830 revolt were concentrated in counties which relied on the 'top-up' system of parish relief (as discussed in the first chapter). For example, before 1834, unemployed paupers in Selborne on outdoor relief received an allowance of 6s for a man and wife. Extra money was given for each dependent child, so a family received from 8s to 12s depending on how many children they had. Selborne was one of the parishes where a workhouse was demolished. Giving these ungrateful labourers parish relief was obviously an incitement to idleness, lawlessness and downright rebellion.

The new Poor Law greatly curtailed the payment of outdoor relief and 'family allowances'. Relief should only be given to workers who were very ill or urgently needed help. In practice, parishes continued paying some sort of outdoor relief, particularly in manufacturing areas. If a mill closed down, so many workers were thrown out of work at once, it was impossible to house them all in a workhouse.

A succession of good harvests following the introduction of the new Poor Law helped smooth its passage at first in rural areas. However, the new legislation had profound implications for children in rural districts. Workers felt obliged to take work at whatever wage farmers offered rather than go into the workhouse. (Labourers could be jailed as 'vagrants' if they refused 'gainful employment'). Families with young children bore the biggest brunt of the new restrictions. The government effectively forced parents to send their children out to work.

Sussex farmer James Hudson told an 1836 committee on agriculture that before the Poor Law reforms, labourers overburdened with children refused to let them go into the workhouse. They insisted on receiving parish relief at home. 'Children have been kept at home in idleness, and not put to any employment whatever; now they are willing to let them get parish work on all occasions'.[27]

James Jacobs of Westbourne (Sussex), who had six children under the age of twelve, faced dire poverty under the new regimen. The failure of the turnip harvest in 1835 meant he couldn't get his usual seasonal work. So Jacobs set off to find a job, taking his two eldest daughters with him. They walked sixty miles before they found any employment: picking hops for three weeks. The mother and youngest children left behind found work in the fields; the children alternated between school and work.

The Poor Law Commissioners were delighted by the increase in child labour. Dr J. P. Kay (later Kay-Shuttleworth) said approvingly: 'Children are trained to habits of industry at an early age now that the allowance system does not discourage their employment.'[28] Boys in Bedfordshire formerly considered too young to go labouring with their fathers were now 'constantly seen hedging and ditching' with them.[29] Women carried their babies in their cradle to the fields so they could work, instead of staying at home to look after them.

Parents became anxious for children to hold on to their jobs. A child who upset their employer by being naughty or telling a lie could look forward to a beating from an angry parent when they got home.

A schoolmaster at the National school at Frant warned the new Poor Law was affecting children's schooling, as they were: 'beginning to be taken much younger to work than formerly… therefore they will not have the opportunity of receiving so good an education as heretofore.'[30]

While the Poor Law Commission congratulated itself on the success of its measures, a great deal of resentment built up. William Cobbett declared that a destitute man could now only obtain parish relief 'upon such terms that he must become the vilest of slaves before he can obtain it'.[31]

The Times (17 May 1844) commented on the agricultural labourer's loss of dignity and vulnerability: 'The present system is to strip the labourer of every shadow of right, protection, and property – to make him a labourer and nothing else. Thus naked and helpless, he is beaten down by a tremendous competition for work and wages. He has lost all claim to work, and is forced to get it in a scramble'.[32]

Discontent led to more hayrick fires in Bedfordshire in December 1843. There were widescale arson attacks in Suffolk and Norfolk in July the following year. Young men felt they had no future in the countryside, and they drifted away from the land to the towns, where they had more hope of finding work.

In 1843, almost a decade since the new law came into force, the assistant Poor Law Commissioners made a special report on the employment of women and children in agriculture. The full impact of the 1834 reforms were now fully apparent.

As the Poor Law Commission had hoped, the restriction of outdoor relief led to a wage rise in rural districts, but it was only a tiny increase. One of the most obvious consequences of the new law was an immense increase in the employment of women and children.

Labourers' earnings had sunk so low (in Wiltshire, 8s to 10s per week depending on the season) that few families could subsist without the wife and children working. It was far more common for children to work than their mothers.

In the eastern counties, women and children were exploited under the 'gang labour' system. This was confined to a small geographical area, but the children's sufferings caused an outcry.

The gangs were a way of getting labour-intensive work such as turnip harvesting done as cheaply as possible. The system first grew up during the mid-1820s and was flourishing by the early 1840s.

The parish of Castle Acre near Litcham, in Norfolk, became notorious for its gang system. Castle Acre overflowed with surplus workers owing to nearby landowners' intransigence. Landowners had stopped building new housing on their estates. This saved them money, kept the rates down, and prevented labourers gaining a 'settlement' there under the Poor Law. (This was known as a 'closed' parish).

As the old cottages fell down and were not replaced, their inhabitants were displaced into neighbouring 'open' parishes like Castle Acre. Here they settled in whatever housing was available, often rackety hovels built by local tradesmen hoping to make a quick profit. As more labourers arrived in the village, competition for houses meant that rents spiralled upwards for these 'wretched dwellings'. The labourers took whatever work they could get.

The closed parishes, then, suffered from an acute labour shortage, but local farmers had a 'pool' of potential workers they could call on in Castle Acre whenever work needed doing.

The farmer sub-contracted the work to a 'gang-master' who engaged to do the work for a fixed price. The gang-master chose his own labourers and set their wages. Adults and children of both sexes were hired, and obviously the less money the gang-master paid in wages, the greater his profit.

The farmer got his work done extremely cheaply, so he was naturally keen on the gang system, and the practice quickly mushroomed. When word spread the only way to get work was to live in Castle Acre, even more labourers flooded in (including some very 'bad characters') so they could join a gang.

The gangs travelled wherever they were needed, even if the farm was several miles away from their home parish. This was very hard on the children in the gangs, as it made their working day incredibly long.

If bad weather meant the gang could not do their work, they were sent home empty-handed. The gang-master paid by the task, not the hours worked. 'Children of six years old have to walk five, six or seven miles to their work, and then, if it rains, to walk back again without earning anything'.

Mrs Sculfer, a mother of six living at Castle Acre, said many children started in the gangs when they were six years old. Her two oldest girls (age fifteen and seventeen) worked in the gangs 'pulling turnips'. The girls' hands got covered in blisters. They earned 8d per day. No other work was available for them. 'My eldest girl has a thorough dislike to it. She almost always goes crying to her work…I wish I knew of any place I could get for her'.

Boys and girls of all ages were mixed together in the gangs, and there were suggestions they got up to 'wickedness and immorality'. Labourer Samuel Peeling said: 'It has ruined many a girl; it's a very bad system'.[33] Gang children did not get the chance to go to school as they began work at such young ages.

The 1843 report also looked at the disgusting state of rural labourers' housing. Many cottages in rural areas had only one or two bedrooms. Overcrowding led to disease and high child mortality. One Dorset village had over forty cases of typhus at one time.

The report's revelations caused a great deal of embarrassment to reformer Lord Ashley. Some of the most revolting hovels were in Dorsetshire, home of the Shaftesbury estates.

Dr Edward Spooner was a medical officer for the Blandford Poor Law Union. When typhus fever was raging in the area, he found a family of ten living in a three-roomed cottage (one downstairs, two small rooms upstairs): an old man, his wife, two middle-aged daughters, a son and his wife, and their four children. The floor was earthen. The whole family suffered from typhus. Few new cottages were being built despite a growing population, and the old ones were left to tumble down.

Conditions were no better for agricultural workers in other parts of Britain. Cobden condemned the small cottages or 'bothies' of Scotland: 'more wretched hovels… are not to be found among the wigwams of the uncivilised African'.[34] (Presumably Cobden meant native American Indians, the reporter may have misquoted him.)

The 1843 report put Lord Ashley in an extremely awkward position. Not only was he MP for Dorsetshire, but the Shaftesbury family was a big landowner in the county. He had never really got on well with his father, the sixth earl, who was a harsh and uncaring landlord to his Dorset tenants.

In recent years they had become somewhat reconciled. When Ashley made some of his rare visits home to Wimborne St Giles, he could kid himself that all was right with the world. Everywhere looked neat, tidy and prosperous within a few hundred yards of the park gates. The nearby village was described by Somerville as 'one of the sweetest little villages in all England'. It had a church with an energetic vicar, Robert Moore, who took great care of his parishioners. But Somerville could not help noticing: 'the farm labourers are as badly provided on the St. Giles estate as elsewhere, save those where the clergyman's benevolence is diffused'.[35]

Ashley had not been in favour of the 1843 commission when first mooted. He felt it was a ruse by his opponents in government to distract the nation from factory reform. However, when the damning report on squalid rural housing was published, Ashley's eyes were fully opened at last. The rift between Ashley and his father deepened.

A Dorset clergyman, Sidney Godolphin Osborne, piled more pressure on Ashley with a series of letters to the *Times* confirming the report's veracity and demanding action. This letter was a real gift to Ashley's enemies in parliament.

A chastened Lord Ashley told a meeting of the Agricultural Society at Sturminster in November 1843 that he: 'ought not to be lynx-eyed to the misconduct of manufacturers, and blind to the faults of landowners.'[36] His audience consisted of farmers considered responsible by many people for the grinding poverty endured by their unfortunate peasantry, so he tried to be tactful, whilst steering them towards more charitable stewardship.

Ashley said their county had become notorious for the poverty of its labourers and the filthy state of their cottages. While not immediately admitting the truth of the report's allegations, he felt strongly that if the charges were proved true (and they had been made by a government officer), it was their Christian duty to set matters right.

This speech enraged the sixth earl, who told his son to mind his own business. There was no money available to build new workers' cottages on his estates. (Ashley knew full well his father had spent hundreds of pounds that year on a new greenhouse and other luxuries). And the speech angered Ashley's political opponents, who felt he should roundly condemn these terrible living conditions, and set an example on his home turf.

Anti-Corn Law campaigners John Bright and Richard Cobden now had a wonderful stick with which to beat the land-owning classes; the misery of agricultural labourers was proof positive the Corn Laws did not bring prosperity to the land.

In a speech at Covent Garden, Cobden declared Ashley: 'had not done justice to his constituents by going to Stockport and Manchester to find objects of benevolence, while so many were to be found close at home.'[37]

On 16 March 1844, the famous debate between Ashley and Bright on factory legislation took place, in which Bright pointed an accusing finger at Ashley about the state of Dorsetshire labourers, as discussed in Chapter Six.

Ashley knew full well his position was untenable but felt unable to admit his impotence at home, and clear his name in public, either from fear of his parent, or family loyalty. When his father died in 1851 and Ashley succeeded to the earldom, he was dismayed to find his estates were greatly encumbered with debts. He had no money to make the improvements he wanted.

Child labour in the countryside was not confined to husbandry. Families turned to domestic industries and handicrafts to boost their income. Children worked for long hours in close, stuffy rooms in the straw-plaiting, shirt-button making, glove-making and pillow-lace industries.

Cheap machine-lace had greatly depressed the prices for pillow-lace, but the latter still gave employment to thousands of women and children in Oxfordshire, Bedfordshire, Buckinghamshire, Northamptonshire, and Devonshire. The processes involved in embroidering and finishing pillow-lace were similar to those of machine-lace.

The children worked in lace 'schools', which were really workshops. They started learning the trade when they were eight years, although children as young as five were recorded. Young children in Bedfordshire worked for about eight hours a day, for which they earned just a penny or three halfpence. An older teenager earned 3s 6d per week for working up to fifteen hours a day. Sitting in a stooping position over the lace cushion all day gave the girls lots of health problems, and the delicate work ruined their eyesight.

Friedrich Engels thought this was far too high a price for society to pay 'for the fine ladies of the bourgeoisie' to wear lace. No matter what suffering was caused, the 'wives and daughters' of the middle classes would 'deck themselves with lace as before.'[38]

Making wire-buttons for shirts was another family income booster in counties like Dorsetshire. A mother and her children could earn three to six shillings per week. Parents were very unwilling to lose this money by letting their children attend school unless they took their work with them and made buttons between lessons. Wire shirt-buttons went out of fashion by the 1850s (pearl buttons were preferred,) and great hardship was caused when the women and children lost their employment.

Young girl glove-makers at Yeovil liked the independence of working at home, despite working long hours. The West Country was an important centre for this time-consuming and labour-intensive craft. Some processes were done in factories, and others in the artisans' own homes, where they were helped by their families.

First, men workers tanned, cleaned and dyed animal skins to make them into leather supple enough for gloves. They started out in the trade as errand boys when they were about eight years old. Boy apprentices stretched and cut out the leather ready for sewing. One of the most difficult parts of the trade was learning how to cut the leather into the correct shape for gloves. Leather was too expensive to waste, so apprentices did not begin practising this skill until they were at least fourteen. They earned 1s 6d per week or more depending on how long they had been apprentices. The boys stood for long hours and worked in poorly ventilated rooms. They enjoyed very little time off for rest and recreation.

After the leather was cut into shape, the glove halves were 'put out' to women and children, who sewed the gloves together at home. The children, who were paid by the dozen, were supervised by their parents or 'teachers' as in the lace schools.

Girls learnt to sew the gloves when they were about six or seven years old. In summer they worked from six in the morning until eight at night. The sewn gloves were sent back to the leather-cutters for finishing off. The youngest girls only earned sixpence to one shilling per week, but as a local doctor remarked, 'it all helps in a family'.[39] The girls sewed gloves for all their working lives, until their eyesight began to fail.

Householders in Yeovil complained it was almost impossible to hire girls as domestic servants because they preferred the independence of glove-making. The girls only considered going into service when trade was really bad.

Country children were not perceived by philanthropists and reformers as needing 'rescue' like factory and workshop children, even though they worked hard. William Cooke Taylor thought that 'hand-weeding corn, hay-making, stone-picking, potato-planting, potato-picking, or bean-chopping' was far more tiring than factory work. Factory children worked longer hours, but they earned more, and did less 'continuous' toil.[40] Few people proposed that rural children should stop earning a living because their work was so obviously vital to family income.

The lack of employment opportunities for girls until they were in their teens meant they spent longer at school than boys, who were taken out of class at ten years old so they could begin farm work. Girls, too, were taken out of school if needed on the farm for harvest time or potato-picking. And large numbers of country children were never going to get a decent education as long as they were sent to lace or other handicraft 'schools' at an early age to earn a tiny wage.

But rural children were seen as a low priority, even though the 1843 report drew attention to abuses such as the gang system. The question of rural children's work and schooling was set aside for over two decades.

Chapter 10
Sweeps and Slaveys

When my mother died I was very young,
And my father sold me, while yet my tongue
Could scarcely cry, 'Weep! weep! weep!'
So your chimnies I sweep, and in soot I sleep.
(*The Chimney Sweeper*, William Blake, 1789).

Legislation on its own was not enough to protect child workers. It was pointless for parliament to enact laws to eradicate evils, if the laws were so toothless that society could ignore them with impunity.

Generations of climbing boys endured decades of misery because of society's callousness. Several peers and members of parliament were determined to block progress if it hit them in the pocket. Reactionary die-hards such as Lord Lauderdale were not prepared to lift a finger to help the most vulnerable members of society.

No more than a few thousand children were involved in chimney-sweeping, but the cruelty endemic in the trade was a reproach to Britain's conscience.

The chimneys of Georgian and Victorian houses needed sweeping regularly. If soot from a coal fire accumulated inside a chimney, it did not work properly, and smoke blew back unpleasantly into people's rooms instead of going up the chimney. If too much soot collected inside the flue, the chimney could catch fire.

Early in the eighteenth century, chimney-sweeps in England began sending small boys (or girls) armed with brushes to climb up inside chimneys to clear them of soot. Some chimneys, particularly those in rich men's houses, were extremely complex in design to ensure that they worked efficiently. The chimney system at Carlton Hall, the mansion of Yorkshire peer Lord Beaumont, was just one example of these three-dimensional mazes with tight bends and turns. Chimney flues sometimes had long horizontal sections; some sections were shaped as a semi-circular arch. The worst chimneys were difficult even for a small child to navigate, and were extremely narrow in places: some were only nine inches (22.5 cm) square. Tiny children were specially prized as climbing boys.

Young children were sold like slaves to master sweeps by their parents, who received a tidy sum for their offspring. Some parents just gave their children away (perhaps if they were illegitimate), glad to be spared the cost of their upkeep.

The sweeps also used their own children, or took apprentices, but they did not always bother with formal indentures. One sweep at Windsor used his three daughters to climb chimneys. When they grew up, they became 'journeymen' sweeps and dressed as men.

It was not unknown for sweeps to kidnap boys of the right age and size and press them into service. Sweeps prowled around the workhouses, where a grateful overseer would be only too pleased to offload a pauper child onto a new master, no questions asked: a fate only narrowly avoided by Charles Dickens's fictional 'Oliver Twist'.

Using small children in chimneys was by no means a universal practice. The fashion did not reach Edinburgh until the 1790s. It was unknown in European towns except for Paris, and was starting to gain ground in large American cities.

'Climbing' was an extremely dangerous job. Children were sometimes sent up while the chimney was still blisteringly hot, or a fire was still burning in the grate. A plank of wood was placed on the fire so the boy had somewhere to rest his bare feet. Cases were recorded where boys were forced to climb up burning chimneys to put out the fire.

If a chimney was too narrow to climb easily, and the boy came back down again, the master sweep forced him to strip naked, and threatened him until he went up again. Boys got stuck in the narrow flues, or lost in the bewildering twists of the dark, choking passages. If a chimney had not been swept for a long time, soot piled up in large drifts inside, or fell down without warning on the boys as they climbed. An unwary child venturing into these soot heaps would suffocate, unless he had the presence of mind to extricate himself in time. If a boy panicked, and the sweep did not have another boy to go in after him to help, there was no way of getting him out without demolishing part of the chimney.

Climbing boys breathed, ate, and slept covered in soot. Their eyes were inflamed by the soot, and their knees and elbows were covered in sores. Their spines, arms and legs became deformed from climbing the narrow passages while they were still growing. All day long, often over long distances, the boys lugged around heavy bags of soot and the weighty dust-cloths used to protect householders' furniture while chimneys were swept. (Soot was valuable. It was sold as manure, not thrown away).

Some boys were given straw to sleep on. For many others the soot-bags were their only bedding. It was most important the boys washed regularly in order to prevent sweeps' cancer of the scrotum ('sooty warts') which was fatal if not caught early enough. Several sweeps died because they were too afraid to submit to the surgeon's knife.

The better class of master sweeps looked after their boys with reasonable humanity. They coaxed the boys up the chimneys by offering them a pork pie or other treats, and washed them regularly. London sweep James Watson fed and clothed his apprentices well, and took them to Sunday school, making sure they were well washed first.

Unfortunately, respectable sweeps were outnumbered by itinerant sweeps who wandered from town to town looking for work. They picked up boys wherever they could, and slept anywhere they could find shelter, like cellars or sheds. These brutal, uncaring and ignorant sweeps were some of the lowest dregs of society. The worst cruelties were perpetrated by ex-journeymen sweeps, who took up the trade because they knew no other life. Sweeps who had never climbed a chimney themselves had no empathy with the boys. They beat them if they did not work quickly enough. If a boy was timid, perhaps because the chimney was too hot, they stuck pins into his feet to 'encourage' him to go faster.

In theory, climbing boys enjoyed the protection of the law. Jonas Hanway (the campaigner on behalf of pauper children) and others proposed legislation in 1788 to make it harder for sweeps to abuse the boys. Hanway's Act limited a sweep to a maximum of six apprentices. Sweeps were not allowed to take apprentices unless they were at least eight years old. But a sweep could send his own child up a chimney regardless of age.

The 1788 Act was widely evaded. The parents who sold their children to sweeps lied about their age. Since many sweeps did not bother to formally apprentice the boys, these children were not covered by the Act, and their masters could not be prosecuted.

Humanitarians were moved by the climbing boys' plight. A mechanical chimney-sweeper was invented in 1803 by a Surrey carpenter, Mr Smart. One of the first societies to improve the boys' conditions and promote the use of sweeping 'machines' was formed in the same year. This machine could clean 'ninety-nine' chimneys 'out of a hundred' so there was no need to use children.[1] Smart's invention was a long and flexible system of hollow tubes, connected by a cord inside, with a collapsible brush at the far end. The brush could be opened out or closed up by the sweep as appropriate as he cleaned the chimney. A great many sweeps did not like using the machine because it was hard work. If they sent a boy up a chimney, the child did all the hard graft, not his master, who rested and chatted to the servants while cleaning was taking place.

Mrs Elizabeth Montagu (1720–1800), leader of the famous 'Blue-Stocking Club' of learned literary ladies, was a patroness of the chimney-sweeps. She held a yearly celebration for them on the lawn of her house in Portman Square, London. The story goes that a little boy belonging to one of her relatives was kidnapped by a sweep when he was only three or four years old. Some time later, on a May Day, Mrs Montagu was having her chimneys swept, and the sweep's boy was recognised as the missing child.

Another version of the story identifies the boy as Edward Wortley Montagu, son of Lady Mary Wortley Montagu, the renowned traveller and pioneer of smallpox vaccination. Lady Mary was related by marriage to Mrs Montagu. Edward hated his life at Westminster School; he ran away and became a chimney-sweep's boy. One day a gentleman spotted him while walking in the street, and took him home to his father.

On May Day each year, Mrs Montagu gave a feast of roast beef and plum pudding to all the climbing boys in London to give thanks for her relative's safe return. After the boys had enjoyed their dinner and dance, they were given a present of a shilling each.

The boys would have welcomed this feast. Many masters half-starved their children, which had the double advantage of saving money and keeping the boys nicely undersized. The boys were so hungry they begged or stole from the houses they swept. Charles Richmond was a chimney-sweep's apprentice at Marylebone. In December 1791, he was convicted for stealing clothes. He told the court his master forced him to steal when no-one wanted their chimneys cleaning, and beat him if he refused.[2]

If the law was properly enforced, it made a real difference to children's lives. In August 1809, Henry Doe, a master sweep at Marylebone, was fined £5 by Bow Street magistrates for having an apprentice under the age of eight. (This little boy was only about five or six years old). While the child's mother was away for several months, his father, a plumber named Mr Millet, sold his son for three guineas to the sweep.

When the mother returned, she was horrified to find her child had disappeared, and even more upset when she heard what happened to him. She tracked down her son, but Doe refused to return him without the three guineas originally paid for him. The distraught mother sought advice from a solicitor, who instantly summonsed the sweep. The magistrates fined Doe, and ordered him to return her son to her.[3]

Magistrates were forced to act if a child died, or a case of dire abuse came before them. In April 1815, master chimney-sweep T. Young was convicted of extreme cruelty to his apprentice at Dublin. This little boy was so badly injured he could barely speak, and was carried into court in a nurse's arms. Young had burnt straw underneath the boy to make him climb the chimneys quickly. When he reached the top of a chimney, Young pulled him back down again by a cord tied to his leg. The child was covered with sores from this treatment. Young deliberately threw him into a tub of water to make his sores smart. The magistrate ordered Young to be flogged from the gaol to the Exchange (and again after two months), and to two years' imprisonment.[4]

The *Edinburgh Annual Register* reported the trial of another chimney sweep in July 1816. William Moles (or Molys), at Hicks Hall, Middlesex, had brutally assaulted his five-year-old apprentice John Hewlings. John broke his leg after Moles dragged him out of a chimney so violently that he was slammed against a marble hearth. The child died from this injury shortly afterwards.

Moles was originally charged with the boy's murder, but was acquitted at the Old Bailey. He was tried again on a charge of assault; several people testified they saw Moles thrashing the little boy. (One witness passing by the sweep's house was so alarmed by the screams and cries he heard from inside that he kicked down the front door. He discovered Moles and his wife beating John, and remonstrated with them, but they were unrepentant. They said they could do as they liked with their property). Moles was found guilty, but the harshest punishment the court could inflict was a two-year prison sentence.

Following cases like these, Henry Grey Bennet, a Radical MP and determined campaigner for the climbing boys made several attempts to tighten up the law.

An 1817 select committee uncovered several cases of boys burnt to death or stuck in chimneys, even when there was no deliberate cruelty by their masters. A Wakefield lad, twelve-year-old Joseph Fisher, was terribly burnt and died four days after climbing a chimney while a fire was 'stirred up' in a neighbouring house.[5] The neighbours' chimney was connected to the one he was cleaning. The boy's master accused the neighbours, Benjamin and Hannah Byrom, of deliberately stirring up the fire. They were tried for wilful murder at York Assizes on 17 August 1811. The Byroms stoutly maintained their innocence: the sweeps should have warned them they were cleaning the chimney. The couple were acquitted.

The death of eleven-year-old Joseph Holt illustrates the peril the boys faced from complicated chimney systems. Joseph climbed up the chimney of a house in Orchard Street, Westminster, and got lost inside. His master, Mr Hope, instantly sent for a builder to break into the chimney to rescue his apprentice, but they could not find him. By the time they realised Joseph had accidentally got into another chimney which joined onto the first one, he was dead.

Smart's sweeping-machine had been invented over a decade earlier, but only fifty or sixty were used in the London area. Thomas Edmunds, a London sweep, testified he swept over thirteen hundred chimneys in one year using Smart's invention. Many respectable London surveyors and builders said chimneys could be cleaned perfectly well by machines 'with few exceptions'. The older style, awkwardly-shaped chimneys could be adapted for machine-sweeping if special 'trap doors' were inserted so soot did not pile up in the wrong place as the machine swept inside.

Some master sweeps petitioned the committee, reiterating their belief that machines were 'impracticable'.[6] They attributed the children's miseries to the narrowness of the flues they had to climb, and called for changes to building regulations: chimneys should have a minimum size of nine inches by fourteen.

Bennet introduced a sweeps' Bill in 1817. He wanted master sweeps stopped from taking on child apprentices younger than fourteen, and apprentices banned from climbing chimneys. Bennet's bill fell by the wayside when parliament closed for recess, so he tried again the following year, and again in 1819 after another select committee uncovered more harrowing tales of woe. This bill survived its passage through the House of Commons after some heated debate.

The MP for Barnstaple, Francis Molineux Ommaney, declared all the climbing boys he had ever seen looked blissfully happy and full of glee. (Ommaney was a parish overseer. He was worried about the burden on the rates if guardians could not apprentice boys to sweeps).

Bennet retorted that anyone walking along the street could see their 'miserable, distressed, dejected' appearance. Alderman William Wood remarked: 'If glee of countenance could ever be discovered through the covering of soot, it must have been occasioned by recent escape from imminent peril in a chimney'.[7]

Bennet's efforts were stymied once more when his Bill met stiff opposition from the House of Lords. Lord Lauderdale ridiculed the 'zealots' who wanted to help climbing boys. He accused them of putting their safety before that of the general public, who needed protecting from chimney fires. The indefatigable Bennet tried again, this time proposing tighter regulations instead, since any hope of banning the boys' use was clearly doomed. Thanks to Lauderdale, the Lords threw out this Bill, too.

It was left to private individuals and the humane societies to do what they could to help sweeps such as William Cooper. William was apprenticed by his father to a sweep, Mr Davies, in 1805. William was ten, but his father lied about his age. He said William was nine years old, because he knew Mr Davies wanted an apprentice for seven years. The sweep would only have taken William for six years if he knew his true age.

The first time Davies sent William up a chimney, he encouraged him, saying there was plum pudding and money at the top for him. William scraped all the skin off his knees and elbows when he began climbing, and was very sore for the first month. His master beat him with a brush if he could not clean a narrow flue. When William was sent up to extinguish a kitchen chimney fire in Holborn, his leather breeches caught fire. He was burned on his body and thighs.

William Cooper's story had a happier ending than many other boys. (His friend 'Stuttering Tom', who was apprenticed to another sweep, died from 'sooty warts'). When William's indentures finished, he found a job looking after gentlemen's horses. Later, he entered the chimney-sweeping trade as a master sweep, and found premises at Black Horse Yard, Rathbone Place, London. William wanted to use his son as an assistant but did not want him to suffer as he had.

Cooper applied to the society for helping climbing boys.[8] It supplied him with one of Smart's sweeping-machines. William had to repay half the cost, but the society's aid meant his son was saved from climbing the chimneys. The boy carried the brushes and helped to work the machine.

In 1827, another sweeping-machine (an improved version of Smart's) was invented by Joseph Glass (1793–1868), a bricklayer at Cripplegate, London. Glass was awarded a prize of £200 by one of the humane societies. Joseph spent many years trying to protect climbing boys, and helped prosecute ruthless masters.

In addition to the humane societies' work, writers like Richard Ayton called attention to the many 'wretched little slaves of chimney-sweepers, a numerous class of beings most infamously oppressed, whom it is not too serious to call a reproach to the country'.[9]

More horror stories led to yet another select committee. Again, master sweeps insisted that boys were indispensable for cleaning complex chimney systems. Chimneys, for example, for still-rooms and laundry-drying rooms, sloped at acute angles in alternate directions inside, forming a kind of zig-zag shape.

The most difficult chimneys were in the mansions of noblemen and peers. They could not be swept by machine without physical alterations which cost money. The Bishop of London's residence in St James's Square, Lord Brownlow's in Belgrave Square, and Apsley House, home of the Duke of Wellington, were among those criticised. Public buildings like the Admiralty Office (which had forty-five flues) had chimney systems impossible to sweep thoroughly by machine.

The Act of 1834 tightened up apprenticeship regulations. Boys must give their consent to being indentured in front of two magistrates. A minimum chimney size of fourteen inches by nine inches was again called for, but since legislators neglected to make anyone responsible for enforcing the Act, this was a complete waste of time. As late as the 1860s, new houses in breach of the regulations regarding chimney size were built in towns like Bradford.

Philanthropic efforts were not confined to petitions on the climbing boys' behalf. The *British Magazine and Monthly Register* reported news of a special school for climbing boys in Brighton. The school was founded in 1835 after an attempt to shoehorn the boys into classes with ordinary children met with failure. No-one wanted sooty urchins dirtying their nice clean classrooms, so the local vicar, Rev. H. M. Wagner, stepped in and established an evening school for the boys. The wealthier inhabitants of Brighton subscribed five pounds each to furnish a room with books and desks where children could study in their work-clothes. (The children were so dirty that any attempt to put them in clean ones was deemed futile). Evening classes were held three times a week at the National School.

Each child was lent a dark coloured smock to put over his clothes to keep the desks clean. Soap, water and towels were kept in the classroom in case the boys hadn't had time to get clean. The boys were taught the three 'R's and received religious instruction.

The school was a great success. The boys won prizes for good conduct, and it is pleasant to discover they 'were treated with kindness, to induce them to attend the school.' The writer estimated over 2,000 boys worked as chimney-sweeps in large towns in England.[10]

Many climbing boys did not go to any school, not even on Sundays, unless they were lucky enough to have a good master. Joseph Allen, a thirteen-year-old Wolverhampton boy, said: 'I go to school every Sunday on Queen Street'.[11]

When the boys grew older, they stuck to the only trade they knew. Around the age of sixteen, boys got too big to climb chimneys and struggled to find work. If a sweep took them on as a journeyman assistant, wages were very poor: around two shillings per week plus their 'victuals'. This pittance was barely enough to keep them in shoes (they walked miles every day). To make ends meet, they stole the younger climbing boys' pennies which they had earned, or gambled with them until they took all their money.

Lord Ashley first became interested in the climbing boys in 1840, when the 1834 regulations were due to expire. (At this time Ashley already had his hands full fighting for factory reform). Ashley strongly supported the Whig government's new measures aimed at ending the boys' misery once and for all. The 1840 Act, which came into force on 1 July 1842, did not permit anyone below the age of twenty-one to climb chimneys. Sweeps were not allowed apprentices younger than sixteen. Master sweeps faced fines between five and ten pounds if they broke the law.

At first, thanks to prosecutions brought against sweeps by the humane societies and campaigners, the number of climbing boys decreased. Towns like Bath, Leicester, Edinburgh and Glasgow successfully banished their use. Highly active societies in the Midlands, Birmingham, Staffordshire, and other areas promoted the use of machines. The Wedgwood family of Etruria virtually wiped out the use of climbing boys in the Potteries.

But within a few years, numbers crept back up again, particularly in London, as master sweeps realized they could get away with murder. Like all previous attempts, the 1840 Act was doomed to failure without satisfactory means of enforcement. If a sweep was challenged about the small boys accompanying him, he said they were not for climbing chimneys, just to carry his brushes and bags of soot. Once the sweep was inside someone's home, no-one had the power to enter and check if the boys went up a chimney.

The biggest hurdle of all was public prejudice against sweeping machines. People would not be budged from the belief that boys were the safest way to clean chimneys. They were terrified of chimney fires. Servants were dead against sweeping-machines because the master sweeps gave them tips or 'perquisites' for their 'trouble' while the chimneys were swept. And the sweeps told them that machines would leave soot all over their nice clean furniture.

Magistrates charged with upholding the law were either convinced machines did not work, or knew their own chimneys needed modernising, and refused to pay for the necessary alterations. They insisted that boys were used in their own homes, and often refused to convict when sweeps were prosecuted. If a sweep was brought to book, his fellow sweeps clubbed together to pay his fine, so the law was useless as a deterrent.

Little changed until the 1860s. The British public remained unmoved by the climbing boys' plight. Meanwhile, twenty-three more children died in chimneys, suffocated by soot.[12] There was a shocking case at Manchester in 1847, when a seven-year-old boy died after being repeatedly forced up a hot flue by his master, John Gordon. Gordon was convicted of manslaughter and transported for ten years.[13]

As the death toll mounted, Lord Ashley (now Lord Shaftesbury following his father's death) tried again in 1851 to get the law changed, but was unsuccessful. Two years later, Shaftesbury became chairman of a Climbing Boys' Society formed to raise public awareness, and gather more evidence of the dangers the boys faced. He reintroduced his 1851 bill, but was met by implacable resistance in the House of Lords.

Lord Beaumont was one of Shaftesbury's bitterest opponents. Interestingly, Beaumont's Yorkshire residence, Carlton Hall, was highlighted as one of the worst chimney systems to clean in Britain. The architect was Lord Beaumont himself. One tower alone had twenty-three chimneys, and the passageways inside had baffling changes in direction. The man employed to sweep them, Richard Harrison, was petrified whenever his son climbed them. Harrison kept track of his son's whereabouts as he ascended, ready to break into the chimney stack and rescue him if necessary. It was estimated the Carlton Hall chimneys would cost no more than ten shillings to adapt so they could be swept by machine.

The Lords did not like their dirty washing (or rather perilous chimneys) being aired in public like this, and the bill was quietly dropped. However the bill, with some revised clauses, was allowed through by the Lords in 1854. Then it was given the kiss of death by the Commons during its second reading. Lord John Russell and others opposed the bill's wording, arguing it would stop sweeps having any assistants for their work. Shaftesbury, greatly upset and disheartened, brought in another bill twelve months later, but was obliged to let the matter drop when that too failed.

However, Shaftesbury successfully appealed for climbing boys to be included in a Children's Employment Commission set up in 1861. The commission found that the law was 'inoperative in most parts of England' apart from the metropolis and some big towns. Several thousand children still illegally climbed chimneys, and their numbers were rising. In Ireland, the law was ignored. The situation in Scotland was much healthier; local authorities and police firmly put down any use of climbing boys.

Parents had not stopped selling their children to sweeps; five pounds was a good price. In England, 'great and unnecessary suffering' was endured by boys as young as five or six years old. They began work at three or four o'clock in the morning (so the fireplace could be used by the household later in the day), and were on their feet for twelve to sixteen hours per day.

Dreadful cruelty was used to toughen the boys' soft skin for their work. Mr Ruff, a Nottingham sweep, explained: 'This is done by rubbing it, chiefly on the elbows and knees with the strongest brine... close by a hot fire. You must stand over them with a cane, or coax them by a promise of a halfpenny, etc., if they will stand a few more rubs.' When the boys first went up a chimney they came back 'with their arms and knees streaming with blood'.

Richard Stansfield, a sweep for thirty-five years, claimed: 'In learning a child you can't be soft with him, you must use violence. I shudder now when I think of it'. Stansfield began as a climbing boy at the age of five, and was so badly treated that he ran away, but his master caught him.[14]

The masters did not have things all their own way. The scourge of the sweeps was 'poacher turned game-keeper' Peter Hall, a former master. When one of Hall's apprentices died after becoming stuck in a flue, he was very upset, and determined to stamp out the use of boys. Over a twenty-year period, Hall successfully obtained 400 convictions of master sweeps. The sweeps 'were very much afraid of him' and hid their boys away if they heard he was in town.[15]

The commission recommended that the police in England should prosecute master sweeps as in Edinburgh and Glasgow. Sweeps should be licensed; no boys under sixteen should be employed in chimneys; and sweeps found guilty of cruelty must face a prison sentence. Because magistrates had proved reluctant to impose a hefty five pound fine on master sweeps, they suggested reducing the minimum fine to forty shillings.

Shaftesbury worked hard to change public opinion, helped by writers like Charles Kingsley (*The Water Babies*, 1863). Kingsley (1819–75) vividly recreated the torments suffered by climbing boys in his story of Tom and his evil master Grimes.

In 1864 Lord Shaftesbury piloted a new Act through parliament to regulate the industry. Shaftesbury told the House of Lords the best master sweeps favoured stopping the use of boys: 'It is the householders, and especially the great people, who keep it up, declaring that no power on earth would induce them to allow a machine to enter their premises'.[16]

The Act banned sweeps from employing children younger than ten years old except at their own place of business. Magistrates could impose a prison sentence where necessary, but Shaftesbury, when framing the legislation, seemingly had not understood the reasons why previous legislation proved useless. No-one was given powers to enforce the law, so another chance was missed to put an end to the boys' sufferings.

Two years later, the Children's Employment Commissioners produced another report. This Act, too, proved totally inadequate. There were 2,000 climbing boys aged between five to ten years in England; Yorkshire alone had 200 sweeps' boys. The 'disgraceful scandal' of parents selling their young children to sweeps continued.[17]

Almost another decade passed before Lord Shaftesbury finally made progress following the deaths of several more little boys. Gateshead sweep Thomas Clark was given six months' prison with hard labour for manslaughter after eight-year-old Christopher Drummond suffocated in the flue of a greenhouse in September 1872. Less than three years later, twelve-year-old George Brewster died on 12 March 1875 after ingesting a large amount of soot while sweeping the flues at Fulbourn Lunatic Asylum, Cambridge. His master, William Wyer, was found guilty of manslaughter and sentenced to six months in jail with hard labour.[18]

Shaftesbury was aided by a crusading newspaper campaign in the *Times*. The publicity shamed even the House of Lords into submission, and Shaftesbury's Act of 1875 successfully made the statute books. Master sweeps' licences must be renewed annually and could be withdrawn if the sweep was caught breaking the law. The police were finally given powers to enforce the regulations and issue licences.

It was almost a century since the first law was passed (1788) attempting to curtail this shameful practice. Shaftesbury's doggedness in pursuing this seemingly hopeless cause had paid off at last.

It seems surprising that domestic servants had so little sympathy for the climbing boys, but in that class-conscious society, they rather looked down their noses at them for being so dirty.

Domestic service was the biggest employer for girls aged ten to fourteen. There was a huge demand for servants in those days of labour-intensive households. Girl servants greatly outnumbered boys. In 1841 there were over 1,100,000 female domestic servants (all age groups) in the United Kingdom, and around 300,000 male indoor servants.[19]

In the county of Middlesex (including London,) around 9,000 boys and young men under the age of twenty worked as domestic servants, compared with 28,500 girls and young women under twenty.[20] (This figure may be an over-estimate because the census returns included farm servants mistakenly listed as domestic servants). Boys worked as pages, or did menial jobs such as gardening, cleaning boots or knives, or helping in the stables.

The servant population increased as Britain's population grew: the number of girls aged ten to fourteen employed as domestic servants almost doubled from 50,000 in 1851 to over 89,000 in 1871.[21] The decline in demand for live-in farm servants boosted the number of girls looking for work as domestic servants in towns.

Middle-class families (almost without exception) employed at least one servant, more if they had sufficient means. Having a servant moved one up the social scale, no matter how much penny-pinching was needed to pay her wages: 'almost every tradesman and farmer, though with scarcely a shilling to call his own… every clerk, and every such person, begins by keeping a servant'.

William Cobbett reckoned that a household in the 1830s with an income of £150 to £200 per year, even with two or three children to provide for, could afford a servant girl. A London maidservant cost over thirty pounds per year, with her board, food, lodging, a fire for her room, etc.[22]

Statistician and political economist George Richardson Porter estimated it cost on average about £35 per year to keep a female servant in the early 1850s.[23] This was beyond the reach of most working-class families. Even mule-spinners on thirty shillings a week struggled to afford a servant, and only a tiny percentage did so.

In the smallest households, every bit of household drudgery was done by a maid-of-all-work or 'slavey', as she was aptly nick-named. When Charles Dickens's father was imprisoned for debt in Marshalsea prison, his wife and the youngest children moved in with him. But they somehow contrived to keep on their maid-of-all-work to help with the laundry.

Domestic goddess Mrs Beeton wrote pityingly of the maid-of-all-work: 'Her life is a solitary one, and, in some places, her work is never done'. A family's 'slavey' was up with the lark long before they were awake. She had no rest until they were all tucked up in their beds again. Her duties included cleaning out the hearths and lighting the fire, and all the cleaning, dusting and polishing. She did the cooking, laundry, waited on the family and made the beds.

Their daily lives were subject to the mistress's temper. A 'slavey' was 'subject to rougher treatment than either the house or kitchen-maid, especially in her earlier career; she starts in life, probably a girl of thirteen, with some small tradesman's wife as her mistress, just a step above her in the social scale; and although the class contains among them many excellent, kind-hearted women, it also contains some very rough specimens of the feminine gender…the mistress's commands are the measure of the maid-of-all-work's duties'.[24]

The mistress of the house was advised to set a good example to her young servants so they did not pick up bad manners: 'With the mild and good [mistress] they become softened and improved; but with the dissipated and violent, are too often disorderly and vicious'. A live-in servant received food, clothing (or uniform), and lodging in addition to their wages, which varied in quality according to whether it was a 'a good place' to work.[25]

Domestic service was an occupation much favoured by parish overseers and charities keen to offload pauper children. Training in domestic skills such as needlework or laundry work was given to girls in workhouse and charity schools. The Shrewsbury House of Industry instructed its girls in 'cookery, housewifery, washing, scouring, and such other work as may best qualify them for service'.[26]

Early in the nineteenth century, girls apprenticed out as domestic servants by the Foundling Hospital who did not 'give satisfaction' to their masters were apprenticed to manufacturer Samuel Oldknow. He found them work in service. Morrice Lievesley, secretary of the Foundling Hospital, reported that over fifty girls were transformed into 'useful members of society' by Oldknow. In fact, Lievesley added, in rather sinister fashion, 'he has never failed'.[27]

Girls were also employed as 'nurses', looking after their mistress's children. Worryingly, children as young as five were 'sent out to nurse' in Oldham in 1843 – a rather tender age to be responsible for someone else's children. At Wolverhampton, parish apprentice boys were made to 'nurse infants' if they were too young to do useful work in the forges.[28]

In 1861, approximately 900 children aged five to nine and 15,000 youngsters aged ten to fourteen were 'nursemaids' in Britain. One can only hope that mothers chose good, steady girls to care for their offspring. These young nurses probably got experience looking after siblings at home before looking for a situation.[29]

Whether a pauper youngster was apprenticed out to a chimney sweep, miner, weaver, or bound as a domestic servant, parish overseers showed little interest in the child's welfare once they left the workhouse.

A sensational court case in 1851 led to immense public anger and a change in the law. Eminent lawyer George Sloane and his wife Therese lived in chambers at Pump Court, the Temple. One day in early December 1850, a neighbour's servant caught sight of Sloane's servant girl Jane Wilbred. She was desperately thin and emaciated, and appeared close to death. Jane was filthy, dressed in rags, and covered in sores.

The Sloanes were confronted by their outraged neighbour Mr Phillimore, who insisted that Jane must leave them. Mrs Sloane tried to grab Jane, saying she would take her back to the workhouse. But Phillimore, who was also a barrister, said Jane must stay in his care. He sent for a doctor. Mr Sloane, seeing which way the wind was blowing, said he would pay for Jane's medical treatment.

When a doctor examined Jane, he found she weighed less than sixty pounds (about twenty-seven kilograms). A girl of her age and height should have weighed at least 100 pounds (fifty kilograms). The police were called in and Sloane was arrested. Details of Jane's treatment emerged in the press after Sloane's initial court appearance. When he appeared again before Guildhall magistrates, an angry mob gathered in the streets, and a riot broke out. Twenty police constables were needed to protect Sloane during his journey from the court to prison.

Mrs Sloane fled across the Channel to Boulogne, where she stayed under an assumed name. She was tracked down by two London detectives, and the French police deported her to England. She was arrested at Folkestone harbour and committed to Newgate to await trial. The *Illustrated London News* (1 February 1851) reported Mrs Sloane was 'dressed rather shabbily, and altogether presented a most wretched appearance.'[30]

After being treated in hospital, Jane recovered sufficient strength to testify against her employers before the magistrates. She was born in 1834, and put in the West London Union workhouse after losing both parents while still a little girl. When she was fourteen, Jane was apprenticed to Mrs Sloane and her husband as a maid-of-all-work. The master of the workhouse asked Jane to let him know how she got on in her new place, and Mrs Sloane said she would let Jane visit the workhouse at the end of her first month. But Jane never came back, or wrote to the parish overseers.

At first she was treated kindly. Jane was fed well, and given meat three or four times a week. But when the Sloanes' pet linnet died, Jane was blamed, and that was when her ill-treatment began. She was regularly beaten and starved. While the Sloanes enjoyed roast beef dinners, which Jane served at table, her only meal was a basin of broth per day. These cruelties, however, were just the tip of the iceberg of other acts of revolting sadism. Therese Sloane was the main culprit, but her husband joined in the abuse. Jane did not run away, because she did not know where to get help.

The Sloanes were tried on 5 February 1851. They were found guilty of assault and sentenced to two years in Newgate prison. The magazine *Punch* commented angrily that if Jane Wilbred's property had been damaged, rather than her person, 'then would the law have arrayed itself in tremendous terrors; then would it have announced imprisonment – transportation it might be, with daily slavery. But it was only human flesh which was striped [beaten]; only human feelings that were outraged; and the evil-doers, the evil not being worked upon property, that have the milder punishment.'[31]

George Sloane's mind and body were broken down by the disgrace. He died in August 1852, just over a year after being convicted.

Several issues were raised by this case. West London Poor Law officials were initially reluctant to prosecute the Sloanes for ill-treating Jane, because they believed that special permission from the Poor Law Board was required first.

Another problem was the status of the law regarding servants. The Sloanes could only be charged with starving Jane on a count of withholding nourishment to an 'infant of tender years'. Jane was a teenager, and therefore too old to be an 'infant', so the judges acquitted the Sloanes on that part of the indictment. The *Times* was appalled: it seemed Jane could be 'starved with impunity'.[32] She had no protection under the law.

A few days after the Sloanes were convicted, judgment was given against the Birds, the farming couple found guilty of assaulting apprentice Mary Ann Parson (as we saw in the previous chapter). During the same month at Brentford, rector R. A. Johnstone resigned his post, following his conviction for a criminal assault on a servant girl.

Following high profile cases like these, the Servants and Apprentices Protection Act was passed in 1851. Magistrates were given greater powers to intervene in cases of cruelty involving servants and apprentices below the age of eighteen. For the first time, it was an offence for a master or mistress to wilfully neglect their servants or apprentices (if bound by indentures) by not giving them sufficient food and shelter. If convicted, the master or mistress faced a three-year prison sentence.

Parish overseers must keep a register of children under sixteen apprenticed out as servants. Persons appointed by the parish should check on children twice yearly. If the child's master or mistress lived more than five miles from their 'home' parish, the apprentice's new parish was responsible for regular checks on his health. Unfortunately, the law was completely ineffectual. Children were just too frightened to give evidence against their masters, and parish overseers turned a blind eye to any problems. Attempts were made in July 1863 and 1868 to broaden the Act's remit, but came adrift in parliament, in the time-honoured fashion.

There do not appear to have been any major campaigns to improve the servant girl or boy's lot. 'Domestics' were too convenient. We have seen how difficult it was to protect the climbing boys, who cleaned legislators' chimneys a few times a year. Any interference with the 'slaveys' who kept people's homes running smoothly would have been doomed.

Although vast numbers of children and youngsters worked as domestic servants, it was not a popular choice of job – pretty much a last resort. Domestic service was often the only work available in rural districts.

Servants voted with their feet. When Henry Mayhew conducted his massive survey of the labouring poor in London in the early 1860s, he discovered that many young street-sellers and beggars were ex-domestic servants who had run away after being badly treated.

In manufacturing areas, especially the textile towns, there was a real shortage of domestic servants. Girls who spent their earliest years pin-making or working in factories were 'totally unsuited' to domestic work.

It was a truism that women and girls greatly preferred factory work to domestic drudgery. In Elizabeth Gaskell's *North and South*, newcomer Margaret Hale finds it almost impossible to hire a servant girl in Milton, a northern manufacturing town, because they all wanted 'the better wages and independence of working in a mill.'[33]

By the dawn of the twentieth century, the number of female domestic servants under fifteen plummeted to fewer than 65,000 as young girls found more congenial work in shops and factories.[34]

Chapter 11
Candles of Hope

Whether a child worked down a mine or made nails in a workshop, climbed chimneys and ploughed a field, she or he had little time for school except on Sundays. Thousands of non-factory working children were left in ignorance, as we have seen.

In all the trades and industries discussed so far, the lack of working-class children's access to schooling regularly worried investigators. There was no national body to ensure that children received an education.

The provision of working-class schools had long been controversial. Some politicians (and many working-class parents) believed that education was a complete waste of time for children facing a future as factory fodder or down a mineshaft.

Some upper-class writers had social and political reasons for deterring the working classes from broadening their minds. If workers learnt to read, they might be seduced by seditious or inflammatory political pamphlets. This was a recurrent fear for a Britain mesmerized by the bloody excesses of the French Revolution.

A succession of working-class flashpoints in the early decades of the nineteenth century underscored this view. The Luddites smashed machines in the textile districts; an uprising in Derbyshire was quashed; the Peterloo 'massacre' caused headlines, and so on. Workers were evidently dissatisfied. How far would they go to demand change?

Wider access to education was therefore considered a dangerous luxury in some reactionary quarters. Even Sunday schools were viewed with dark suspicion. Magistrates in north-west England seriously considered banning them during the feverish Radical agitation for political reform in England in 1819 (the year of Peterloo).

If the lower classes were educated, they might want to 'better themselves' instead of spinning cotton, hewing coal, or labouring on the land. If that happened, who would do all the work? The upper classes could hardly be expected to keep the wheels of industry turning. Heaven had ordained that the working-classes should do all the hard toil that society needed.

There was a growing school of thought, however, that education (particularly religious instruction) would damp down sedition, not fuel it. If workers could read the Bible, they would become thankful for their 'blessings', and learn their proper 'place' in society.

But the 'devil was in the detail'. Reformers who favoured schools for poor children held widely differing views on how much education they should receive, and the form it should take.

Over the years, many different types of institution grew up: Sunday schools, workhouse schools, charity schools, dame schools, 'common day' schools and 'public' schools.

The Sunday School movement was founded by Robert Raikes in the 1780s. While on a visit to the pin-making district of Gloucester, he was shocked to see 'wretchedly ragged' children playing in the street. When he 'lamented their misery and idleness', a local woman told him that hordes of tiny pin-makers swarmed around the neighbourhood on Sundays, when the pin factories were closed. The children spent their time in 'noise and riot' and 'cursing and swearing'.[1] Raikes set up a Sunday class to get the children off the streets and into church, and the idea quickly spread.

Some parishes gave poor children vocational training, like the school of industry at Shrewsbury discussed in Chapter Two. John Forster wrote an account of a very successful one in Kent, established in May 1796. The school had room for sixty children. They learnt how to spin, knit and weave.

Before the school's foundation, the parish had had great trouble finding masters willing to take workhouse children as apprentices. But as the school's reputation grew, its pupils were in high demand. By the time they reached twelve years old, most children had left school and been apprenticed out into trade or domestic service. The scheme helped to reduce the poor-rates and turned the children into 'blessings to their parents, and useful and valuable members of society.'[2]

'Dame' schools were child-minding services rather than educational establishments. Parents paid a few pence for their young children to attend. Class sizes could be anything between twenty and fifty children. They learned their 'A B C' in close, confined rooms with little ventilation. Some Liverpool and Manchester schools were in cellars. 'Common day' schools were for older children, and cost a little more: up to 9d per week.

The standard of teaching was very poor in most of these schools. Sometimes children shared their class with dogs and chickens. Teachers had no formal qualifications, and often carried on a trade like hatting, or selling foodstuffs, while in charge of the class. Discipline was maintained by a 'whack' from a rod, cane or birch.

Charity schools like the 'Blue Coat' institutions in cities like London and Chester aimed to give children enough education so they could be apprenticed out. Sunday and charity schools were normally free.

'Public' schools were paid for by public subscription (the converse of today's 'public' schools such as Eton and Harrow). The two main bodies providing 'public' schools followed the 'National' and 'Lancasterian' systems. The National Society, founded by Andrew Bell in 1811, was staunchly Anglican. The rival Lancasterian Society, founded by Joseph Lancaster in 1808, was for the children of Dissenters. (It was renamed the British and Foreign Society in 1814).

These schools used variants of the monitorial system in which the teacher taught one set of pupils a lesson, which they in turn taught to a second set of children. Learning was by rote, and of dubious quality by modern standards, but rather better than the dame and common day-schools.

Corporal punishment was not normally used, but teachers used some very odd disciplinary methods to modern eyes. For example, in Lancasterian schools, troublemakers had their arms bound behind their back, or were put in a basket which was hauled up to the ceiling out of the way.

To sum up, working-class parents who wanted to send their children to school had some choice, but the overall quality was poor. And there were parents who wanted their children to receive an education. At Bristol in the early 1840s, working-class parents shelled out over £12,000 annually for their children to attend dame and common day-schools.[3]

The most forward-thinking pioneer of working-class education was Robert Owen, who opened a school for his young mill-workers at New Lanark in 1816. He employed a combination of the Lancaster and Bell monitorial systems. Robert accepted children as young as three years old in his school. He believed this was better for them than playing in the streets all day and picking up bad habits. The youngest children attended an infants' school. Classes were held outdoors in fine weather or indoors if wet. The infants were taught 'mutual kindness' and good habits by example and practice. They learnt through play, too.

Owen's school had 444 children in 1816, of which 279 were between six and ten years old.[4] The children were said to be happy, healthy, and fond of school and their teachers. After two or three years in the infant class, the children went into an upper class where they learnt the three 'R's; the girls also learnt sewing. Children were given exercise such as dancing, and the musically inclined learnt singing or perhaps a musical instrument. When they were ten years old, children left the school to work in Owen's mills (or other local employment), but stayed on longer if parents did not need their wages. After leaving the day school, about four hundred children went to evening classes and Sunday school (which also catered for day scholars).

Not all mill-owners were as interested in educating their young workers as Owen. The government hoped that the 1833 Factory Act would increase the number of factory schools. Although the Act specified that factory children aged nine to thirteen must have two hours' school each day, no money was made available for this. Factory inspectors were authorised to found schools where they felt they were needed, but no funding was available.

In 1835 over 47,000 children under thirteen were employed in cotton, wool, worsted and flax factories. Only 17,000 of these children received the prescribed two hours' schooling each day (the 1833 Act was not yet fully in operation). Another 9,000 children under thirteen worked in silk factories, but none of these children had to attend school.[5]

The quality of factory schools depended on how much a mill-owner was prepared to spend. At the Marshalls' flax mill in Holbeck in 1838, where 'no expense' was spared, over half of the 287 child workers under thirteen could read the Testament. (The mill employed over 880 workers under eighteen). But Holbeck was an exception.

Factory inspector Robert Baker said that there were only a dozen good factory schools in the 500 mills he inspected in the West Riding of Yorkshire. Many mill-owners felt the government was 'picking their pockets', and just paid lip service to the Act. Classes for factory children were 'taught' by the engineman, or the overlooker, his wife, a local shopkeeper, or whoever they could rope in.

One school attendance certificate for a child signed by a 'teacher' read: 'This to sertfy that 1838 thomas Cordingley as atend martha insep school tow hours per day January 6'.

In another school, the factory clerk wrote out the school certificate, and the teacher signed his name with his 'mark'. Baker found children receiving instruction from the 'fireman' in his coal-hole as he fed the engine fire with fuel.[6] The children's books were covered in soot. Instances such as these led factory inspectors to push hard for a national system of education.

Robert Hyde Greg, the opponent of factory reform, commented in 1837 that a general system of education for all children could be a good way of protecting them from exploitation. He rather naively believed that if children spent some time at school every day, this would safeguard them from being overworked. (There was still scope for them to be overworked before and after classes).

A national system of education was still a long way off. Decent schools and properly qualified teachers were desperately needed. In 1833, the government began an annual grant of £20,000 for building schools. Each school had to raise half the cost itself, which meant poorer areas were unlikely to see any benefit from the scheme. The National and British Societies both received money from the pot, but the lion's share went to National schools run by the Established Church.

Six years later, a special government committee was set up to decide how public money should be used to fund education. The first secretary was Dr James Phillips Kay (later Kay-Shuttleworth), one of the Poor Law Commissioners. He worked incredibly hard to improve education for the working classes.

The middle classes could not agree on how to fulfil the need for more school and better teachers. Religion was a great divider, not healer. Anglicans wanted schools and teacher-training kept firmly under the established church's watchful eyes. Nonconformists vehemently objected to any Anglican interference over their children's education. Secularists wanted religious teaching kept out of school altogether. The working classes were given little say on the type of education they wanted for their children.

Successive governments tried to grapple with the education problem, but whenever they embarked on a programme of reform, their frail barque was capsized by waves of opposition from warring religious groups.

A government scheme to set up a state-run teacher-training college was overturned by antagonism from Anglicans and Dissenters. So, Dr Kay and Poor Law Commissioner E.C. Tufnell set up their own private college at Battersea. Religious groups were shamed into following suit and set up their own training colleges. The Battersea scheme was a great success, but expensive to run, and in 1843 it was taken over by the National Society. This was a start, but many years passed before professionally qualified teachers became the norm rather than the exception. When the 1851 census was taken, hundreds of teachers signed their name on the forms with an 'X'.

Education for workhouse children was just as problematic. The Poor Law Commission of 1834 recommended they should have lessons in reading and writing from a proper teacher instead of one of the inmates, as in the past. But no professionally trained teachers were yet available.

Some parish guardians objected to providing writing as well as reading classes; learning to read was sufficient education for workhouse children. The Board of Guardians at Bedford wrote to the Poor Law Commissioners in 1836 on this score, but not, they claimed, on grounds of economy. They were worried that providing both skills would mean queues of paupers banging on their door, desperate to put their children in the workhouse so they could have a good education.

The commissioners acknowledged it was possible poor children might be 'enticed into the workhouse', but people's 'distaste for the necessary restraints of workhouse discipline' made this unlikely.[7] (This was an understatement – people hated the workhouse). Ordinary day schools for workers' children would be far more attractive to parents than the workhouse, with its social stigma. If workhouse children received a substandard 'pauper education,' they were less likely to find a job in later life. Children who could write and read would be far more employable. But parish guardians continued to drag their feet. Education for workhouse children was not a priority.

The factory inspectors, who were charged with ensuring factory children had an education, made urgent calls for more schools. Leonard Horner, writing in October 1842, singled out the cotton district of Ashton-under-Lyne, Dukinfield and Stalybridge (total population 55,000) for criticism. (Horner was now inspector for north-west England). The cotton industry had brought unprecedented growth to this area; over eighty per cent of the population were textile workers.

Horner estimated that thousands of children in the area had parents who could only pay a few pence for their education. Several thousand more parents could not afford any fees. Ashton's population was 25,000, but there was no 'National School, no school of the British and Foreign School Society, nor any other public day-school' for working-class children.[8] (Horner later discovered that there was a church school at Hey Chapel and a Roman Catholic school at nearby Stalybridge, but this was still wholly inadequate for such a large population).

At Dukinfield, a National Society grant provided funds for a classroom for 100 boys, but at nearby Stalybridge, a newly built National school was in debt before children had even enrolled. Two local cotton-masters contributed to its costs, but the school was unable to open owing to lack of funds.

Overall, the educational picture was pretty grim. The high proportion of young people (nearly half the population was under the age of twenty in 1841) combined with the scarcity of good, accessible schools for working-class children meant there was a vast sea of ignorance.

The sheer scale of the problem was highlighted by the 1843 Children's Employment Commission. Nationally, regardless of occupation (mines, trades or factories), many children 'never go to school, and have never been at any school'. In manufacturing areas, 'there is not a single district in which the means of instruction are adequate to the wants of the people'.[9] Schools had accommodation for less than one-third of the population. In the Birmingham area alone, over half the borough's 45,000 children aged five to fifteen years old did not go to school.[10]

The commission reminded the government of the lack of decent teachers. Where children did have the opportunity to attend day school, far too many teachers were 'wholly unqualified for their office'.[11]

Most children relied on Sunday schools for education. But even children who had spent several years at Sunday school could not read properly or spell. When investigators questioned them, children allegedly 'able to read' only knew the letters of the alphabet. (One wonders how many of them were so tired that they dozed through Sunday classes).

Britain was nominally a Christian country, so the commissioners were greatly upset by the scores of children ignorant of the Scriptures and Bible stories. One Yorkshire collier girl told them: 'Jesus Christ was born in heaven, but I don't know what happened to him. He came on earth to commit sin'.

Another girl, who spent three years in Sunday school but had never heard of the Apostles, asserted confidently: 'Jesus Christ died for his son to be saved'. One sixteen-year-old Wolverhampton boy thought: 'Jesus Christ was King of London a long time ago'.

The commissioners concluded that Sunday school education was so ineffective, children received as little benefit as if they had never been to school at all.[12] Children lacked even the most elementary general knowledge. Some Black Country children had never heard of London. They did not know the name of the Queen, and had never heard of British heroes such as Wellington and Nelson. However, they had an encyclopaedic knowledge of the lives and careers of highwayman Dick Turpin, and notorious criminal and serial prison escapee Jack Sheppard. Both these dubious role models ended their careers dangling at the end of a hangman's rope.

Dishonest employers or shopkeepers could easily swindle working-class children who had little understanding of arithmetic. They had no working knowledge of the coin of the realm they received as wages. One seventeen-year-old did not know how many farthings (¼d) were needed to make twopence, even when they were put in his hand for him to count.

The commission highlighted the problem associated with workers of very tender years. Even if enough 'abundant and excellent' schools were suddenly provided with the aid of a magic wand, they would be 'wholly beyond the reach' of many children because they began work at such young ages: 'from five, six, seven and eight years old'.[13]

The moment a child was old enough to earn a shilling or two, parents' only interest was in 'eatable profit', and they took them out of school.[14] Lancashire block-printers who were on very good money (twenty to thirty shillings per week) could easily afford the twopence fee to send their child to school, but there was no contest when she could earn 2s 6d per week at the print-works.[15]

Parents salved their conscience by sending their children to Sunday school. But it was difficult to persuade children who had spent all week down a mine or in a factory to spend their only day of rest in Sunday school. A Staffordshire boy said: 'I do not go to church or chapel; we are worked too hard for that. On Sundays I get up at ten and take breakfast. I put on Sunday clothes and walk about in summer; in winter I sit by the fire'. A Yorkshire lad agreed: 'I work here in the dark six days, and I can't shut myself up on Sundays too'.[16] (John Fielden once startled his God-fearing listeners in the House of Commons by commenting on the inhumanity of browbeating working children into spending their one day off in the week inside Sunday schools).

Evening classes were not the answer. Children were too tired to go to school when they finished a long shift. Mothers felt it was cruel to make their children, especially the younger ones, go to class when they had just spent at least twelve hours working and were physically exhausted.

The problem was most acute for children who toiled in coal and iron mines, as one Yorkshire mother commented: 'It's hard when the bairns have fallen asleep by the fireside, after their supper, to wakken [sic] them up to go to school.'[17] In Scotland, it was more common for working children to attend evening classes, but here too, colliers' children did not go.

Parents who had never been to school themselves did not see any point in sending their children. Investigator Mr Grainger discovered that Midlands parents on a good wage were 'utterly indifferent to the moral and physical welfare of their offspring. It would be a serious error to mistake this indifference for despair arising from distress and misery'. When trade was good, Birmingham mechanics 'were each earning from £2 to £5 or £6 per week', but instead of saving for the future and 'promoting the welfare of their families, these large wages were but too often wasted in vice and extravagance'.[18]

Parental apathy was not universal. As we saw in an earlier chapter, north-east miners campaigned to shorten their sons' working hours so they would have more time for school. The pitmen of Northumberland, Durham and Scotland wanted boys aged ten to fourteen to go to school under the 'half-time' system like factory children. Lancashire and Cheshire miners also wanted some kind of compulsory education for their children.

Parents in metal-mining districts (tin, copper, lead and zinc) made considerable sacrifices to send their children to school. They took pride in their children's education and were keen for their children to do well. A large majority of children went to a day school, and began work when they were older (age ten or twelve in Cornwall) than in coal districts.

These children's labour was not as severe as in coal mines, and they attended evening classes after work. The schools in metal-mining districts were not always of a high standard, but much better than in coal-mining areas, and children benefited accordingly.

One very good free school was run by the London Lead Company for their workers at Nenthead, Cumbria. Children aged six to eleven learned the three 'R's, natural history and geography; girls were taught sewing and knitting. During winter months, when no ore-washing was done (it was too cold), boys up to the age of fourteen also went to classes. The firm insisted on their children attending Sunday school in addition to weekday classes. Children were presented with a Bible when they reached a certain standard in religious knowledge.

At Leadhills in south Lanarkshire, the school for poor workers' children was so good, one observer claimed they enjoyed a 'better system of intellectual culture than even the middle-class children of England generally'.[19] The miners of Leadhills had long been renowned for their cultural awareness. In 1741 they had set up their own lending library (the first workers' library in Britain), which boasted 1,800 volumes by the 1840s.

Scotland's factory schools had a very good reputation. The Catrine and Stanley mills had excellent schools. At New Lanark, Robert Owen's scheme had borne fruit, although he left the business in 1827. (Owen had lost all his money funding utopian schemes). Factory inspector James Stuart commented in 1843 that of the 1,000 people working in the town's cotton industry, 'there is not a single uneducated person, not one who cannot read and write, and who does not know something of arithmetic'.

By contrast, there was a dearth of decent factory schools on Leonard Horner's beat. Only sixteen of the 117 factory schools under his supervision were 'good', and 860 children received a decent education there. Of the 6,872 children employed in mills in his area, over 3,000 attended factory schools. Others went to dame schools, National and church schools of various denominations. Most of these schools were atrocious, even though children paid around 2d per week each for instruction. Horner estimated that: '4,500 are getting no education whatever' even though they had school attendance certificates. Factory inspectors had 'no power to interfere to put a stop to this discreditable mockery of education'.[20]

The Chartist riots of the late 1830s and early 1840s made the government and reformers even more anxious to provide better schools. As always, Lord Ashley spoke up strongly on behalf of the children. He quoted a speech from a Chartist leader: the 'intemperance and vicious habits' of the working classes were 'the fault of the aristocracy and mill-owners, who had neglected to provide the people with moral improvement'.

Ashley warned that uneducated children might grow up into godless, lawless and seditious subjects. 'We owe to the poor of our land a mighty debt....There are many hearts to be won, many minds to be instructed, and many souls to be saved'.[21]

In 1843, Sir James Graham tried to broaden access to education for working children as part of his ill-fated factory bill. He wanted factory children's schooling increased to three hours per day. Mill-owners would get financial help to build schools. Once the schools were up and running, they would be maintained by the poor rates. (This funding suggestion did not go down well with rate-payers).

But Graham made a grave tactical error. He wanted factory schools to be supervised by the Anglican church. School committees must include the local clergyman and two churchwardens, and the schoolmaster must be vetted by an Anglican bishop.

An unholy row broke out. Furious Nonconformists did not want Anglicans to have any influence on how their children were taught in school. The deeply religious Lord Ashley was in the opposite camp. He was convinced that state education should be supervised by the Anglican church, and was not prepared to give many concessions to the Dissenters.

Following months of argument in parliament, and a monster petition against the bill by Nonconformists, the government beat a hasty retreat. The bill was shelved, and with it the question of a national system of education. It was left to churches and voluntary groups to build more schools. They rallied to the cause, determined to plough their own educational furrow without government interference. The nation's children were the biggest losers in this battle for their hearts and minds.

The 1844 Factory Act established the half-time system for factory children. They must attend school every day, either in the morning or afternoon, and go to work at the opposite end of the day. (Alternatively, they could work on three alternate days for ten hours per day, and go to school on the other days). This Act gave inspectors new powers to check on factory schools. If an inspector found a schoolteacher unfit to teach from 'gross ignorance' or perhaps 'immoral conduct', he could annul school certificates signed by the teacher.[22] Employers now had a greater incentive to employ good teachers, since it was not legal for children to work without school certificates.

The following year, 45,000 factory children in the north-west attended school five days a week under the new Act's half-time system. Horner was pleased to see an improvement in the schools in north-west England, and hoped mill-owners running the few remaining bad factory schools would be shamed into cleaning up their act.

The 1844 Act also gave inspectors powers to use fines paid by erring manufacturers to pay for new factory schools, or to buy equipment such as new books or maps for existing ones. The National School at County End, near Oldham, was given funds to enclose a piece of land so that children could have a playground.

The issue of religion came to the fore again in November 1845, when Horner commended Mr North, general manager of the North Shore Mill Company in Lancashire, for his 'enlightened views' and model factory school.

This factory, 'one of the largest and best conducted' in Horner's district, was owned by J. Aspinall Turner, J. Garstang and R. Ford North. It was the only cotton mill in Liverpool, employing over 850 workers, including sixty-eight children under thirteen, and 378 young people.

Mr North provided a schoolroom in a 'large, well-ventilated apartment' and a Sunday school. About 200 children attended the day school: those employed in the mill, and the offspring of workers living nearby. Around 300 adults and children went to Sunday school. Attendance was only compulsory for half-timers under the age of thirteen years. The Sunday school teachers were volunteer mill-workers.[23]

Horner hoped his report on the North Shore Mill would inspire other factory owners to emulate its example. Unfortunately, it stirred up a hornet's nest of criticism.

The Roman Catholic clergy of Liverpool were outraged because North Shore factory children and parents were 'encouraged' to attend the (Protestant) Sunday school, even though many were reportedly Catholics. (Children over thirteen years old and older workers were not ordered to attend – 'persuasion only' was used – but how many workers would feel brave enough to remonstrate with their employer?)

The Catholic clergy rushed to protect their flock from 'these gross violations of the rights of conscience'. Local vicar George Brown and others petitioned parliament in March 1846 to express their dismay that Horner had recommended North Shore as a model for other factories to follow. They begged MPs 'not to give any sanction to the obnoxious principles' illustrated in Horner's report. Factory workers must have 'perfect religious freedom'.[24]

The controversy died down when Father Newsham, a local priest, persuaded the directors of North Shore Mill to relax the Sunday school rules so Catholics would not be deterred from working for them.

There was still no legal compulsion for owners of non-textile factories to educate their child workers, even though schools had potential benefits for employers as well as workers. Educated workers were more orderly and careful.

The factory schools at Price's Patent Candles showed what could be achieved by a caring employer, however. The managing director was James P. Wilson, described by an admirer as 'one of the best men living'. He was extremely religious, and cared deeply for the health and moral welfare of his youthful workers. Wilson said his philanthropic schemes were inspired by the life and works of Dr Arnold of Rugby.[25]

The firm had a two-acre site by the banks of the Thames at Vauxhall Bridge, and another large works at Battersea. The family business, founded in 1830, was run by the sons of its founder, William Wilson.

Price's candles were originally made from coconut oil and tallow. The candles were cheap to buy, and burnt brightly and clearly. In the 1840s, the firm expanded and took over Samuel Child's night-light works at Brompton. The night-light manufacture was moved to Vauxhall. The Vauxhall factory was enormous. Another night-light factory (Albert's) at Belmont was taken over by Price's, and moved to new premises under the arches of the South Western Railway.

By the early 1850s, Price's switched to making candles from palm oil. The candles were marketed as an 'ethical' product. Palm-oil exports were more profitable for African producers than slavery, which still thrived even though it was banned in Britain and the colonies since 1834.

The palm-oil ships unloading their freight at Vauxhall were known locally as the 'African Blockading Squadron'. Every Price's candle burnt was said to 'put out a slave'.

The candle factory would find it difficult to market itself as an 'ethical' concern nowadays because of its heavy reliance on child labour. Children often worked nights from 6 p.m. until 6 a.m. The 'patent' candles were made by huge machines which processed the fat into giant 'cakes'. The cakes were melted in vats, and the liquid poured into moulds (unlike traditional candles made by repeatedly dipping a wick in tallow or wax). Boys helped move the cakes of fat to the vats ready for melting, and children packed the candles in boxes.

When the firm took over Samuel Child's night-light factory, it acquired another complement of child workers (their nimble fingers were well-suited to making night-lights). A writer who visited the factory thought the production line, with its 'little army of boys in clean blouses and caps' and 'long rows of girls in pinafores' looked like a school-room.

Boys punched out cardboard and tin components to make 'cups' to hold the fat in the night-lights. Some fixed wicks in the lights, and others filled the cups with the fat or 'stearine.' Girls plaited cotton wicks for the night-lights. In very warm weather, the stearine became too difficult to handle in the mid-day heat, so the children came into work at four o'clock in the morning and worked for four hours. They returned at six o'clock in the evening and worked for another couple of hours.

The factory school began in a humble way. Wilson claimed the project began when some children developed a thirst for learning and wanted to learn how to write. (It seems likely Wilson was being modest, and he suggested the idea to the boys). They practised their handwriting with scraps of paper and worn-out pens begged from the counting house. Their foreman encouraged them, and when more boys joined in, Wilson provided them with some makeshift, easily moveable desks. The boys set these up at night for studying after clearing away the candle-boxes.

George Wilson, James's brother, gave them books as prizes, and the children's literacy greatly improved. The boys were proud of their achievements and keen to run their little school themselves. At first the Wilsons did not interfere beyond giving them some 'copy-books, spelling-books, and testaments', and helping boys with their spelling.[26] In the winter of 1848, James cleared out the upper floor of an old building at his own expense for use as a school-room, and built an iron staircase to it for easy access.

When more boys joined the night school, the pupils found it was not easy running a large class by themselves, so they asked James Wilson to take charge. To encourage more boys to come to school after a long day's work, Wilson gave tea-parties for the scholars, and this simple treat was a great success.

Wilson founded schools for the night-light children as well as the candle workers. (Their former employer, Samuel Child, sent the Brompton children to evening classes at the nearby National school, but Wilson was unimpressed by the quality of education they received there.) The school for night-light workers was situated under a railway arch. Boys and girls were taught separately. The night shift boys were given 'breakfast' (or more accurately, their supper!) in the morning when their shift ended.

Customer demand for night-lights was highly unpredictable: orders suddenly flooded in without warning. Formerly, the neighbourhood children were called into the works at short notice to help out, then were sent back to the streets when the orders were fulfilled. This was obviously very unsettling for the children, so Wilson founded a day school for them. When fresh factory hands were needed, they were chosen from the most diligent scholars.

The children were 'very eager' to become proficient enough to start work so they could take home money for their parents. All parties benefited. The children received a free education, and the Wilsons had a pool of labour they could draw on, (and who they knew personally and could trust) when needed. When children were no longer needed in the factory, they went back to school instead of roaming the streets. By the early 1850s, the schools catered for over five hundred scholars.

The boys particularly enjoyed using the works' cricket field provided by the Wilsons. The manager, men and boys all played together happily. Wilson organised baths at the factory, so workers could clean off candle grease after their shift, and built a swimming pool. Young workers were treated to annual excursions such as a trip to Guildford by train, or to Herne Bay. For many candle children, this was their first ever visit to the seaside.

James Wilson paid for his innovations from his own pocket. When he reported on his expenditure in March 1852 for the firm's shareholders, they were so impressed by Wilson's benevolence they reimbursed all the money he had spent and took over the schools' running expenses (around £1,200 p.a.).

Wilson used the money from the shareholders to build a chapel and engaged a permanent chaplain. In 1853, the Wilsons constructed another factory at Bromborough Pool (near Birkenhead) with a model village and school. Bromborough was close to Liverpool, the main port for palm oil, and it was more economic to make candles there.

When Wilson's 'educational report' for the shareholders was published, there was immense public interest in newspapers and magazines. Seven thousand copies of the report were initially printed, but this was insufficient to satisfy demand. The report's sale acted as an advertisement for the firm and sales of Price's candles rocketed.

People bought the candles as a matter of conscience. James Wilson was swamped by letters of congratulation and encouragement from well-wishers, including factory inspector Robert Baker, and writers Harriet Beecher Stowe and Mrs Gaskell.

Why did such humane employers like the Wilsons continue to make children work nights? (They worked alternate night shifts, one week on, one week off). The Wilsons could not do as they liked with the firm; they had a duty to their share-holders and workers. If night-work was abolished, the factory would be less competitive, and cost the share-holders a lot of money.

James Wilson wrote: 'My brother and myself live in hopes of seeing this entirely done away with in the course of years… at present it would require so heavy an outlay, that we feel it would be out of the question to propose it.' When factory inspector H.W. Lord visited Price's candle factory at Battersea in the early 1860s, Wilson showed him round the site. He explained their dilemma on night-work, and expounded his belief that 'external compulsion' (government legislation) was the best way to abolish night work.[27]

Unfortunately, Wilson's philanthropic activities were almost snuffed out during a trade slump a couple of years later. The firm's shareholders got cold feet at the huge expense, and school funding was sharply curtailed.

Wilson's educational schemes were said by contemporaries to have the same effect on commercial philanthropy as the invention of Stephenson's 'Rocket' had on the birth of the railways. His care for his workers set other manufacturers thinking and wondering how far they should look after their employees.

John Bagnall and Sons owned Golds Hill Ironworks and Collieries at West Bromwich. In 1853, two junior partners in the firm were inspired by Wilson's efforts and set up night schools for their workers. They gave lessons themselves with the aid of some volunteer teachers. After a few months, a schoolmaster and two women teachers were hired. The firm spent £6,000 (a tidy sum then) on a building for use as a church and school.

In the meantime, factory inspectors were puzzling over the best way to win over parents. How could they persuade them to spend a few pennies on their children's education instead of making them bring home a wage?

If parents were given incentives, maybe they would keep children in school longer before sending them out to work. School prizes (money, or books like the Bible) proved popular. These awards were sponsored by industrialists and landowners like the iron and coal-masters of south Staffordshire. Over an eight-year period, three boys at the Bagnall schools won £4 each, thirteen boys and three girls won £3 each, one boy and four girls won £1, and nearly fifty boys and girls were awarded a Bible.[28]

The prizes idea quickly spread to north Staffordshire and Dudley. The London & North-East Railway Co. in Crewe, the Weaver Navigation trustees, and mining districts of Shropshire, Durham and Northumberland, all set up similar schemes. School prizes were 'a hit' with many parents, and the school-leaving age rose in some places like Wolverhampton.

Prizes were insufficient to overcome parents' prejudices in the coal and iron districts of south Staffordshire, however; the families targeted by the original scheme. A three or four-pound prize, which was not guaranteed, could not compete with the lure of regular wages. Seven-year-old boys were taken out of school by their parents to work in the rolling-mills, or down the pits, where boys under ten (the Mines Act was still flouted) could earn four to six shillings a week.

All these philanthropic efforts, however admirable, barely scratched the surface of the education problem. Reformers would never tip the scales in favour of education against wages so long as parents paid for their children's schooling.

Professor William Stanley Jevons (1835–1882), writing in the 1860s, put the facts baldly: 'At present it may almost be said to be profitable to breed little slaves and put them to labour early, so as to get earnings out of them before they have a will of their own. A worse premium upon improvidence and future wretchedness could not be imagined.'

Jevons called for a national system of education, even if it meant depriving parents of their children's earnings. The time had arrived, now that the country was so prosperous, to invest in the nation's future, even if it was expensive in the short term. 'If we cannot do it now, we can never do it; and wretched, indeed, must be a kingdom which depends for subsistence upon infant labour'.[29]

Chapter 12

Mangling The Operatives

So far, successive governments had been distinguished only by their timidity over the issue of children's working conditions. To recap, factory legislation was never intended to outlaw child labour, just to curtail the worst abuses.

Reformers had made little progress so far. While politicians crossed swords over the 'Ten Hours' issue, children in the bleaching, finishing and calico-printing trades worked disgracefully long hours.

Early critics of factory reform repeatedly drew attention to its extremely narrow and seemingly arbitrary remit. Mill-owners felt it was totally unfair to limit children's hours and the age they could start work in their factories, when a calico-printer could work children of any age for as long as he wanted.

In the early 1840s, children as young as eight regularly worked the same shifts as adults in Lancashire, Cheshire, and Yorkshire calico print-works. A standard 'day' was twelve hours, but when demand was high printers began at six in the morning and worked all night if necessary.

The 'tear' boys and girls ('tearers' or 'tierers') helped block-printers by preparing a surface of wet dye ready for the printing-block. A child used a flat brush to transfer dye from a pot to a circular frame covered with a woollen cloth, which they brushed evenly with the dye. The printer placed the block onto the wet cloth to take up the colour, then pressed the block down firmly to make the pattern. Children stood for many hours performing this monotonous task.

Leonard Horner began campaigning on behalf of print-works children in 1840. He spoke to a mother of eight children whose husband had deserted her. Her twelve-year-old son James, 'a delicate looking boy', began at the print-works when he was about six years old. His mother said she had often carried her son to work at midnight in the middle of winter. James worked from midnight until two the following afternoon. He took bread and butter and tea to work for a snack at 4 a.m. Breakfast was brought to him at 8 a.m. He had nothing else to eat until he finished in the afternoon. The night shift lasted for two weeks, after which James switched to a 6 a.m. start.

Some print-works used a 'twelving' system. The children's shifts were from twelve noon until midnight, when another set took over until twelve a.m. the next day. This gave the printers a fair share of daylight hours. They were fined for bad work, and made more mistakes while working by gas. The children stayed late if there was a shortage of tierers.

A mill-owner complained to Horner. He could not get enough workers, because children got far higher wages at the local print-works 'for working any number of hours'. When the 1833 Factory Act came into operation and cotton masters sacked the youngest children, they were 'immediately employed' at nearby print-works.[1]

Calico-printing was chiefly carried out in Lancashire, Cheshire and Derbyshire. There were a few works in Kent, the west of Scotland, and Dublin. Over 11,000 workers under eighteen were employed in Lancashire print works alone.

The 1843 Children's Employment Commission estimated that over 5,600 children under thirteen were employed in the north-west and Derbyshire, plus at least another 5,000 in print-works in Scotland.[2] Printing was performed by machinery as well as the traditional block-printing by hand.

Working conditions varied according to the different stages of the printing process. The stove rooms, where wet cloths were dried, were incredibly hot and humid, with temperatures reaching 110°F. The girls who worked there often fainted from exhaustion. Temperatures in the block-printing rooms were cooler: sixty-five to eighty degrees Fahrenheit. Night work and long hours were still customary, and child 'tearers' often fell asleep at work. Children had little opportunity to go to school even though the block-printers, who earned good wages, could easily afford the fees.

Incidentally, one of the commissioners who studied the productivity of the print-workers noticed that in busy periods, when printers did fifteen-hour shifts, they spoilt far more fabric than usual. The masters, worried by the loss in production, shortened their hours slightly, and the number of mistakes dropped back to normal levels. This put the nail in the coffin of Nassau Senior's (already discredited) theory that a manufacturer's profits were made during the final hour of production.

Lord Ashley had recently toured the manufacturing districts again. He visited calico-printing works, and went down a coal mine to see conditions for himself. After the 1843 commission's report was published – 'records of suffering, ignorance, and shame' – Ashley was determined to change the lives of the children and workers he had seen.

However, the general public, which had leapt to the defence of the colliery children, was left completely unmoved by the report. In the face of this indifference, Ashley knew he had little hope of achieving any protection for print-workers. Therefore, when in 1845 he introduced a bill to protect print-works children, and those in bleaching and associated trades, he confined his measure to children under thirteen. Ashley quoted extensively from the 1843 report in his speech. He told the House of Commons he would never stop fighting for the nation's child workers as long as any part of 'this mighty evil' remained.[3]

Some MPs were indifferent to his proposal. Calico-printers like Richard Cobden were downright hostile, and the House was deeply suspicious of Ashley's stated determination to interfere in many other industries.

Ashley was partly successful. The Print Works Act of 1845 banned children under eight from working in print-works. Females and boys aged nine to twelve were not allowed to work between 10 p.m. and 6 a.m. Children must have a statutory amount of education: thirty days in a six-month period. A year after the Act's introduction, Leonard Horner reported happily that 'the great evil of employing children of a very tender age is at an end'.[4]

But the government refused to regulate the bleaching, dyeing and finishing trades where children also worked long shifts. Manufacturers claimed they could not fill rush orders if hours were restricted.

All the other industries (apart from mines) covered by the Children's Employment Commission were left completely unregulated. Calico-printing children were the only ones to receive protection from the state. Lord Ashley felt deeply frustrated and helpless in the face of the great forces ranged against him.

Ashley was forced to turn his attention again to the question of factory hours. The cotton mill-owners were up to their old tricks, running rings round the inspectors. Factory legislation was so poorly worded that inspectors found it impossible to stop manufacturers overworking their young employees.

Mill-owners had brought back the 'relay system' prevalent in the early 1830s. The factory 'day' officially ran from 5.30 a.m. in the morning until 8.30 in the evening. Although women and young persons were limited to ten hours' labour, these hours could be worked any time during the factory 'day'. The masters constantly 'shuffled' workers and shifts like a pack of cards, and sent child workers in and out of the factory at odd times. Inspectors could not check how long a child had really worked. Ashley and the inspectors tried to tighten up the law in the teeth of opposition in and out of parliament.

The problem lay not with the Ten Hours Act of 1847, but the 1844 Factory Act which it amended, and was still in force. Without going into the legal complexities, an ambiguity in the legislation meant that some magistrates agreed with mill-owners who claimed it was lawful to work 'relays' of children. The factory inspectors disagreed, and brought a test court case to prove it.

However, in the cotton towns of north-west England, factory inspector Leonard Horner faced real problems because JPs would not convict mill-owners prosecuted for illegal working. Mill-owners working legally lambasted him for not enforcing the law, because they lost custom to masters working longer hours. The mill-owners working relays accused Horner of being overly strict. Consequently, the Ten Hours Act was hardly worth the paper it was printed on.

Ashley and the short time committees were devastated. All those years of heartbreak and campaigning for a ten-hour day had gone up in smoke. John Fielden died two years after the Ten Hours Act was passed, his health shattered by the long fight to achieve the bill. He was greatly disheartened when the new law did not work as well as hoped.

Lord Ashley was weary and disillusioned. It was now 1850: seventeen years since he first started campaigning for factory workers. He was very busy with the Ragged School movement; he was a member of the Board of Health trying to clean up Britain's festering slums; and his sixteen-year-old son had died the previous year. It seemed as if the factory question would never be settled.

When some mill-owners suggested they might give up the relay system in return for a ten-and-a-half-hour factory day, plus an earlier finishing time on Saturday, Ashley felt it was time to compromise. He insisted, however, a ten-and-a-half-hour day should only be put in place if the operatives agreed.

This proviso was overlooked by the short time committees, who saw only that Ashley had 'wobbled' over the Ten Hours issue. A storm of protest broke over Ashley's head. The factory hands did not trust the mill-owners' olive branch. They believed the mill-owners intended to keep the relay system. Ashley was demonised, and no longer the workers' darling.

The government's Factory Act of 1850 *increased* women's and young persons' hours to ten-and-a-half-hours a day. Their factory 'day' ran from six in the morning until six at night (with an hour and a half for meals), except on Saturdays, when they finished at 2 p.m.

But children under thirteen were not included in this new factory 'day'. They still worked their allotted six-and-a-half hours any time within 5.30 a.m. and 8.30 p.m. After the women and teenagers went home for the day, the men were kept hard at work with the aid of relays of child helpers. The factory hands' suspicions were proved correct.

The inspectors soon found this law was being evaded, too. Mill-owners refused to co-operate. On 7 June 1852, two inspectors who tried to visit Mr Sumner's mill at Glossop, and check on his working hours, had the mill doors slammed in their face. Within minutes, the inspectors were surrounded by an angry mob of men from the mill and forced to hide in a nearby hotel.

The only way to crack down permanently on the relay system was to close the legal loophole which permitted relays, and limit factory children's working day. In 1853, an Act was passed which specified children could not work before 6 a.m. or after 6 p.m. As Lord Shaftesbury said (Ashley succeeded to the earldom two years earlier) factory legislation was in 'good working order' at last.[5] Women, children and teenage boys all started and finished the factory 'day' at the same time.

Many thousands of children and young people were now covered by factory legislation. By 1856 there were 46,000 children under thirteen employed in textile mills, and 72,200 boys aged thirteen to eighteen. The proportion of child workers under thirteen had fallen from thirteen per cent in 1835 to just over six per cent. Females were in the majority: 387,800 women and girls over the age of thirteen (counted together for statistical purposes) comprised over half the total workforce of 682,500 people.[6]

Although Lord Shaftesbury had fallen out with the short time committees, he did not cease campaigning for children in industries related to textiles. In 1854 he proposed a bill to regulate bleachworks, which prompted another select committee, headed by Hugh Seymour Tremenheere. Girls and boys worked 'for fifteen, sixteen, eighteen or more hours per day'. The Bleach Works report of 1855 recommended that workers should have the same 'day' as factories.

Mary Ann Niblots had worked at Blair and Sumner's bleach-works at Bolton for two years: 'I am going on thirteen... I come to work sometimes at five, sometimes at seven, eight or nine o'clock'. When there was a rush job to do, 'I come at twelve o'clock at night, and generally go home at tea-time next day. I sometimes have sore feet'.[7]

Tremenheere believed there was no necessity for such excessive hours. They were primarily owing to last-minute orders. If bleach-masters' customers were warned they must give longer notice, the work could be spread out more evenly. As soon as the bleach-masters realized they faced regulation, though, they promptly banded together and lobbied parliament. They thwarted several efforts to regulate the bleaching and finishing trades. It was not until 1860 that the first Bleach Works Act brought the trade under the Factory Acts, except for open-air bleaching 'fields' where fabric was bleached out of doors. The Act was hedged about with many provisos and was not as successful as campaigners hoped.

Meanwhile, factory inspectors had another major war on their hands over the hundreds of workers mutilated or killed by unsafe machinery every year. Leonard Horner and his colleagues were thoroughly sickened by having to report so many needless deaths. But when the inspectors tried to change working practices to reduce the death toll, they faced a storm of criticism. What right had these interfering busybodies to tell mill-owners how to run their factories?

The biggest casualties in this battle were the workers, young and old. Even if they survived their terrible injuries, they faced a lifetime of poverty if they lost the ability to earn a full wage.

Employers did not have to pay any compensation to workers injured on their premises. Some employers voluntarily paid up, but others had to be shamed into it. In 1838, fourteen-year-old Alexander Dunn stood on some boxes to oil a drum at Crawford & Smith's flax factory at Montrose. One of the boxes gave way under his weight, and his leg became trapped. Alexander's leg was amputated below the knee; he bore the operation 'with fortitude'. Alexander was in hospital for nine weeks. All he received from his employer was his wages and an extra thirty shillings.

Luckily for Alexander, the Forfar town clerk, Mr Roberts, heard about the accident and prosecuted the mill-owners on his own initiative. Crawford & Smith caved in. They gave £50 to Alexander and paid Mr Roberts's £18 legal costs (the child was treated free at Montrose public infirmary, so there were no medical bills).[8]

Unguarded shafts rotating at high speeds caused horrific fatalities and injuries. Lancashire mills seem to have been particularly prone to this problem, possibly owing to the sheer number of mills and operatives concentrated in the county. Small wonder that Friedrich Engels thought Manchester factory workers looked as if they lived 'in the midst of an army just returned from a campaign'.[9]

Lord Ashley actively pursued mill-owners in the courts on behalf of injured children. The first case he brought was against James Haworth, owner of a mill at Shaw Clough, Rossendale. In January 1840, sixteen-year-old Mary Howarth was 'fearfully mutilated' when she was caught up by an unguarded upright shaft.[10] She broke both her thighs, an arm and leg, and her head and body were badly bruised. She survived the accident, but was still using crutches months later. Haworth declined to pay Mary any compensation and even refused to pay her medical bills. The day after Mary's accident, a guard for the shaft was finally erected. It cost just five shillings.

Leonard Horner mentioned the girl's plight to Lord Ashley. There was currently a select committee investigating the effectiveness of factory legislation, and he hoped Mary's story would speed up the introduction of a law to box off machinery.

Lord Ashley took legal action against Haworth, acting as 'a friend' of the girl. Mary's father, who was working in the same room and witnessed his daughter's accident, was ready to act as a witness. He told Horner that the mill-wright who constructed the shafting had advised it should be boxed off.

At first the mill-owner tried to bluster out the affair. He swore he would have his day in court, but as the time drew near, he got cold feet. Haworth travelled all the way to Cowes on the Isle of Wight, where Lord Ashley was staying, to beg him to drop the legal action. He offered compensation to the girl.

Lord Ashley promised to stop the prosecution if Haworth paid £50 compensation to Mary, her surgeon's bill of £15 10s, and all of Lord Ashley's legal expenses. Haworth had to pay his own legal costs, and for his journey down to Cowes. Ashley made him sign a letter of apology with an undertaking that in future all potentially dangerous machinery in his mills would be securely guarded. (Ashley wanted to publish the letter as a way of raising publicity for the issue).

Factory inspector T. J. Howell reported another case taken up by Lord Ashley. This time the case came to court. Seventeen-year-old Elizabeth Cotterell (Cotterill) was badly hurt when her clothes were caught up in unfenced upright shafting at Samuel Stocks & Son at Heaton Mersey. The machinery was revolving at sixty revolutions per minute, and Elizabeth was trapped for up to five minutes before the machinery was stopped. She was horribly mutilated. Stocks didn't pay her any compensation; he deducted 1s 6d from her wages for the part of the week she hadn't worked. Elizabeth's medical care cost her a great deal of money at a time when she was unfit to work.

Lord Ashley pursued Stocks & Son 'as a friend' of Elizabeth under common law: a person had a duty of care to their neighbour. If Ashley had simply given Elizabeth the funds to prosecute the case herself, she would have been liable for all the legal costs if the case failed. Instead it was Ashley who risked a possible legal bill of hundreds of pounds on her behalf.

At Liverpool summer assizes in 1840, Samuel Stocks pleaded 'Not Guilty'. When the court heard it would have cost just ten shillings to securely cover the shafting, the judge ordered Stocks to pay £100 damages to Elizabeth; £40 costs were awarded to Lord Ashley.[11]

However, the publicity surrounding this prosecution did not inspire manufacturers to prevent similar injuries. A few months later, in early December, a Bolton newspaper reported three fatalities (all under the age of eighteen) within a few days of each other. The youngest was fourteen-year-old Isabella Gibly. She worked at Cartwright's mill at Whalley Banks, Blackburn, and was standing near an upright shaft when her dress got caught up.[12]

The *Times* reported on 29 December 1840 that there was so little remaining of poor Isabella's body it was not thought worthwhile to bury her in a full-size coffin, just a box.

Even when a manufacturer fenced off a shaft, sometimes the workmanship was so shoddy, it was still a potential menace. In January 1844, factory inspector Mr Ewings reported the case of Ellen Ravenscroft, a seventeen-year-old piecer at Euxton, near Preston. She was 'torn to pieces' after becoming entangled when working near shafting covered by a flimsy tin casing.

The following month, a sixteen-year-old working in a mill engine-house at Guest's mill near Manchester was hanged when his worsted scarf was snagged by upright shafting. Leonard Horner believed that there were hundreds of shafts insecurely guarded. He thought this inattention was probably more owing to 'habitual carelessness' by mill-owners than penny-pinching.[13]

William Baker, a silk throwster at Derby, strongly believed that compulsory fencing of all machinery would be an 'unnecessary and vexatious expense'.[14] He thought that only machinery which operatives were likely to go near in the ordinary course of their work should be safeguarded.

The Strutt family in Derbyshire took a more enlightened view. Anthony Strutt invested a great deal of money over several years to ensure his mills at Milford were safe workplaces.

The 1844 Factory Act at last put the onus on manufacturers to safeguard their machinery. Children were banned from cleaning it while it was in motion. Factory accidents must be reported. This was a major success for Ashley and the factory inspectors. The provisions of the Act came into force on 1 October that year.

No children, young people, or women were allowed to clean any part of the mill-gearing while it was moving. (The mill-gearing and shafts put the spinning or weaving machinery in motion). Every fly-wheel powered by steam or water, and all parts of steam engines and water-wheels, and every hoist or teagle (lift) near where young people worked, or which they might pass close by, must be securely fenced off.

A very important provision of the 1844 Act prohibited children and young people working between the fixed and traversing parts of a self-acting mule while it was in motion. The moving carriage of the self-acting mule was powered by steam or water. It moved with relentless force until it struck against the fixed part of the machine. (Mules worked by hand were slightly safer for children to clean, because the operative could instantly stop the machinery).

The mule-spinners ('minders') who supervised the self-acting machines were supposed to stop the moving carriage so the scavengers could clean underneath the mule. Children swept up the dust and filaments which fell from the cotton while it was being spun. Spinners were paid by piecework, and it saved time if the scavenger quickly nipped underneath the machine instead of waiting for it to stop.

Self-acting spinning mules continued to claim young lives after the 1844 Act because of operatives' carelessness or indifference. The better mills pinned up notices displaying the relevant clause of the Act. At first sight the operatives, not mill-owners, were at fault when they ordered youngsters to clean machinery while it was moving. But Horner was convinced that mill-owners could do more to stop accidents.

Alternative technology was available. A recently invented automatic scavenger-roller, which automatically cleaned under the self-acting mule, meant there was no need for children to go underneath the machinery. In March 1849, Leonard Horner was notified by a Blackburn surgeon of the death of fourteen-year-old

Emanuel Gill. Emanuel died instantly when crushed by a self-acting mule at John and Thomas Sparrow's mill, Blackburn. This was the third death in Blackburn from similar causes in a short space of time. Horner was especially angry because in the previous three years he had seen an automatic scavenger-roller used at several mills.

Horner prosecuted the Sparrows and alerted local press when the case came to court in April. The minder, Dewhurst Robinson, swore he had never known anyone in the mill to go under the machinery before when it was in motion. The magistrates didn't believe him. The Sparrows were fined two pounds for breaching the act, plus another two pounds for not notifying the accident, and costs.[15]

A clause of the Act permitted the inspectors, if they felt part of the machinery appeared likely to injure workers, to hang up a warning notice to that effect. If the manufacturer did not fence it off and a worker was injured, the factory owner was liable to a fine of between £10 and £100. If inspectors served one of these notices on a mill-owner, and the mill-owner disagreed that the factory machinery was insecurely guarded, the master could take the matter to arbitration.

As Horner pointed out, it was very difficult for someone who wasn't an expert mechanic (or factory owner) to say if fencing off any machinery which seemed dangerous would interfere with its proper working. So he kept a careful watch on the accident returns from surgeons. During the next twelve months, he received many reports about hand injuries from the cog-wheels at the end of throstle frames (cotton-spinning machinery). Sometimes operatives were so severely injured, they had their fingers amputated.

Horner sought expert advice from a Manchester machine manufacturer and discovered these cog wheels were already boxed off in several factories. He ordered all his inspectors to serve warning notices in every factory where this type of cog wheel was unguarded. Most Lancashire mill-owners complied. A notable exception was John Bright Bros. of Rochdale (the firm owned by the famous Radical politician) who insisted on going to arbitration. With the help of William Fairbairn, the famous engineer, Horner persuaded the judge it was practical and necessary to fence off the cog wheels in Bright's factory.

Unscrupulous manufacturers exploited any possible legal loophole. In 1851 inspector Robert Baker summonsed W. Hill, a Leeds flax-spinner, for not fencing off his machinery securely after seventeen-year-old Mary Freeman badly injured her hand. Baker had previously notified Hill the gearing in his factory was in a dangerous state.

However, when the case came before the magistrates, Hill proved the machinery which injured Mary was brand new. It was not installed until after Baker's notice was served. The magistrates agreed with Hill that the 'danger sign' only applied to machines in the mill seen by the inspector, not the new one, even though it was virtually identical to the older ones already deemed unsafe. The magistrates' decision made it impossible to successfully prosecute Hill. The master made some amends. He gave Mary's mother five shillings per week to make up the loss of her wages, and promised to pay the girl some compensation.[16]

This judicial decision meant that inspectors were faced with a logistical nightmare. They visited hundreds of different mills. It was not humanly possible to identify which machinery was new every time they made a return visit. The only way around this was to frame future legislation compelling manufacturers to make all parts of the machinery as safe as possible in the first place.

One of the biggest controversies surrounding the 1844 Act arose over high-level shafting. When the Act came into force, mill-owners argued it was pointless spending money to fence off shafting over seven feet from the floor. It was (in theory) well out of workers' reach.

Terrible accidents still occurred, though, no matter how inaccessible and seemingly innocuous high-level shafting appeared to be. Workers sometimes needed to access the shafting to oil it, or to lime-wash the walls (a requirement of the Factory Acts). Dreadful injuries occurred if people became entangled.

Home Secretary Lord Palmerston acted after receiving the factory inspectors' returns for April 1853. They reported six deaths and 370 accidents caused by machinery over the previous six months. Palmerston wrote to the inspectors in June insisting on a change of tactics. He bluntly told them to enforce all clauses of the 1844 Act requiring machinery to be securely guarded, instead of waiting for an accident to occur, and then prosecuting the mill-owner concerned.

The inspectors agreed. On 31 January 1854 they issued a circular to all factory owners. Over the previous three years, 128 accidents (including thirty-five fatalities) had occurred owing to high unguarded shafting. On average forty people were killed or injured each year from unfenced shafting. The inspectors warned they would no longer countenance any evasion of the Act's provisions regarding fencing.

This warning caused a major revolt amongst mill-owners. They descended in a body on Palmerston. They argued it would be hugely expensive to fence off machinery that employees did not go near in the ordinary course of their duties. As a result of the masters' bullying tactics, Palmerston backed down, and told inspectors not to insist on these shafts being guarded. He suggested other ways of protecting factory hands, such as only allowing adults to do any jobs near high level shafting.

Dr T. K. Chambers, in a lecture to the Society of Arts, commented on the fencing controversy. Inventing ways to stop workers coming into contact with machinery were all very well, but no-one ever suggested ways of altering the machinery's operation: 'making the monster itself less fearful is never thought of'.[17]

Inspector T. J. Howell remarked that mill-owners saw the fencing clause as an 'arbitrary capricious regulation… contrived by the inspectors…in a spirit of vexatious interference with the "rights of capital"'. But the law was made 'for the protection of all'. Children were employed from the age of eight and could not be expected to be as careful as older workers. 'Death and mutilation for life is rather too severe a punishment even for heedlessness and indiscretion'.

As Howell tactfully put it, 'considerations of expense' had 'unconsciously warped' the mill-owners' opinions on fencing. The 'rights of capital' were clearly more important to masters than their workers' right to life.[18]

The factory inspectors' half-yearly report for October 1854 lists five children under eighteen killed by factory hazards in Leonard Horner's district. An unnamed twelve-year-old boy, Ann Harrison (eight) and Harriet Brown (seventeen) were killed by an unguarded upright shaft in separate accidents. Two other children were crushed by a self-acting mule.

The inspectors' efforts were not helped by magistrates' lack of support. Two adults were killed by unfenced horizontal shafts in north-west England that autumn. Henry Glenny (twenty-two) got his foot caught by a strap in an Oldham factory. The strap lapped around the horizontal shaft driving the machinery, and Glenny was killed instantly. When inspectors prosecuted the mill-owner, some of the magistrates who heard the case were factory owners themselves. They dismissed the case without any explanation, even though the Act was clearly contravened.[19]

Barrister Thomas Tapping, noting that over 1,780 injuries and deaths from machinery were reported in the six months ending on 30 April 1855, sadly concluded that the laws for 'the protection of the lives and limbs of operatives have failed in their intended effect'.[20] Tapping suggested stiffer penalties: manufacturers should face prison sentences as well as fines.

The most intransigent mill-owners were in Lancashire, with a few honourable exceptions. Mill-owners in the rest of the country, particularly Yorkshire, co-operated with the inspectors' suggestions for secure fencing.

The Lancashire mill-owners dug in for a lengthy battle. On 6 March 1855, over 100 firms banded together to form a Factory Law Amendment Association (later the National Association of Factory Occupiers). Its avowed aim was to force a change in the Factory Acts. It soon became clear that the mill-owners really wanted to sweep away the whole system of factory regulation and inspection.

The war of words between manufacturers and inspectors spilled out into newspapers and popular magazines. In April 1854, journalist Henry Morley wrote an unsigned article 'Ground in the Mill' for Charles Dickens' *Household Words*.

He recounted the ins and outs of the high-level shafting controversy, and lamented the 'yearly sacrifice' of factory hands to 'the commercial prosperity of Great Britain'.[21] Morley kept the issue in the public eye with several hard-hitting articles. He dubbed the mill-owners' society 'the National Association for the Protection of the Right to Mangle Operatives'.[22]

In 'More Grist to the Mill,' on 28 July 1855, Morley warned of the association's secret agenda. The mill-owners were raising a 'fighting fund' of five thousand pounds. They would pay legal costs and fines for any member prosecuted for not fencing off his machinery. They wanted the inspectors' powers of interviewing operatives in private to be repealed. Certifying surgeons should answer to JPs, not factory inspectors. No shafts over seven feet above the ground should be fenced off. The association quickly retracted its intention to pay fines when it discovered this was illegal, however.

The mill-owners' chief 'spin doctor' was author Harriet Martineau (1802–76). Harriet was the daughter of a Norwich silk manufacturer whose business failed during the banking crash of the mid-1820s. She was a great supporter of technological marvels, and seemingly genuinely believed that all cotton manufacturers were benevolent gentlemen with a paternal interest in their workforce. Mill-owners were well known, according to Martineau, for their 'intelligence, beneficence, public spirit, and devotedness to the cause of popular advancement'.

Martineau claimed that mill-workers killed by unfenced machinery 'threw away' their lives 'through disobedience and wanton exposure of themselves to danger'. She compared factory accidents with railway accidents: 'Is every drunken vagabond who lies down in the track – every deaf old man who chooses the railway for his walk – every fidgety traveller who steps out while the train is in motion… to be regarded as the victim of the railway proprietors?'[23] Martineau launched a vitriolic attack on Leonard Horner's work as a factory inspector (the manufacturers' association wanted him sacked).

Morley and Dickens slammed Martineau's rhetoric as 'preposterous'. In 'Our Wicked Mis-Statements', they outlined Martineau's pamphlet for their readers and combatted it point by point. They refuted Martineau's statistics on accidents, citing figures from the latest factory inspectors' reports. Morley's and Dickens's sole aim was to 'take thought for the operative working amidst dangerous machinery…it is strictly within the province of the law to protect life.'[24]

Lancashire mill-owners kept up the political pressure, and got their way with the 1856 Factory Act. The new Act said that mill-gearing, like machinery, only needed securely fencing off unless women, young persons and children were likely to come into contact with it. They did not have to fence off shafts 'out of reach'. The inspectors had lost.

The 'National Association for the Protection of the Right to Mangle Operatives' had won a resounding victory, but never achieved its chief aim: to tear down the Factory Acts or render them useless. However, the Act's passage was a sad day for workers.

That same year, at John & William Slingsby's cotton mill near Skipton, Yorkshire, eighteen-year-old William Ellison paid a terrible price for the inspectors' defeat. Ellison climbed a ladder to replace a strap on the drum of an unfenced horizontal shaft over ten feet above the factory floor. The strap touched the rotating shaft, and instantly got entangled, taking Ellison with it. He died from multiple fractures of his chest, arm and legs. Shortly after the accident, the mill-owner fitted a strap hook to every drum in the factory. (A strap hook was a method of catching a loose strap so it did not cause an accident).[25]

To be fair, some workers were careless; they were very young. And some manufacturers acted promptly once they were alerted to a problem with their machinery.

For example, in the mid-1860s, the process of printing lithographs by steam was first introduced to north-west England. When a new steam printer was installed at Smith & Barnes' printing-works in Brazennose Street in Manchester, the young lads working there simply could not resist tinkering with this exciting new machine. Less than three days later, some boys had their fingers crushed in the cog wheels, and a bigger tragedy was only narrowly averted.

Mr Smith (one of the owners) said the boys had been playing: 'one boy actually climbed the strap while it was in motion, and another put his arms around the upright shaft…he was flung round, but luckily not seriously hurt. Those have now all been guarded against; the cog wheels have a small tin boxing fitted over them. Of course no fencing could be built to stop a boy climbing a strap in motion, but I think that was a warning to them; they will not try again, though no serious injury resulted; the fright was considerable, indeed the whole place was frightened, men and all, but the boy was only very sick after it, and came to work as usual the next morning.'[26]

One problem area where manufacturers also took decisive action was the high-pressure danger of boiler explosions. Steam boiler technology was far from perfect, and the engineers who tended boilers did not always have sufficient training for dealing with the awesome power of steam.

Boilers blew up with alarming regularity, endangering the lives of the workforce and people living nearby. At Bradford in late November 1850, several teenagers were amongst the dead and injured after a massive boiler explosion at C. Waud & Co.'s mills. The boiler was less than twelve months old, but had no safety valve. When the engineer opened a valve at the wrong moment, he was killed instantly. Four hundred people (men, women and children) were at work when the disaster happened. They cowered under the machinery as an immense shower of bricks and metal rained down on the glass panes of the mill roof. Margaret Donnell (seventeen) died from her injuries shortly afterwards.[27]

A few days later, on 29 November, twelve people died in the aftermath of another huge explosion at Firth Bros.' woollen mill in Halifax. The force of the explosion demolished part of nearby Lilly Lane mill, where thirty young people and children were employed. One of the mill-owners, Samuel Firth, shooed youngsters out of the engine-room earlier in the day because he suspected it was about to burst. The engine-tenter (minder) Joseph Helliwell and Firth were charged with manslaughter, as they knew the boiler was old and unsafe.[28]

Another twenty people were killed on 17 March 1851, including fourteen-year-old Mary Ann Wright, in a boiler explosion at Henry Marsland's Park Mills, Stockport. One week later, another eight people were killed at a Manchester calico-printing works.[29]

After this spate of accidents, Lord Ashley raised the issue in the House of Commons in 1851. The safety of steam engine boilers was not covered by the Factory Acts. The only action that factory inspectors could take if they saw an obviously dangerous boiler was bring it to the mill-owner's attention. They did not have powers to interfere.

Ashley asked if steam engine boilers could be brought within the remit of the factory inspectorate. The home secretary, now Sir George Grey, felt this was totally impracticable. It was fairly easy for an inspector to give an opinion on whether factory machinery was properly fenced off, but the safety of a steam boiler was something 'no inspector could well determine'.[30]

Now, manufacturers invested a great deal of capital in their mills. An explosion destroyed mill buildings and stopped production as well as wasting life and limb. They took decisive action. In the mid-1850s in Manchester, an Association for the Prevention of Steam Boiler Explosions (later the Manchester Steam Users' Association) was founded. The association set up a system of boiler inspection by expert engineers. It proved extremely useful, and similar schemes were set up in other large manufacturing towns. If only mill-owners had been as united and far-sighted in safeguarding their employees in other respects, many lives could have been saved.

The factory inspectors were also very concerned by some appalling accidents in the flax 'scutching' mills of Ireland.

The flax plant has a very stiff, woody stem, which must be removed before the soft, pliant fibres inside can be used to weave cloth. This was done by 'breaking' and 'scutching' the stems.

When these processes were done by hand, flax stems were first 'broken' (weakened) by crushing a bundle of them between the jaws of a large wooden device, rather like the mouth of a crocodile. Next, a worker separated the shards of unwanted outer stem from the fibres by repeatedly striking them with a special scutching tool. After scutching, the flax was 'heckled'. It was straightened, separated and cleaned of any remaining dirt and fragments of bark, until the fibres were silky and glossy ready for spinning.

Machines did the processes of breaking, scutching and heckling far more quickly and efficiently than by hand. In very large factories like Marshall's immense steam-powered flax mill at Leeds, all these processes took place under one roof.

But in Ireland, many scutching mills were housed in tiny sheds in remote country districts. These sheds were attached to corn-mills. The miller provided power as a service to local farmers, who sent their wives and children to the mills with the flax they had grown.

Workers fed bundles of flax stems into massive grooved rollers powered by the mill-stream. These machines were highly efficient at swallowing up the workers, many of whom were under eighteen. If a bundle of straw got wrapped around a boy's hand, or a girl's dress get snagged, or she put her hands just a fraction too near the machine, they could lose one or both arms in an instant.

The farmers' wives and children were not used to factory work: 'Every season, in autumn and winter, persons wholly unaccustomed to machinery are taken from field labour to feed these rollers; and as the machinery is entirely unprotected, and the persons quite unacquainted with the dangers they incur, the accidents are, in number and kind, wholly unexampled in the history of machinery'.

At Kildinan near Cork, local surgeon William Dwyer reported that between 1852 and 1856, workers suffered six fatalities and sixty mutilations in just one mill. Another doctor, William White, wrote: 'In many cases a quarter of the body is torn from the trunk', resulting in 'death, or a future of wretched incapacity and suffering'.[31] Similar accidents were recorded in Coleraine and Armagh.

Ventilation was also a big problem in these mills. The scutching process generated huge amounts of dust, and the sheds had low roofs. Dust got into the operatives' eyes and lungs. They suffered from eye disease, coughed and spat blood.

The 'scutchers' were only saved from long-term damage to their health because scutching was seasonal work, and they got a breather while working in the fields for several months. The young girls and women who bundled up the flax into handfuls ready for the scutching machines did not suffer as much from the suffocating dust, because they worked outside.

Robert Baker tried to get flax scutching-mills included under the factory acts in 1850, but his efforts were unsuccessful. The government decided that flax scutching was an 'agricultural operation' because it took place in rural districts, and the mills were left unregulated.

The inspectors grew more worried as the number of scutching mills and workers increased: there were over 1,800 scutching mills in Ireland by 1862. After a ten-year-old girl at Armagh lost an arm and foot in 1865, Baker raised the issue again in the inspectors' reports.

Baker wrote to two major scutching machinery makers in Ireland for their opinion on whether scutching was a manufacturing or agricultural process. Both firms agreed it should be covered by the factory acts. MacAdam Bros. of Belfast said they had 'no doubt' scutching was a 'manufacturing operation'.[32] However, the government would not budge. Scutching mills would have to wait until inspectors could change its mind. All that the inspectors could do was to persist in their campaign to bring as many industries as possible under the umbrella of protective legislation.

Chapter 13
A Change of Heart

By 1860, factory legislation had been in place for almost three decades. Lord Shaftesbury felt the time was ripe to once more campaign on behalf of children and young people outside the Factory Acts.

He was deeply concerned. In the two decades since the last Children's Employment Commission report, several old trades had disappeared and new 'dangerous' industries such as lucifer match-making had become widespread. Mines, print-works and bleach-works were now regulated, but over 150 trades were not covered by legislation.

In 1861, Shaftesbury requested another Children's Employment Commission. Between 1863 and 1866, the Commission published five voluminous reports into pottery, glass-making, millinery, iron and steel-works, paper-staining, fustian cutting, percussion caps and cartridges, lace, hosiery, and scores of other trades.

Being a potter was still a very unhealthy occupation. In Stoke-on-Trent, over half the men over the age of twenty who died from lung disease were potters.

Fortunately, signs of change were visible: manufacturers had come round to the idea of regulation. Half a century earlier, Josiah Wedgwood II asked for the industry to be 'let alone'.[1] Now twenty-six masters (nearly all the major employers), including Wedgwood & Sons, and Minton & Co., wrote to the secretary of state stressing the need for legislation.

The masters had discovered that over a quarter of child workers could not read. Children were taken out of school early (before they were ten), so their parents could send them to work. The better manufacturers could not act on their own, because others in the area would never agree to join them. 'The employment of children at such an early age is injurious to health, stunts their growth, and causes in many cases a tendency to consumption, and distortion of the spine… legislative enactment is wanted to prevent the employment of children at such an early age, and secure to them at any rate a minimum of education'.[2]

Distressing as conditions were in the potteries, workers in the lucifer match industry were threatened by a truly harrowing industrial disease. At the time of the 1843 Children's Employment Commission, lucifer match-making was a recent development. In 1833, a method was found of applying highly toxic 'white' phosphorus directly to match-heads. Large numbers of impoverished children and young people made lucifer matches. The Commission noted the lack of ventilation in the factories, and the prevalence of long hours. The children were 'pale and sickly-looking', but major illness was not mentioned.[3]

However, in 1845, a Vienna doctor drew attention to a terrifying condition affecting phosphorus workers. Five years later, the London Medical Officer of Health, Dr Letheby, reported cases of the disease in Britain. 'Necrosis of the jaw…one of the most terrible (illnesses) that can afflict humanity', caused 'intolerable' pain.

Tooth decay was an early warning sign of the disease. The jawbone of the worker slowly died, and their gums became covered in abscesses. Some people had to have their whole lower jawbone removed; many died. John Bell, an adult worker at Thomas Todd's Bethnal Green Road factory in London, lost his jawbone to necrosis: 'It's like everlasting pain…no-one can describe it'. 'Phossy jaw', as the disease was known, was largely preventable if proper ventilation and washing facilities were provided for workers.

By 1863, over 1,600 children and young people were employed in the industry, which was concentrated in London, plus a few firms in Manchester, Newcastle and Norwich. Most workers were employed by ten large firms, but about 400 worked in small garrets. The small manufacturers were the most lackadaisical regarding safety, but even some big firms did not do enough to protect their small workers. The children most exposed to danger were the boys who 'dipped' bundles of matchsticks in the mixture containing phosphorus, and the workers who hung up the bundles to dry. They breathed in deadly fumes every day. Youngsters ate their meals in the same rooms where phosphorus was used, which made it even likelier they would contract the disease.

Charles Garner (fourteen) and his brother John (twelve) worked at John Baker's works in Bethnal Green. Both boys' voices were hoarse, and their clothes 'shone' at night from the chemicals impregnated in the fabric. Charles had already lost a couple of teeth. John, a 'pale unhealthy looking' boy, had very bad teeth: 'They ache all day and all night sometimes'.

There was no need for this terrible suffering. Bryant & May had recently opened a new factory at Fairfield, Bow: 'a nicely conducted place'. Their 'new safety' matches were made with red phosphorus, much safer than ordinary white phosphorus, but many manufacturers refused to use it because it cost over twice as much. At this time their child workers appeared 'happy and contented'.[4] (Much later in the century, Annie Besant and others launched a major campaign to help Bryant & May's match girls form a union to combat their slave-like working conditions).

Children's working conditions in other industries were still highly dependent on their employers' attitude. Birmingham was the chief centre for Britain's steel pen manufacture. The two biggest works were Joseph Gillott & Co., and Hinks, Wells & Co.

The enormous factory of Hinks, Wells & Co employed over 500 hands. In 1851, the factory used two and a half tons of steel to produce 35,000 gross of pens weekly from best quality Swedish iron.

Strips of steel were placed in metal boxes and 'roasted' for twelve hours in a large stone oven. Rough edges were removed from the steel strips, which were soaked in 'pickle' or vitriol (dilute sulphuric acid) to clean them. Then the metal strips passed through the rolling-mill several times until they reached the required thickness. The men working the rolling-mill had boy helpers to 'catch' the metal as it passed through the rollers. Many more processes were required to create a finished pen from the thin ribbons of steel: cutting out, pressing, 'bronzing' (tempering), scouring, grinding and so on.

The boy helpers in the rolling mill wore filthy clothes 'soaked' with grease. Their shirt sleeves were stained yellow from the 'pickle'. There was nowhere for children to wash their hands except a tub of dirty water. When the metal cut their hands, the 'pickle' made the lacerations smart.

Jack Parden (eleven) had 'very ragged' clothes. He had had 'bad eyes' ever since he started working there. His hands were often cut by the metal but 'Mother will not let me lose my place over my hands'.[5]

At John Mitchell's pen factory on Newhall Street, two workrooms were 'cellars unfit for human habitation'. The air stank from vitriol and one boy working there, fifteen-year-old Frederick Parkes, had big 'holes' in his hands and clothes from the chemical. He had stopped going to Sunday school because his clothes were always in rags.

By contrast, Joseph Gillott & Co's immense factory on Victoria Street had 'clean, fresh and airy' workrooms. Mr Gillott employed hardly any children under thirteen. There were 'very many' teenage girls at work, but most of the workforce were young women. The steam press used in the manufacturing process had a special guard to stop workers losing their fingertips.[6]

In the glass industry, boys did not start work as young as formerly, although investigator J.E. White found one nine-year-old boy, Johnnie Mathers, working as a shovel holder at James Hartley's Sunderland works. (A 'shovel holder' held a shovel in front of another glass worker's face to protect him from the intense heat while gathering the glass 'metal' from the furnace).

Johnnie said: 'We are called [to work] at any hour of the day or night... When I am off working sometimes I am sleeping and in bed, and sometimes I get a play'. He earned 3s 6d per week. Johnnie was taken on at the works at such a young age from 'mere charity'. His father was killed in a colliery accident, and his mother was 'badly off'. Managers insisted that the boys' parents wanted their sons to work as young as possible, not the works owners.

White had real difficulty interviewing the glass-house boys because they ran about so much. The glass-blowers shouted angrily at him if their work got held up, because they were on piece-work.

Boys' work was considered essential to keep costs down. Some glass firms tried to give the boys' jobs to men, but found their wages bill was too high.

Previously, the 1840s commission had found little evidence of ill-treatment in the glass-houses. But in 1865, White quickly became convinced the glass-house boys were beaten far more than necessary, sometimes for no fault of their own. One Sunderland manager said he often stepped in to take a boy away from his father's supervision, and give him to another man to train up. The father 'seems to expect more of him than he would from a stranger, and to be too harsh'.[7]

White interviewed Joseph Hood (17), a taker-in from a Birmingham glass-house who was ill in hospital. Joseph had heart disease caused by rheumatic fever. He had worked at a glass-house for four years, and said the men were 'rough brutes' who often beat the boys, but 'we do not tell the master; they would beat us worse then.'[8]

An anonymous lad (White did not identify him in case he was punished) worked at a large northern flint-glass works. The men were unkind to the boys and 'skelped' (hit) them. 'When you spoil a few things you get called so [sworn at]… they tell you to go to the "damned place". I was at school, but I was so pleased to get work here before my schooling was done… and now I would be glad to get away. No one knows nothing [sic] before he comes into a glass-house… You soon learn things here. Boys think it would be so pleasant to come and get money, but it would be a [sic] vast better for them to stay at school'.[9]

At Birmingham, famous glass firm Chance Bros. invested much effort into educating their workforce, after discovering how few of their young workers had literacy and numeracy skills. The firm built 'large and handsome' schools near the works, and made it a rule for all workers under eighteen to attend evening class.[10]

The millinery trade, however, had not mended its ways. All voluntary efforts by the industry to regulate itself had completely failed – very worrying, as it was a major employer. In England and Wales, 600,000 women, young people, and children were employed as dressmakers, milliners and seamstresses. There were 112,000 millinery workers in Ireland, and 51,000 in Scotland.[11]

Ridiculously long hours had not disappeared. In one 'first class' Edinburgh millinery house, girls worked twenty-two hours per week longer than factory workers were permitted. Employers still caved in when customers made emergency orders.

Madame Jacobi ran a family business on Bond Street: 'As it is, if I refuse a lady, she goes to my neighbour, who takes her order; so I cannot refuse without displeasing her, and perhaps may lose her custom, because she thinks me disobliging.' (It was customary in the millinery trade for the manageress to use a French name. One wonders how many 'Madame Jacobis' were really plain Mrs Smith or Brown).

Economics played a part. Milliners felt compelled to use girls as cheap labour. Their wealthy clients demanded (and got) long credit, sometimes thousands of pounds over several years. Mistresses were worried that shorter hours would erode their profit margins and resisted the idea of legislation.

But a change in attitude was evident here, too. The better employers admitted that over-long hours were unprofitable, as girls were too tired to do decent work.

Madame Jacobi and other managers felt that legislation would give them a level playing field: 'we should be all alike; and the ladies, when they know that it is necessary, would give us a little more time; their orders would be executed quite as quickly as they are now.'[12]

Mr Macintosh of Swan & Edgar (a well-known store on Regent Street) agreed: 'nothing but an Act of Parliament will be of any use to restrict the hours of work.'

There was some good news: the advent of the sewing-machine removed the worst drudgery involved with millinery, needlework and 'slop-work' like shirt-making and tailoring. Wages were rising where machines were used. Girls began as machinists around the age of fourteen. Mrs Gilling, a Cheltenham dressmaker, said 'I am quite sure my machinists, who used to be hand-workers, have improved in health' since using machines.[13] She could afford to pay them higher wages now that production had gone up. Girls and young women worked late nights at some firms, however.

The Children's Employment Commission estimated that 1.4 million children, young persons and women workers would benefit from protective legislation. The revelations of the disgusting conditions endured by so many of the nation's children at last led to action. When the Commission reported back in 1843, its evidence was met with indifference. This time around, there was a flurry of protective legislation.

What caused this momentous change?

The Victorians were immensely proud of Britain's industrial achievements and the growth of Empire. It was inevitable that industry – the source of Britain's wealth and power – was endlessly discussed in newspapers and magazines. The old idea that people's lot in life was ordained by heaven and they should give thanks for it, no matter how bleak, came under fire.

Writers like Thomas Carlyle (1795–1891) discussed the 'condition of England' question. Why did the 'dumb millions of toilers' endure such 'dire misery'?

The nation had lost its soul in the pursuit of profits. It was time to build a fairer society for all. In *Past and Present* (1843), Carlyle pilloried the profit motive and the gospel of laissez-faire. The government could do far more to improve living conditions for workers and their children. Whenever a 'vested interest' gainsaid reform by saying 'I will lose profits', then society should answer: 'Yes, but my sons and daughters will gain health, and a life, and a soul'.[14]

Social comment was a favourite leitmotif with novelists and poets. Elizabeth Cleghorn Gaskell (1810–65) drew attention to the class divide in her novel *Mary Barton* (1848), an impassioned plea for greater understanding between masters and workers.

Charles Dickens's *Hard Times* (1853–4), set in the imaginary industrial 'Coketown', also explored the class divide. Politician Benjamin Disraeli's novel *Sybil* (1845) discussed the 'Two Nations' of rich and poor, and their lack of mutual understanding, as if they were 'inhabitants on different planets'.[15] Charles Kingsley looked at the plight of rural labourers in his novel *Yeast* (1848), and the sweated trades in *Alton Locke* (1850).

Frances Trollope (1780–1863) was an early critic of child factory labour in her novel *Michael Armstrong* (1840), a sentimental and shocking tale inspired by apprentice Robert Blincoe's 'Memoir'. Its uncompromising portrayal of factory life caused much queasiness amongst middle-class reviewers.

People began to question the diktat that children must work. Children should have a time of innocence, a time to learn and explore the world around them. Working-class children should not be doomed to toil in their earliest years. Elizabeth Barratt Browning's poem *The Cry of the Children* (1842) was a passionate call to end working children's suffering:

> The young fawns are playing with the shadows,
> The young flowers are blooming towards the west;
> But the young, young children, O my brothers,
> They are weeping bitterly! –
> They are weeping in the playtime of the others,
> In the country of the free.

Charles Dickens placed children and their experiences in the heart of novels like *Oliver Twist* (1837), *David Copperfield* (1849–50), and *The Old Curiosity Shop* (1840–1). The dark days and loneliness he endured in his early years, slaving away in the blacking factory, never left him. His memories gave him a unique insight into the childhood world he lost when forced into the world of work.

In a brilliant scene in *The Old Curiosity Shop*, Dickens parodied the different expectations for working-class and middle-class children. Little Nell, who earns a living at 'Jarley's Wax-Work', is castigated by stuffy schoolmistress Miss Monflathers for not slaving in a factory.

Monflathers tells Nell it is 'naughty' of her to be a 'wax-work child' when she could 'have the proud consciousness of assisting, to the extent of your infant powers, the manufactures of your country; of improving your mind by the constant contemplation of the steam-engine; and of earning a comfortable and independent existence of from two-and-ninepence to three shillings per week? Don't you know that the harder you work, the happier you are?'

One of Monflathers' teaching colleagues reminds her of Dr Isaac Watts' *Divine Songs for the Use of Children* (1715):

How doth the busy bee
Improve each shining hour,
And gather honey all the day,
From every opening hour…

In books, or play, or healthful toil,
Let my first years be past,
That I might give for every day,
Some good account at last.

An angry Monflathers declares that only 'genteel children' should spend their first years 'in books, or work, or healthful play'. Their 'work' should be 'painting on velvet, fancy needlework, and embroidery'. Girls like Nell must 'work, work, work'.[16]

Victorians looked back to Rousseau's and Wordsworth's ideas of childhood as a time of precious innocence. A great flowering of children's literature infiltrated the puritan moralism of the previous century, with stories of fantasy and imagination like Lewis Carroll's *Alice in Wonderland* (1865).

But the facts of life had not changed. Unlike working-class children, middle-class children did not work during their youth. It was accepted that they should be educated. Of course, boys and girls were schooled differently according to Victorian ideals of gender: females were doomed to a future life of cosy domesticity. A childhood without toil was a dream, but scarcely an aspiration, for working-class children who knew that their families depended on their wages.

The work ethic had not disappeared. As late as the 1890s, the anonymous author to a *Boy's Book of Trades* for young people wrote: 'Those who imagine that the necessity for labour is only an evil must be either grossly ignorant or wilfully wicked. Whoever wastes his life in idleness, either because he need not work in order to live, or because he will not live to work, will be a wretched creature, and at the close of a listless existence will regret the loss of precious gifts and the neglect of great opportunities'.[17] Hogarth, Hannah More and Sarah Trimmer would have smiled benignly.

Workers often expressed a wish they had been able to stay at school longer. James Caldecott, a foreman at an Ardwick factory in the 1860s, began work in a mill as a half-timer when he was seven years old. After he left the mill and stopped going to school he 'soon forgot all he had ever learnt'. When James grew up, he went to evening classes and the local mechanics' institute so he could get an education.[18]

Thirteen-year-old Charles Everidge, who worked in a Wolverhampton steel toy factory until eight o'clock at night, said he wished that he finished work earlier so he could 'go to night school'.[19]

The concept of healthy 'playtime' for workers of all ages was gaining ground. In the 1840s, public parks and libraries sprang up so workers had somewhere to go during their time off other than the pub. Mill-owners like Joseph Strutt gave Derby a magnificent arboretum to improve townsfolks' health.

Titus Salt, who founded an alpaca wool business at Bradford, built an immense factory (then the largest in the world) in the beautiful Aire valley in 1853. The 'new and busy town' of Saltaire he constructed for his workers was equipped with comfortable housing, schools, a 'literary and philosophical institution', a cricket ground, bowling-green and an 'abundance' of playgrounds.[20] His operatives had somewhere to work, rest and play (but no pub).

Attitudes in industry had changed for the better. The untiring efforts and quiet tact of the factory inspectors had gradually accustomed industry to a measure of state intervention.

Inspector R. Whately Cooke-Taylor reported that the once hostile factory hands had come around to the idea of inspection. It was now 'a recognised success' and a 'source of increasing satisfaction to the operatives'.

Even the masters had grudgingly come to terms with it. People no longer feared that 'ruinous consequences' would automatically follow if more industries were regulated, as they did less than two decades earlier.

The 'once violent opposition' of mill-owners to factory legislation had proved 'fallacious and groundless'.[21] The doom-mongers who prophesied businesses would close, and textile districts become a wasteland of derelict mills, were wrong. The spectre of lost production was a complete chimera. Shorter working hours meant that factory hands were less tired and more productive.

A Preston firm which reduced the factory day by an hour in 1844 found to its amazement that production remained the same.[22] The factory hands, who were paid by piecework, earned the same money in eleven hours as they used to over a twelve-hour day. They were more alert, and made fewer mistakes. They had more leisure time for evening classes, too.

Politicians were forced to eat humble pie. In the spring of 1860, the Bleachworks bill was being debated in the House of Commons. Sir James Graham, who had so often stonewalled or watered down factory legislation, made a 'confession' to the House of Commons. 'Experience had shown to his satisfaction' the nay-sayers were mistaken. Factory legislation 'contributed to the comfort and well-being of the working classes, while it had not materially injured the masters'.[23]

Factory reform of the textile industries, once the establishment's bugbear, was now held up as a shining example to unregulated industries. Legislation had brought enormous benefits, and therefore unregulated industries would benefit from reform, too.

This is not to say manufacturers became fans of regulation en masse. When fresh legislation was mooted, the more hard-line manufacturers lobbied parliament as they had always done, predicting ruin and unemployment. However, they now found it less easy to control public opinion.

All these factors had a 'trickle-down' effect which made it easier to change working conditions. Public opinion had shifted. Workers' lives were more important than profits. The dragon of laissez-faire was not dead, but some of its fangs had been drawn.

Hurdle after hurdle fell for reformers as one by one, industries were brought under the factory acts. The machine lace-making industry (the subject of a special investigation by Hugh Seymour Tremenheere in 1860) was regulated by the Lace Act of 1861. Only lace-making in factories powered by steam or water was regulated, however. Lace-dressing and finishing processes were excluded from the Act, and there were other special exemptions. (As we saw earlier, lace-dressing and finishing processes such as 'drawing' were done by hand, mostly by women, young persons and children in workshops or private houses.)

Three years later, the Factory Acts Extensions Act of 1864 brought pottery making, lucifer match-making, percussion-cap making, cartridge-making, paper-staining and fustian-cutting under regulation.

In the potteries, some manufacturers' forebodings about restricting children's labour quickly proved unfounded. The Cochran family, who owned the spanking new Brittania Pottery in Glasgow, were 'a little fearful at first' regarding the Act, but 'so far we have got on wonderfully well'.[24]

The inclusion of fustian-cutting in the Act was a real milestone: the first time a domestic industry was made subject to inspection. Fustian-cutting (fustian was a hardwearing fabric) was done in people's homes as well as factories. This was a much-needed reform. Fustian cutters liked to observe 'Saint Monday' and even Tuesday at the beginning of the week ('play days') and their child helpers worked up to twenty hours a day at the end of the week so their masters could make up the time.

The 1864 Act 'commenced a new industrial era'.[25] There seemed no limit to which industries could be regulated. Three years later, the Factory Act Extensions Act made blast furnaces, copper mills, iron and steel mills, metal manufacture (where powered machinery was used), glass, paper, tobacco and other industries subject to inspection. The 1867 Act applied to all workplaces in the designated industries employing more than fifty people (a new legal definition of a 'factory').

The 1860s commission had reported that the worst conditions, and youngest workers, were found in workshops. Children endured 'protracted and injurious labour in small, crowded, dirty, and ill-ventilated places of work…'[26]

Pillow-lace (hand-made lace) and straw-plait (used to decorate bonnets, or make hats) were made in 'schools' which employed very tiny children. The schoolmistress kept a big stick ready to ensure children completed enough work for their parents to sell. When J.E. White investigated straw-plait schools, some infants were too young or timid to answer his questions properly, and he relied on the schoolmistress to make sure he wrote down their testimony correctly.

At Houghton Regis, George Tompkins (three and a half) was the youngest 'plaiter' there. He only made a yard or so of straw-plait in a day. Mary Scrivener (four) made five yards of plait before dinner, and five after. 'I have my "five" to do, and if I have not done it, I have to stop or to do it at home. I earn no money, but aunt sells my plait. I have no mother'.[27]

The Workshops Regulation Act of 1867 finally brought child workers employed in handicrafts, including in private houses, under the Factory Acts. Any place employing less than fifty people was defined as a 'workshop'. The infamous millinery trade and cottage industries like lace, hosiery, straw-plaiting and glove-making were just a few of many employments covered by workshops legislation. As in factories, children's labour was limited to six-and-a-half hour day; women and young persons to a twelve-hour day. Children under eight were banned from workshops.

Other clauses were far less stringent than for factories. Children could work any time between 6 a.m. and 8 p.m.; women and young persons could work between 5 a.m. and 9 p.m. Proof of children's age was not required. Eight- to thirteen-year-olds must have ten hours' education per week.

Because of the huge numbers of premises involved, the government decided not to give factory inspectors the task of ensuring workshops complied with the new Act. Instead, local authorities were asked to police the Act.

Lord Shaftesbury estimated that the Factory and Workshop Acts of this year brought an extra 1,400,000 women, children and young persons under protective legislation. These Acts were imperfect, but they finally established the principle that children in factories and workshops were entitled to state protection.

In the late 1860s Robert Baker, now Chief Inspector of Factories, looked back over his thirty-four years spent as an inspector: 'Remembering as I do when there was no Factory Act, except that of 1802 – when the little secular education that factory workers obtained was in the Sunday school – when children of the tenderest years were employed fourteen or fifteen hours a day, often at night – when factory cripples were…constantly seen in the manufacturing districts, and when human life indeed was held in small comparison with commercial profits', each leap forward had proved 'providential in every sense.'

Robert felt that 'The great principles of the Factory Acts' were now recognised as the best way of bringing education within the workers' reach, producing 'the happiest effects on the people.'[28] Baker was certain that the long fight to reform working children's lives had all been worthwhile.

One of the newly regulated industries was brick-making, the focus of a major 'children's crusade' to rescue small workers. A building boom had greatly increased demand for the humble brick.

Every brick-maker's child was born 'with a brick in its mouth'.[29] (That is, they started work at an early age). Bricks were made from clay mixed with fine ash (usually four parts clay to one part ash). If the clay contained too much sand, some ash was replaced by coal-dust or 'breeze'. Children sifted the coal-dust before it was added to the clay.

After mixing, the mass of clay was taken by barrow to a 'pug-mill' worked by a horse. The clay was thoroughly chopped and kneaded by metal knives inside the pug-mill to form a homogeneous mass. In some works, children 'tempered' or kneaded the clay with their hands and feet instead. The 'pugged' clay was carried by boys and girls to the bench where the 'moulder' (brick-maker) worked. Moulding was often done by women. This was very cold, damp work, particularly in wet weather.

The moulder employed up to four children at a time. First, a young lad or girl cut up the clay into large lumps, each slightly bigger than the brick mould. The moulder dipped the mould in sand, covering the inside with a fine layer of sand. Next, she smartly smacked the clay lump into the mould so that every nook and cranny was completely filled. The moulder scraped off any excess clay using a flat piece of wood, and gently removed the brick from the mould. Children carried these 'green' bricks on wheelbarrows to a drying area.

When the bricks were dry, children took them to the kiln or 'clamp' for firing. The fire in the kiln was lit through flue-holes, which were covered up once the fire was well alight. The children looked after the kiln (an even temperature was important for good quality bricks), adding extra coal if needed. They 'punched out' the flue holes with hammers or crowbars when it was time to 'draw' the kiln, or if the kiln had gone out too soon and needed to be cleaned out and re-lit.

Twenty years earlier, the 1840 Children's Employment Commission had visited brickyards but were not unduly alarmed by conditions there. Liverpool children worked long hours: from four in the morning until nine o'clock at night in the summer months. They earned good money: 10s to 12s per week. One ten-year-old boy carried a total of 7,000 bricks per day, and walked up to twenty miles, but appeared 'in perfect health'.[30]

J. E. White visited the Midlands for the 1860s Commission. An estimated 20–30,000 children worked in brickyards and brickworks; their ages ranged from three or four years old up to age sixteen. White considered it a 'healthy employment' as children were in the open air all day, although brick-making was tiring and 'extremely dirty' work.

At Stourbridge, brick-making was a thriving local industry. Fireclay ('white') bricks for furnaces were made in addition to ordinary red bricks. Each fireclay brick weighed 9lb when wet, and 7¼lb when dry. Girls called 'pages' 'carried off' the bricks from the stove to the kiln and then out again; they were paid 8d to 10d per day.

Sarah Ann Smith was a page at Edward Pearson's fireclay brickworks. The girls carried six bricks at a time. Sarah once shifted 1,550 wet bricks in one day. Her working day began at 6 a.m. or earlier and continued until dark.

When White visited Baker & Co.'s firebrick works at Moor Lane, Brierley Hill, he arrived as a kiln was being 'drawn' – emptied of dried bricks. It was still 'like an oven inside.' Girls and women formed a human chain to empty the kiln, which held over 17,000 bricks. It took a day and a half to empty it. Workers tossed the bricks two at a time to one another until the end of the chain, where a cart waited for the bricks.

White commented on the good health and intelligence of twelve-year-old 'angel' Ann Elizabeth Powell. 'Her energy of manner and evident love of work, and her utter absence of all tone of complaint were remarkable'. He calculated that she caught and tossed over 36 tons of bricks over the working day.

Ann said she 'never got beaten, and never got tired, not [even] when staying late. I hope I shall never get tired of work. My mother brought me up to be a good worker.' Ann did not know all her alphabet, but had had a little religious education: 'Father reads the Bible out, but he only comes home once [a] week. An angel is very pretty. I wished I was an angel. They live in heaven… to be an angel I must behave very well'. Another girl, Annie Holt (twelve), said she sang at her work 'many a time'.[31] She went to the Ragged School on Sundays.

Conditions in the red-brick works were far more gruelling than the fireclay works. Girls and boys spent their days working barefoot, wringing wet, and up to their knees in mud. Their clothes were mere rags; the children were so plastered in mud it was difficult to tell girls from boys.

Investigator H.W. Lord, who visited brick-works in Middlesex and Kent, felt the children's hours were 'monstrous'. They were exhausted after work and were carried home at night by their parents, but looked 'strong and healthy'.

Lord felt it was unbecoming work for girls. In Staffordshire, girls laboured clad in rags and showing their legs (very shocking to Victorian eyes). They 'learn to treat with contempt all feelings of modesty and decency'.

Although it was laborious toil, girls preferred brick-making to slaving as a maid-of-all-work, the only other employment in their area. Selina Bennett, a nineteen-year-old worker at Oldbury, said 'I would rather be in the brickyard than go to service'.[32]

Carrying damp, very heavy loads of clay for hours was undoubtedly hard on the smallest children, and cases of rheumatism were reported.

Investigators felt that the worst aspect of brick-making was the children's lack of education. They learnt bad language from adult workers (men and women!). Robert Baker had no doubt that it was 'absolutely cruel' to employ children in brick-yards, especially girls. A brick-maker near Tipton declared that 'Not one in ten of the women and children has [sic] been taught to read and write'. They were 'ignorant, untaught, and unheedful of education'.[33]

One foreman said that brickyard children swore worse than navvies (hard to believe – navvies were renowned for their inventive profanity). 'They say "No", when asked if they can read or write, but just ask them if they can swear! Why, that little child, only eight years old, if he is vexed with anything, will damn his two eyes and curse awfully. It is ruining the child for the sake of fourpence a day'.[34]

Jevon Parkes, a parish relief officer at Tipton, admitted that brick-making was 'very dirty' and 'hard work', but said that the girls were 'very respectable, and come out well dressed on Sundays.'[35]

The self-styled 'George Smith of Coalville' (1831–95) lobbied vociferously for the brickyard children. Smith, the son of a Staffordshire brick-maker, grew up in a brickyard. This deeply religious man had an inner conviction that he was God's chosen instrument on earth to save children.

George Smith ran a 'model' brick works at Coalville. Brick-making was included in the 1867 Factory Act, but Smith was disgusted because the new legislation only applied to brick-yards employing 50 people or more. In 1868, he began a newspaper campaign on behalf of the children, and three years later published a pamphlet, 'The Cry of the Children from the Brickyards of England'.

Smith gave an emotive, tub-thumping and lurid account of his childhood. He had endured miserable working conditions, and still bore scars from the beatings he received as a child. He told fearful tales of the brickyards.

Beer-shops and brick-makers were natural allies, and children were encouraged to drink alcohol: even eight- or nine-year-olds. They received their wages in the pub. The masters paid the men, who paid the children after they settled their 'tab' at the inn. The children's wages were 3s to 6s for a seventy-hour week. Boys and girls earned extra pennies from the men by singing obscene songs, fighting each other, or competing to see who could smoke the most tobacco or drink the most beer. Smith appealed to the middle classes to bring the children within the Christian fold. 'Oh, my fellow-men, haste to the rescue! Save the children if you would save England'.

Smith's pamphlet made him famous. He successfully roused public opinion and stirred up plenty of trouble, but his campaign earned him the sack. He became *persona non grata* in Coalville. The brickworks firms' profits suffered, and some parents were very unhappy about losing their children's earnings. The ungrateful brick-makers burnt Smith in effigy.

When an 1871 Act banned girls under sixteen and boys under ten from the brick-yards. Smith was jubilant. Children once employed in carrying heavy clay 'were sent from the brick-yards home and to school.'[36] The girls still needed to earn a living, however, so they found jobs in domestic service instead. Smith went on to campaign for better living conditions for canal-boat children and gipsy children. These children were always on the move, and it was very difficult for them to get any education.

Meanwhile, in the countryside, the battle for reform was stuck in a rut. Children's education was secondary to farmers' needs. One farmer told Mr Hedley, an investigator into rural education: 'At certain seasons we want the children, and *must have them*'.

Hedley said: 'Children begin to have a money value [to their parents] as soon as they shout loud enough to scare a crow, or can endure exposure to the weather watching cows in the lane. At eight years of age they can earn sixpence a day or more'.[37]

The exploitative 'gang system' was still going strong in counties like Norfolk, Suffolk and Lincolnshire. In 1865, Lord Shaftesbury asked if agricultural ganging could be included in the Children's Employment Commission's survey.

Two years later, the commission reported that around 20,000 children worked in 'private' gangs of up to twenty people hired by farmers. They were supervised by the farmer or one of his labourers.

The commission was most worried by the treatment of the 7,000 children in 'public' gangs. Gangs of up to forty people were hired out by gang-masters to local farmers. Children as young as six walked miles to their place of work. Some gang-masters brutally beat the children.

Mrs Antony Adams was a labourer's wife in Denton, Huntingdonshire. 'In June 1862, my daughters Harriet and Sarah, aged respectively eleven and thirteen years, were engaged to work on Mr Worman's land at Stilton'.

When the children got to Stilton, the gang-master took them near Peterborough eight miles away, where they worked for six weeks, walking there and back each day. 'They used to start from home at five in the morning, and seldom got back before nine. They had to find all their own meals, as well as all their own tools [such as hoes]. They...were good for nothing at the end of six weeks'. The 'ganger' persuaded Mrs Adams to send her six-year-old daughter Susan, too. 'She was that tired her sisters had to carry her the best part of the way home – eight miles, and she was ill from it for three weeks, and never went again'.[38]

Mixed gangs were the 'ruin' of some teenage girls, who became pregnant while at work. Young children learned very 'immoral' habits from older workers.

Lord Shaftesbury asked parliament to intervene in April 1867, and the Agricultural Gangs Act of that year came into force on 1 January 1868. It only applied to 'public' gangs. Children under the age of eight were banned, and mixed gangs were not permitted. Girls could not work in a gang at all unless a female gang-master supervised them. Gang-masters had to be licensed.

Critics of the Act foretold it was useless to prohibit public gangs while leaving the private ones untouched, because parents would just send their children to work in those.

Another report on children and young people in the countryside in 1867 drew attention to their lack of educational opportunities. Investigator E. C. Tufnell thought that children under nine should be banned from farm work altogether and sent to school. Since boys were not strong enough to do full-time work on farms until they were about ten, 'a compulsory school attendance' would 'impose no hardship to the parent'.

Another investigator, Mr Tremenheere, disagreed. Children's earnings were too important to rural families in some areas; stopping them working altogether would cause real distress. He felt that a better plan was for children to attend school a minimum number of times per year. The number of attendances could be scaled down as the children reached a certain educational standard.

There was little point arguing over the merits of school attendance, however, if there were not enough schools. Parishes like Battlesden in the Woburn Poor Law Union had no schools at all. Others were reasonably well equipped: the

Heacham area (Docking Poor Law Union) of Norfolk had fifteen schools, most of which were 'well conducted'.[39]

A major issue in districts with good schools was persuading parents to keep the children there long enough to get a decent education. In 1873 an Agricultural Children's Act was passed to address this. Children in rural areas were banned from working until they were eight years old. This rescued children from the private gangs, too.

The Act incorporated some of Tremenheere's suggestions. Children must attend school a specified number of times per year until they were twelve years old, or passed a standard exam. The Act was viewed with acute suspicion by parents and farmers, though, and classrooms still emptied whenever children were needed on the farm.

Chapter 14
Empire Builders

More and more child workers in trade, industry and agriculture were now under the law's protection. Reformers and philanthropists felt justified in congratulating themselves. Great strides forward had been made against all the odds.

Now attention switched to the swarms of destitute children who littered the streets. 'Street arabs' did not go to school. Children earned a living any way they could: begging, running errands, or doing odd jobs like sweeping a crossing through muck-strewn Victorian roads. Sometimes they sold small items like fruit, flowers or matches.

Socialist reformer Katherine Conway lamented 'the weary feet of the children who run errands often for ten hours in the day. Our streets are filled with children selling and begging in one breath…The sight of their pinched faces and shivering limbs has made a mockery of our Christian peace for many a year'.[1]

Henry Mayhew told some street children's stories in *London Labour and the London Poor* (1861). 'Liz', who was nine years old, sold nuts and boot-laces. Her family were very poor, but 'Father would die afore he would let mother take as much as a loaf from the parish'. Liz began selling nuts when she was seven. Her mother told her that even if she only made a penny profit, it could buy her 'a good piece of bread'.[2]

If poor and hungry children could not earn enough to get by honestly, they turned to crime for easy money. They picked pockets and stole. Some resorted to prostitution.

In 1851, a 'den' of juvenile thieves was discovered at Lambeth. The police discovered a 'cave' in the brickwork of the railway arches. The only entrance was by crawling through a small hole. The den was fitted out with a portable stove, cooking equipment, and straw for bedding. Five youths found inside, all 'well-known thieves', were charged with trespass and imprisoned for several weeks.[3]

Respectable folk believed that lawless and illiterate children like these were a menace to society. What was to be done with them? Reformers began waging war against crime, poverty and ignorance on the streets.

Earlier in the century, child 'criminals' over the age of seven faced the same punishments as adults. They could be flogged, imprisoned, transported abroad or even hanged. In practice, judges showed mercy, and most children capitally convicted had their sentences commuted to transportation.

Some people now believed that juvenile crime was linked to poverty. Was prison the answer for child offenders, or was it counterproductive? Maybe locking up children with adult criminals made them more, not less, likely to re-offend. In 1838, the first prison specially designed for young offenders was founded at Parkhurst, although its regime was extremely harsh by modern standards.

One way to remove child beggars and hawkers from the streets was to ship them abroad. Emigration was a popular panacea for the widespread poverty that people saw all around them. Lord Ashley was a keen supporter of child emigration, and successfully pleaded with the government for money to set up a scheme. Later, he supported refuges for homeless children, and ships to train destitute boys to serve at sea.

Charities were set up to help 'juvenile delinquents'. In 1849, the Philanthropic Society founded a 150-acre farm at Redhill to rehabilitate young offenders. About 100 boys aged between eleven and twenty were taught 'the usual farming occupations' by agricultural labourers. The farm's livestock included cows, sheep, horses and pigs.

The Society hoped that boys would acquire good physical and moral discipline. They were taught to look on emigration 'as the great prize of their attainment'. Life on the farm with its relatively kindly regime, and plenty of fresh air must have made a pleasant change for these underprivileged boys: they 'appeared remarkably cheerful and healthy.'[4]

Industrial and reform schools were set up during this period. Industrial schools catered for children under fourteen who got into mischief and appeared likely to end up as career criminals. Reform schools were for older juvenile delinquents found guilty of a crime. A reformatory at Broomfields in Bradford gave ninety children elementary instruction in addition to industrial training. The children boarded at the school until old enough to leave and start work.

Some efforts were made to educate society's poorest children. Schools would not allow children dressed in rags to study. The Ragged School Union was founded in 1844, and Lord Ashley quickly lent his aid as chairman.

Of all Lord Ashley's achievements, the Ragged School movement was the one of which he was most proud. Thousands of children were 'taken from a state of filth and misery, and raised to one of honourable independence.'[5] The ragged schools gave children religious instruction, taught them the three 'R's, and gave them skills so they could find places as apprentices, or emigrate. The movement was important because it fostered the idea that every child, no matter how destitute, should receive an education.

One of the most magnificent ragged schools was at Lambeth. Henry Beaufoy donated a hefty £10,000 in memory of his late wife Eliza (who was keenly interested in helping poor children) to build a school with accommodation for 800 children on Lambeth Walk.

Some ragged schools fed their children. Children could not learn their 'A B C' if they were starving. In Bradford, the Rebecca Street Ragged Schools (1865) provided 200 destitute children with a hot meal every day.

The Westminster Juvenile Refuge and School of Industry gave homeless children a safe place to sleep, and food, as well as an industrial education. Boys learned skills like shoe-making, tailoring, leather-gilding, wood-turning, or French polishing. They were apprenticed out to 'respectable working tradesmen'.[6] Girls learnt needlework and millinery; most became domestic servants. During 1850 to 1851, fourteen boys and girls emigrated to the colonies with the school's help.

The shoe-black brigades, founded in 1851, were an off-shoot of the Ragged School Union. Each boy earned up to 8s 6d per week, a proportion of which was paid into a bank for him. He was given some pennies to spend, and a few pence of his earnings repaid the Shoe-Black Society for kitting him out. The boys' savings paid for them to emigrate.

A number of charities such as Dr Barnardo's and the Salvation Army raised money to send children abroad in the pious hope it was better for them than becoming 'institutionalized' in a workhouse, or workhouse school.

Tens of thousands of children were sent to Canada and Australia as domestic servants or to work on the land. Emigration was very much a one-way ticket. There was little to stop a child being overworked and abused once on the other side of the ocean, and these schemes caused much heart-searching whenever a scandal came to light. Shipping off some of Britain's poorest children to the far side of the world could never be a permanent cure-all, however.

The workhouse was still the last resort for many children, although attempts were made to make them more child-friendly, and improve educational facilities. In the late 1840s, Poor Law Unions were given powers to band together to create schools catering for a large district: the 'barrack schools'.

The idea was to get children away from the 'contaminating' atmosphere of older paupers, including their parents. (Pauperism was thought of as almost a disease which children could catch). Children were given industrial training and literacy skills. Not many 'barrack schools' were built, probably on cost grounds. Poor Law Unions either built new workhouse schools or updated old ones instead. By 1861, 35,400 children were taught in workhouse schools.[7] For children in ordinary 'mixed' workhouses, a kindlier atmosphere was emerging. Play areas were set aside for children, and their diet was improved.

Parishes were still apprenticing out their pauper children. The Jane Wilbred case led to an 1851 Act aimed at stopping cruelty to apprentices, as we saw earlier. In the same year, a controversy arose over the high-handed way some Poor Law Guardians still disposed of surplus children. In January 1851, the *Morning Chronicle* reported that children from St Pancras workhouse had been shipped out to Bermuda (then a penal colony) as domestic servants.

The story broke when Captain Thomas W. B. Burrows, skipper of the brig *James*, approached the overseers of St Marylebone parish and offered to take 'as many [children] as you please' for six pounds a head. Burrows produced a letter of recommendation from the St Pancras board. The Marylebone guardians were appalled by this 'monstrous' suggestion: 'To dispose of children in this way is worse than to transport them.'

St Pancras sent forty-seven paupers to Bermuda: six adults, twenty-six boys, and fifteen girls. Each child's belongings were packed in a canvas sack with an inventory.

The St Pancras officials defended their actions: the scheme was 'a rescue and a great blessing' for the children.[8] The Board of Guardians produced letters from the child emigrants which praised their new homes and asked for more children to come. One wonders if the letters were written under their masters' supervision.

On 6 March 1850, orphan James George (thirteen) wrote to his old schoolmaster at the workhouse: 'I send my kind love to you and all the boys, Half-a-loaf Dabtoe, and the rest. I often think of you all, though you are far from me… please to ask Mr Eaton to send my aunt to the Bermudas…and send me word how my brother Charles George is…'..

Caroline Boyd (eleven) sounded less homesick: 'I have a kind master and mistress…I am treated very kindly indeed, and I am bound for seven years with free will, and I …can earn my own living by working.'[9]

This emigration scheme was illegal, however, because the children were under sixteen. They should never have gone without permission from two JPs and the Poor Law Board. Poor Law investigator Richard Hall commented: 'the directors (guardians) …made good provision for the comfort and welfare of the children. Had they procured for their proceedings the sanction of law, they would have incurred no censure'.[10]

There were now definite symptoms of decline in the repulsive system of parish apprenticeship. People were less willing to feed and clothe a child for years even if they received their labour 'free' in return. In 1844, the law compelling ratepayers to take parish children was repealed, and in 1856 the Poor Law Board ruled that children should not be apprenticed as domestic servants as it was not a 'trade' where they learned a skill. Overseers continued to pay premiums to employers, but the Poor Law Board made it clear they disapproved of this 'state of servitude'.[11] However, the Board was powerless to stop the system. It could only register its distaste.

In 1861, the Liverpool Poor Law Union apprenticed several groups of children to cotton mill-owners in Burnley (Lancashire), and Foster & Fison's worsted mill at Burley (Yorkshire). Children were not supposed to be apprenticed more than thirty miles from their home parish at this date.

Ten Liverpool apprentices, including Susan Henn and David Phillips, were only eleven years old. None of the children were bound for more than six years. Almost all the apprentices were orphans, but the consent of children's parents was obtained if still alive. The Board did little apart from making anxious noises regarding the distance and numbers of children involved. Pauper apprenticeship continued well into the twentieth century.

Education provision for working-class children continued to cause heated debate. The Whig Government under Lord John Russell, which took office in 1846, greatly increased the money given to schools administered by religious and voluntary bodies. Roman Catholic schools were now included in the state grant. Greater emphasis was laid on teacher-training, and the standard of teaching slowly but surely improved, as more qualified teachers entered the system. Education was, however, seen as the best way to turn children into responsible, efficient workers and model citizens, not as a 'right' in itself.

The arguments focused on elementary education, since working-class children were expected to start work when they were ten or eleven years old. Youngsters who wanted to continue their education were limited to evening classes like those organized by the mechanics' institutes. The government had not yet realized that Britain needed more technical and scientific training for workers to keep its place as the 'workshop of the world' in an increasingly competitive global market.

In 1858 a royal commission, chaired by the Duke of Newcastle, surveyed the state of popular education. The standards of privately run 'dame' schools prevalent in town and country had improved little since they were publicly condemned during the 1830s. In the Plymouth and Devonport area, schoolrooms were often so small, 'the children cannot stand in a semicircle round the teacher'.[12]

Religious groups had not lost their enthusiasm for education, and the infant and day schools run by the National Society and British Society were of a higher standard than private establishments.

The Newcastle Commission discovered that while religious groups battled over the right to teach working-class children, their parents were indifferent to the type of religious teaching they received. Parents' priority was the standard of teaching 'whether the school supplied good reading, writing and arithmetic'.[13]

Although more and more money poured into education annually, only just over twelve per cent of the population of England and Wales attended school. Over 2.2 million working class children went to day schools. These comprised 1.5 million pupils attending schools supported by religious bodies; only 47,400 children went to schools funded entirely by taxation. Another 43,100 children went to non-denominational establishments like ragged schools and factory schools.[14]

To put these figures into context, about one-third of school-age children did not go to any kind of school. They spent their time 'idling, playing, or begging on the streets'.[15]

The government grant for teacher-training had not yet had time to increase the supply of qualified teachers. Teachers at Devonport included a former blacksmith, a journeyman tanner and a dockyard labourer. The shortage of teachers was worst in London, where no-one was considered 'too old, too poor, too ignorant, too feeble' to impart instruction to children. The profession was taken up by anyone wanting a job to tide them over a difficult period, like domestic servants who had lost their place, sacked barmaids, and 'persons of doubtful temperance'.[16]

The commissioners made a very perceptive comment on juvenile labour. They noticed that whenever a manufacture became widespread in an area, like the cutlery trade in Sheffield, or the Staffordshire potteries, the division of labour which reduced each manufacture 'to its lowest terms' increased the demand for young workers, because it increased 'the number of minute occupations which do not require the skill or strength of an adult workman'.[17] The factory system, as Andrew Ure noted earlier in the century, continued to promote child labour.

The Commission did not recommend a system of full-time compulsory education for all, however, despite evidence that many children did not receive enough schooling. Families' need for their children's wages was considered a major stumbling block.

If parents were forced to send children to school, they might become a burden on the state: 'Independence is of more importance than education, and if the wages of a child's labour are necessary, either to keep the parents from the poor rates, or to relieve the pressure of severe and bitter poverty, it is far better that it should go to work at the earliest age at which it can bear the physical exertion than that it should remain at school'.

Parents compelled to send their children to school might see them as a 'burden' and treat them harshly. Children only had a 'moral right' to the amount of education their parents could afford. When public money was involved, the state should not dictate how much education a child should have. Parents were only morally bound to give as much schooling to their children as other members of their class considered 'necessary'.[18] It was pointless to equip children with an education above their station in life: working-class children were born to work.

Following the Newcastle Commission report, the government decided it was not getting enough value for the money it put into education. A new 'payment by results' scheme was launched by Robert Lowe, vice-president of the Board of Education. Spending on teacher-training was slashed. Schools received funding depending on how many children passed a certain standard in the three 'R's. Accordingly, the overall quality of teaching declined, as teachers tried to cram children who needed more help with the requisite knowledge.

Thankfully, more forward-thinking ideas began to prevail during the 1860s. Economists such as John Stuart Mill argued that the state should 'require and compel the education, up to a certain standard, of every human being who is born its citizen'.[19] He thought that parents should be fined if they did not send their children to school.

New studies of working-class children's education again highlighted its woeful inadequacy. Over 1.5 million children did not have a school place.[20] Various societies sprang up like the National Education League in Birmingham (1869), which campaigned for universal free secular education. Religious anxieties had not gone away, however, and counter-pressure groups formed to defend the voluntary system.

Neither the National Society nor the British Society wanted to relinquish their important roles in providing education. But they could not keep pace with the growing population, and had insufficient funds to carry on indefinitely.

Therefore, when William Gladstone's Liberal government (which came into power in 1868) brought in a new education bill, the religious societies were forced to adopt a more pragmatic view.

The bill was proposed by William Edward Forster, vice-president of the Education Department. Forster was a Yorkshire worsted manufacturer (it was to his mill where some Liverpool pauper apprentices were sent a few years earlier). He built a school for his factory workers at Burley-in-Wharfedale.

Forster, a well-known supporter of national education, did not view schools for the working classes as a tool to keep them subservient to their 'betters'. He believed all children should have a good grounding in elementary education, which could act as a stepping-stone to higher education.

How could Forster succeed in his plan to introduce a national system when so many others had tried and failed before him? His answer was a 'non-denominational' rather than a wholly secular system for new schools. Pupils were to have 'simple Bible teaching', not formal religious education based on a particular faith.[21]

Forster's chief aim was to build schools in virgin territory untouched by the religious societies owing to lack of money. The Anglicans, Dissenters and other groups were left in charge of their own schools. However, the government made it clear it was no longer committed to building new schools founded on sectarian principles.

The religious societies were given a six month 'holiday' to build schools with state aid. After that, rate-payers in areas with insufficient schools would have powers to elect new 'school boards' to build non-sectarian schools, funded from the rates and the government.

The government would keep paying maintenance costs for existing voluntary schools. This grant was conditional on schools agreeing to an 'opt-out clause', so parents could take their children out of religious education classes. For example, if parents were Nonconformists, and the only school in their area was an Anglican one run by the National Society, they did not have to subject their child to religious teaching that they disagreed with. Religious classes must be held at the start or finish of the school day, so parents could remove their children without disrupting the timetable.

Secularists and Dissenters were bitter about this continued flow of government money to Church of England schools. Quaker John Bright, for one, was hopping mad. If Anglicans were allowed to carry on building for another six months, this gave them time to get an even tighter grip on the nation's children. These groups were proved right when the religious societies launched into a frenzy of school-building.

The Anglicans, for their part, were furious when they heard that the new board schools, paid for by public money, would not include the Established Church's teachings.

Forster's programme of reform was aided by people's worries that Britain was lagging behind foreign competitors. An educated, well-trained workforce was essential so that Britain could compete with Germany and Prussia's military might. Politicians like Robert Lowe also thought the new electorate (the Reform Act of 1867 had extended the voter base to adult male householders) should be better educated, so they could make informed decisions at polling time. However, the consensus of opinion which had grown up following years of reports of widespread illiteracy was probably the biggest factor accelerating reform.

After months of heated arguments from religious societies and secularists, Forster's bill successfully made it onto the statute books. This landmark Act paved the way for compulsory state education. It proved problematic to implement in practice, but was probably the best compromise available in that age of touchy religious sensibilities.

Forster's Education Act of 1870 established the principle of universal education for children aged between five and twelve years old. Parents were still responsible for school fees unless too poor to afford them. School Boards had permissive powers to enforce children's attendance. (There was little point making education compulsory at this time, anyway, as not enough school places were available).

The Act only applied to England and Wales; Scotland and Ireland had their own system of education. (Ireland had had a system of national education since 1831. Scotland's Education Act was passed two years later).

Within a year of Forster's Act becoming law, 300 new school boards were founded, and the number more than tripled by 1876. It took time and money to build sufficient schools, and children had to wait until the late 1880s for enough school places to materialize.

Successive administrations continued to refine factory legislation, but more at the pace of a stubborn old donkey than a steam locomotive. The Factory and Workshop Acts of 1867 had not proved the 'crowning effort of legislative wisdom', as factory inspector R. Whately Cooke-Taylor commented wryly.[22] Local authorities failed to take up the challenge of regulating workshops. Many town councillors, who were workshop owners themselves, were slow to appoint inspectors. Birmingham, Sheffield and other town councils, when asked to implement the Workshops Act, refused point-blank.

In 1871, workshop regulation was taken away from local authorities and given to the factory inspectors to enforce. The inspectors then needed more assistants to aid them with this massive task. By the mid-1870s, the administrative tree was: Inspectors, Assistant Inspectors, Sub-Inspectors, and Junior Sub-Inspectors.

Regulations governing factories were much stricter than for workshops. The inspectors could only advise, not compel, workshop owners to keep their premises clean safe and places for workers.

Inspectors noticed a dramatic decrease in the number of children in non-textile factories (e.g., ammunition-making, engineering, glass-making, metals etc.) after the 1867 Factory Act brought them under regulation.[23]

TABLE 1[24]

	Children	Young males 13 yrs+	Females 13 yrs +	Adult Males	Total Workforce
1868	13,931	48,761	44,840	211,295	318,827
1871	2,247	57,648	51,644	248,245	359,784

Robert Baker thought that this was for the same reasons as when the first Factory Act was introduced in 1833: masters did not want the hassle of form-filling, or providing schools for their child workers. He reported that numbers were already picking up again, however, as masters realized they had nothing to fear, and they increased further over the next few years.

In the early 1870s, factory hands campaigned for a nine-hour day to bring them in line with the working day achieved by trade unionists elsewhere, like in the Glasgow ironworks.

The government compromised with the 1874 Factory Act, which gave women and young persons the ten-hour day which workers had fought for over forty years earlier. The working day in textile mills for women and young persons now ran from six in the morning until six at night (in wintertime, seven until seven), with two hours for meals. This Act raised the age when children were allowed to work in textile mills to ten years (to take effect in 1875).

The 1870 Education Act did not supersede the Factory Acts' requirements for education. The Act's primary aim was to reduce the numbers of poor children roaming the streets, not reduce the numbers of children at work.

It took a long time for education to make inroads in some stubborn areas of Britain. Factory inspector Alexander Redgrave reported that the 1873 Agricultural Children's Act was 'practically inoperative' in some areas. By this time, children employed in handicrafts like straw-plaiting were covered by the workshop acts. Redgrave complained it was 'really impossible to satisfy the poor widow… struggling at straw-plaiting that it is right for her to be compelled to send her child to school in order to earn its one shilling, or one shilling and sixpence per week, while her neighbour's child, earning more upon the land, does not go to school at all.'[25]

Parents in some coal-mining and metal-working areas were still unhappy about schooling, too. Redgrave explained that 'So repugnant is the word "school" to a working man, that I am met with the reply, "If you send my boy to school you must feed him too, for I can't".'[26]

The Black Country was still short of school places because insufficient school boards had been set up. Rowley parish only had eight schools in 1875. Inspector Brewer complained: 'I do not see how I can force into school twenty children out of one street, and leave another twenty out in the same street.' Brewer said there were 'thousands of children' without access to education in the Lye, Halesowen and Cradley area.

Brewer was pleasantly surprised by Halesowen parents. Locals believed that they were 'terribly rough, vicious and dissipated,' yet 130 children regularly attended school half-time. Even children from Islington Street – 'a den of iniquity and drunkenness' – went to school. The nailers' workshops in this street could only be accessed through workers' houses. Brewer had only explored its dark corners twice before, because his appearance was the signal for a 'general stampede' as underage children hid from sight.[27] The inspector planned a return visit, however, as the nailers were spreading rumours he was afraid to venture in.

Workshop regulation began to make an impact, too. Mr Abel, headmaster at Catshill School, Bromsgrove, reported that he had fifty-three workshop children in his school in September 1874. This was a major achievement since: 'Trade being good, many children are taken away from nursing (child-minding) and put to the nail block'.[28] The children in his class had never been to school before. The nailers' children were so ignorant that they were placed in the lowest infants' class. They were incredibly dirty, too. Unless the school teacher nagged them, they only washed their necks on Sundays.

Was the half-time system really such a good idea? Katherine Conway thought that 'The half-time system may be mercy compared to the past', but 'at half-past five on a winter's morning, it is a sorry thing to remember how many little ones… are being waked from their sleep to trudge to their work in a stifling factory and thence, after a hurried meal, into the school'.[29]

The 'bundle-wood' workers were a good example of impoverished children enduring long days owing to the half-time system. Families in some of the poorest areas of London, particularly widows with young children, found employment chopping and bundling firewood.

This was a seasonal trade, briskest during the cold winter months. Thomas Wright (the 'Riverside Visitor') described a visit to a works at Penny Bundle Lane, Deptford in 1879.

The timber for firewood was sourced from Norway. The work was carried out in 'long, narrow, low-roofed structures' similar to covered rope-walks. The wood-sheds were divided into sections or 'berths'. The boss of each berth sawed and chopped the wood. As sticks of firewood fell on the floor, children picked them up and 'piled' them up ready for the bundler, usually female. She tied up the bundles with tarred twine using a special machine. Older boys helped by taking one end of the two-handled bow-saw used for slicing up the wood, or chopping up the wood into sticks.

The 'gang' working in a berth was usually a man, woman and two children, not necessarily related. They worked long hours for meagre pay: 'In the depth of winter the hands usually work from eight in the morning till nine or ten at night, with an hour out for dinner, and half an hour for tea.' 'Pilers' earned about a shilling per day, and bundlers were paid three pence per hundred bundles. (A good workman made around a thousand bundles per day, so a bundler earned about 2s 6d).

The Workshop and Education acts had given these children some education. Wright commented that formerly 'the grim giants Poverty and Greed …wrought their will upon the helpless little ones in very ruthless fashion. Children were taken into the sheds almost as soon as they could walk, kept there hard at work for ten or twelve hours a day, and brought up in the direst ignorance.' Children were not worked so hard now the Acts were in force: 'no child can be taken on as a full-time piler who is under thirteen years of age, or as a half-timer who is under ten years of age.'

Workshop legislation sent these children to school in the morning or afternoon. They worked six and a half hours like factory children. In practice, though, these children effectively 'worked' full-time. Every minute of the children's waking hours was occupied. When they went to school in the morning they had already 'worked an hour or more before going; and on coming out of school at twelve they will have little more than just time to eat their dinners and get back to work again by one. Those who go to school in the afternoon, after having worked all the forenoon, have again to turn into work in the evening… so that, poor little fellows, they fare very badly in the matter of rest and recreation.'[30]

By the mid-1870s, years of government tinkering with factory legislation had left the law in a complex and confusing muddle. In workshops and non-textile factories, children could work when they were eight years old: two years younger than textile mills. A workshop child could perform its permitted six and a half hour shift any time between 6 a.m. and 8 p.m. Women and young persons were allowed a ten-and-a half-hour day in workshops and could start work as early as 5 a.m.

The 1867 Factory Act's definition of a 'factory' and 'workshop' had caused problems. For example, Robert Baker found one building in Birmingham which housed two firms, one making metal items, the other making bone buttons. Each manufacturer hired power (provided by a steam-engine) from the building's owner. The metal firm employed two men and two boys, but was classed as a factory because metals always came under the Factory Act regardless of the 'fifty people' rule. The bone button firm employed forty-five men, women and girls, and was regulated by the workshops act. This employer could run his business over a wider range of hours and faced fewer legislative restrictions than the other master in the same building. Baker recommended that factories and workshops should all come under the same legislation.

Anomalies like these led to a royal commission in 1876 to review factory and workshop legislation. This commission found signs of a gentler attitude towards children; there was less evidence of overwork and brutality compared with the 1860s reports.

The 1876 Commission proved unhelpful regarding conditions for women and children in domestic workshops. Previous reforms were undone. All the previous select committees and factory inspectors' reports might just have been so much waste paper.

Following the Commission's report, the 1878 Factories Consolidation Act addressed some issues raised by the inspectorate. The 'fifty people' rule was axed. A workplace was now defined as a factory or workshop dependent on the type of power used on site. If mechanical power (steam, water) was in use, then the workplace was a factory (with some exceptions). If all the work on site was done by hand, then it was a workshop.

This Act contained a ground-breaking clause: workers injured at work could claim compensation. If a factory owner was fined because he had not guarded his machinery properly, then the money from the fine went to the injured worker or his family. Another forward-thinking development banned children from working in white lead factories.

Despite all evidence to the contrary, the commissioners felt it was not the government's place to poke their noses into family businesses. The new Act permitted domestic workshops far greater latitude regarding hours and working conditions than before. This made it easier for employers to 'sweat' their workers.

Straw-plaiting, pillow lace-making and glove-making (in family houses) were now exempt from any regulation. Katherine Conway thought it was appalling: 'Wherever there is no Factory Act to protect and no Trades Union to resist – in the home industries, such as that of the matchbox makers, the nail-makers… the straw-plaiters, carders of buttons, casers of pins and needles, etc., etc., there the grim tragedy of child workers is still going on with little if any alleviation'.[31]

It is impossible to estimate how many children worked illegally in small workshops. Difficulties of enforcement meant it was all too easy for a file-cutter or chain-maker to work children for long hours in a filthy, badly ventilated workshop. The inspectors did their best to cope. In 1875, Inspector Brewer prosecuted chain-maker Albert Billingham of Sheffield St, Quarry Bank (in the Black Country) for overworking a child. The magistrate told Billingham: 'It is downright positive cruelty, as bad cruelty as though you had stabbed him in the breast.'[32] But it was impossible for inspectors to check on Britain's thousands of tiny workshops: they did not have enough manpower.

Flax scutching-mills were given a special dispensation regarding hours in the 1878 Act. They could run any time of the day or night providing the mill was in use more than six months in a year, or unless they employed young persons and children.

Over two decades had passed since Robert Baker first drew attention to the dangers lurking in the flax scutching-mills of Ireland. The number of mills had declined (from around 1,480 in 1872 to 1,380 in 1875),[33] but workers were still getting caught in scutching machinery.

The 1878 Factory Act at last gave the inspectors powers to ensure machinery in flax mills was properly guarded. They visited each one to check on the state of the machinery, but this was easier said than done in some places. The following year, Inspector Woodgate travelled from Ballyshannon to Gweedore to visit the mills in that area. His journey took over two days by horse and cart, and included a perilous crossing over two sea channels at Lettermacaward, menaced by quicksands.[34]

Young children were slowly excluded from the workforce. Before 1874, half-timers were children aged eight to thirteen years of age. Under the 1874 Factory Act, the age when children were permitted to work in textile factories was raised to nine in 1874, and then to age ten a year later.

The factory inspectors' reports for April 1875 gave statistics for half-timers in textile mills over the previous twenty-five years.

TABLE 2[35]

	1850	1861	1871	1875
Cotton:	14,993	39,788	43,281	66,900
Wool and associated mills:	7,094	5,969	6,021	8,588
Worsted:	9,956	13,178	18,306	29,828
Flax and associated mills:	1,581	3,644	5,562	12,678
Silk:	7,151	7,014	6,928	6,871

(NB. The exclusion of nine-year-olds is unlikely to significantly affect the proportion of half-timers to adults for the 1875 figures, as they were only a small fraction of the workforce).

The proportions of workers in textile mills in 1875 were as follows (percentages have been rounded up):

TABLE 3[36]

	Children	Young males 13 yrs+	Females 13 yrs +	Adult Males
Cotton:	14%	8%	54%	24%
Wool and associated mills:	6%	10%	48%	36%
Worsted:	20%	8%	49%	23%
Flax and associated mills:	7%	9%	66%	18%
Silk:	15%	5%	61%	19%

(NB. Women and girls over the age of thirteen were counted together).

To illustrate how complex factory legislation had become, not all the 'eight to thirteen' age group of silk workers attended school part-time. Under the 1850

Factory Act, which was not repealed until 1878, children over the age of eleven employed as silk-winders or throwsters were classed as 'young persons' and could work full-time. Robert Baker was outraged that this class of workers was able to 'defy the officers of the school boards'; factory legislation was supposed to promote education, not hinder it.[37]

The number of child workers in textile mills peaked some time around 1875–6, when the number of half-timers reached 201,284 children. After that date, half-timers in the textile workforce steadily declined. By 1904, there were 14,568 boy half-timers, plus 17,176 girl half-timers (now defined as under-14s) in textile mills in England and Wales.[38]

Across all industries, after the mid-1870s there was a sharp fall in the number of Britain's child workers. By the summer of 1895, there were 126,896 half-timers working in factories and workshops in England and Wales (all industries).[39]

The half-time system was increasingly criticized by reformers, teachers and members of the Board of Education. They felt that half a day's schooling daily did not give children enough time to learn their lessons properly. Children were reportedly happy with the half-time system, however; it was all part of growing up, and they were encouraged by their parents to look forward to earning a wage.

By the century's end, only three or four per cent of school age children worked under the half-time system. It was very popular with parents in textile districts, however, who resisted moves to abolish it, and the system did not die out until the First World War.

The push to educate the nation's children triumphed at last when Lord Sandon's Act of 1876 put the onus on parents to ensure their children went to school. Four years later, A. J. Mundella's Education Act made school attendance compulsory for five- to ten-year-olds.

This Act greatly boosted school numbers. Children aged eleven to thirteen could leave school on condition they passed a set educational test. Education was still not free. This caused hardship and resentment amongst poor parents until 1891, when the government began giving extra grants for schools which stopped charging fees. This helped to accelerate the introduction of free schools.

The combination of the Education Acts and Factory Acts had a decisive impact on the number of children in school, as the age of first entering work began to rise. The upper age range for half-time workers was raised to fourteen in 1878, so half-timers were now ten- to fourteen-year-olds.

One factor which may have reduced the number of young workers was the tendency amongst parents in manufacturing towns to keep older children at home longer than was customary earlier in the century. They did not want to lose their wages. If older children lived at home until they got married, perhaps when they were twenty or so, there was less necessity for younger siblings to go to work.

Technological improvements also made child labour less necessary. In the countryside, machines took over tasks like reaping and binding. Agriculture lost its importance as the chief employment for boys; they switched to jobs on the railways or in textile industries instead.

Machinery also impacted on domestic trades like straw-plaiting. By 1877, over 1,500 special sewing-machines were used in the Luton and Dunstable area, making home-made straw-plait uneconomic. Factory inspector Mr Wood reported that Bedfordshire villagers were switching to domestic service 'which has been hitherto looked upon with contempt'.[40] Cheap imports of straw-plait from China and Italy killed off the demand for home-made straw-plait, and the plait-schools closed.

Handmade lace saw a similar drop in demand as machine-made lace triumphed and lace schools disappeared. Fortunately, rural families' loss of income from domestic industries and field work was offset by a rise in farming wages. This welcome alleviation of the agricultural labourer's lot owed a great deal to widespread trade union agitation by Joseph Arch and his followers during the early 1870s.

The growth of heavy industry further decreased the number of job opportunities for children away from factories. Steel shipbuilding, electrical and chemical engineering firms wanted adult workers, and children switched to casual jobs like delivering newspapers.

Apprenticeships were still a useful entry point into many trades for the rest of the century. However, traditional apprenticeships were called into question, although some still considered them good training for children. Educators worried that youngsters went into dead-end jobs like machine-minding which did not kit them out for life as future citizens, with no long-term prospects.

School boards grew dissatisfied with the opportunities for youngsters after they finished elementary education. In the 1880s, school boards in Sheffield, Birmingham and other industrial towns set up schools for older children with a broader curriculum than elementary schools. Secondary education for the working classes was becoming seen as essential so that Britain had highly skilled workers to compete with other nations.

By the closing decades of the nineteenth century, the battle for state legislation of factory and workshop children's working conditions appeared to be won. It was no longer a 'live' issue. Society accepted the necessity for some state control to protect children and young people.

The state was now more likely to interfere in people's home lives, once considered sacrosanct. The first society to protect children from cruelty, founded in Liverpool in 1883, was inspired by an American society. London soon followed suit, and these societies lobbied for greater protection for children in their own homes. Lord Shaftesbury, who still actively supported charitable causes despite old age and failing health, lent his aid to the London society.

These societies were also worried by the numbers of children forced by their parents to walk the streets at night selling or begging. Factory inspector Mr Oswald, who looked after the Nottingham area, said he often saw children from six to ten years old selling papers 'till a very late hour every night. I have seen and conversed with little ones between ten and eleven o'clock at night, and when I told them to "go home" they cried, and said that their parents would "beat them if the papers were not sold".'[41]

The National Society for the Prevention of Cruelty to Children was founded in 1889. Thanks to these societies' efforts, the Prevention of Cruelty to Children Act became law later that year. The government now recognized it was necessary to act when children were abused by their parents.

However, an imaginary schoolteacher's report card for the social conscience of the age of capital might read 'could do better'. Progress was far too late in coming. This ostensibly Christian country took over eight decades to rescue the climbing boys, permitted tiny children to be exploited in rural gangs as late as the 1870s, and left generations of children growing up in ignorance while they squabbled over religious education.

The colliery-owning peers like Lord Londonderry who wanted to keep his pits as a 'nursery' for future miners; the manufacturers who put profits first every time that reform was mooted; the uncaring public which left children like chimney-sweeps to suffer for years: all must share the blame. They collectively displayed a failure of imagination where working children were concerned. Children's labour was only curtailed when economically viable. Paradoxically, the man who did most to help the working classes was an aristocrat: Lord Shaftesbury.

'The most eminent social reformer' of the century died on 1 October 1885. Lord Shaftesbury was laid to rest in the family vaults at St Giles. His obituary in the *Times* (2 October 1885) called him the mightiest 'friend of the poor, the degraded, and the outcast'. His 'generous sympathies and ceaseless efforts' on behalf of the working class made him 'one of the most steadfast and powerful friends which the humbler classes have ever had, as well as one of the most trusted'.[42]

For over half a century, Shaftesbury fought valiantly on behalf of working and disadvantaged children and many other worthy causes. The colliery children, factory workers, climbing boys, and children too ragged to go to school: all benefited from his perseverance and compassion. He aided refuges for homeless children, improved conditions for the mentally ill, and found time to set up missions to the costermongers of London.

Lord Shaftesbury did not stand alone in his efforts to help children. Men like Michael Thomas Sadler and Richard Oastler, the doctors and 'fighting parsons' who spoke up for factory workers and agricultural labourers must take a bow, along with mill-owners like Sir Robert Peel and 'Honest' John Fielden. Workers, too, organized marches, and children risked the sack by giving testimony to the royal commissioners. Men like Dr Kay-Shuttleworth laboured for years to give working-class children an education. All played their part.

Factory reform played a huge role in improving conditions for child workers and giving them an education. But the greatest achievement of social reformers was to change society's attitude to working-class children.

State and society now expected all children, now matter how destitute, to attend school. Gradually, legislation excluded them from the workplace. The age when children were legally allowed to work was raised to eleven in 1891 (it came into force two years later). In 1899, the legal working age was raised again to twelve.

Children's wages were still needed in families living below the poverty level. Their parents had to weigh up the risk of being prosecuted for not sending them to school, or hope for the best and send them to work anyway.

A committee which looked into the employment of school-age children calculated that almost 200,000 children (not including part-timers) had some kind of paid employment which they fitted in around school, thus avoiding problems with the law. Children did jobs like delivering milk before school, or running errands after classes finished for the day. Another survey at the turn of the twentieth century estimated that a million children in England and Wales played truant each day so they could help their parents.[43]

Child labour did not disappear. It was shunted into a branch line. A compromise had been reached whereby children combined school and work at a level acceptable to society. Their labour was no longer needed to forge the country's industrial might. Children were now seen as the future citizens, soldiers and sailors needed to keep Britain ahead of her rivals. They formed the construction blocks, not builders, of an Empire where the sun never set.

Timeline of Key Nineteenth Century Legislation

1802 Health and Morals of Apprentices Act.
1819 Act for the Regulation of Mills and Factories.
1833 The Factory Act (Althorp's).
1842 Employment of Women and Children in Mines Act.
1844 Act to Amend the Laws relating to Labour in Factories.
1845 Print Works Act (Lord Ashley's).
1847 Act to limit the Hours of Labour of Young Persons and Females in Factories (Ten Hours Act).
1860 Bleach Works Act.
1861 Lace Works Act.
1864 Factory Acts Extension Act.
1867 Gangs Act (Agriculture). Factory Acts Extension Act. Workshops Regulation Act.
1870 Education Act (Forster's Act).
1873 Agricultural Education Act.
1875 Lord Shaftesbury's Chimney Sweeps Act.
1876 Education Act (Lord Sandon's Act).
1878 Factory and Workshops Consolidating Act.
1880 Education Act (Mundella's Act, for universal compulsory school attendance).
1889 Prevention of Cruelty to Children Act.
1891 Factories and Workshops Act (Minimum age for starting work raised to eleven years old); Free Schooling Elementary Education Act.

Museums

A small selection of Britain's many industrial heritage sites is listed below. Readers are advised to check websites, or contact the museum before travelling, in case any details have changed since going to press.

Cotton

Helmshore Textile Museum
https://www.lancashire.gov.uk/leisure-and-culture/museums/helmshore-mills-textile-museum/
Helmshore Textile Museum, Holcombe Rd, Helmshore, Rossendale, BB4 4NP, Lancashire. Tel: 01706 226459

Museum of Science and Industry
https://www.scienceandindustrymuseum.org.uk/
Museum of Science and Industry, Liverpool Road, Castlefield, Manchester, M3 4FP. Tel: 0330 058 0058

New Lanark World Heritage Site
www.newlanark.org
New Lanark World Heritage Site, South Lanarkshire, Scotland, M1 9DB.
Tel: 01555 661345

Quarry Bank Mill
www.quarrybankmill.org.uk/
Quarry Bank Mill, Quarry Bank Rd, Styal, Wilmslow, Cheshire, SK9 4LA.
Tel: 01625 527468

Science Museum, London
www.sciencemuseum.org.uk
Science Museum, Exhibition Rd, London, SW7 2DD.
Tel: 033 0058 0058

Flax

Gorticashel Flax-Scutching Mill
https://www.ulsterfolkmuseum.org/stories/gortiscashel-flax-mill
Ulster Folk & Transport Museum, Cultra, Holywood, BT18 0EU.
Tel: 0289 042 8428

Silk

Macclesfield Silk Museums
https://www.thesilkmuseum.co.uk/
Silk Industry Museum, Park Lane, Macclesfield, Cheshire, SK11 6TJ.
Tel: 01625 612045

Wool

Leeds Industrial Museum
https://museumsandgalleries.leeds.gov.uk/leeds-industrial-museum/
Leeds Industrial Museum. Canal Road, Armley, Leeds, LS12 2QF.
Tel: 0113 378 3173

National Wool Museum, Wales
https://museum.wales/wool/
Dre-fach Felindre, near Newcastle Emlyn
Llandysul, Carmarthenshire, SA44 5UP
Tel: 0300 111 2333

Glassmaking

The World of Glass
http://www.worldofglass.com/
The World of Glass, Chalon Way East, St Helens, Merseyside, WA10 1BX.
Tel: 01744 22766

National Glass Centre
https://sunderlandculture.org.uk/our-venues/national-glass-centre/
National Glass Centre, Liberty Way, Sunderland, SR6 0GL.
Tel: 0191 515 5555

Mining
National Coal Mining Museum
https://www.ncm.org.uk/
National Coal Mining Museum for England,
Caphouse Colliery, New Road, Overton,
Wakefield, WF4 4RH.
Tel: 01924 848 806

Mining and Metals
Black Country Living Museum
https://bclm.com/
Black Country Living Museum
Discovery Way
Dudley, DY1 4AL
Tel: 0121 557 9643

Pottery
Gladstone Pottery Museum
https://www.stokemuseums.org.uk/gpm/
Gladstone Pottery Museum, Uttoxeter Road, Longton, Stoke-on-Trent, ST3 1PQ.
Tel: 01782 237777

Rural Life
Museum of English Rural Life
https://merl.reading.ac.uk/
University of Reading, Redlands Road, Reading, Berkshire, RG1 5EX.
Tel: 0118 378 8660

General
Young V & A (Victoria & Albert Museum of Childhood)
https://www.vam.ac.uk/young
Victoria & Albert Museum of Childhood, Cambridge Heath Road, London E2 9PA.
Tel:020 8983 5200

Notes

Chapter 1: Forging The Fairytale

1. Hammond, J.L. and Barbara, *The Town Labourer* (Longman, 1978), p.100
2. International Labour Organization website, https://www.ilo.org/projects-and-partnerships/projects/child-labour; https://ilostat.ilo.org/methods/concepts-and-definitions/description-child-labour-statistics/
3. Butterworth, Edwin, *An Historical Account of the Towns of Ashton-under-Lyne, Stalybridge, and Dukinfield* (Ashton, 1842), pp.82, 84
4. Hopkins, Eric, *Childhood Transformed: Working Class Children in Nineteenth Century England* (Manchester University Press, 1994), p.92
5. Census of 2011, National Archives UK Web Archive, https://webarchive.nationalarchives.gov.uk/ukgwa/20160105190821/http://www.ons.gov.uk/ons/rel/wellbeing/measuring-national-well-being/measuring-children-s-well-being/art-measuring-children-s-well-being.html#tab-Population-change. Source: Office for National Statistics licensed under the Open Government Licence v.3.0.
6. Kirby, Peter, *Child Labour in Britain 1750–1870* (Palgrave Macmillan, 2003), p.3; Porter, George Richardson, *The Progress of the Nation* (John Murray, 1851), p.16
7. *Report from the Select Committee on the State of Children Employed in Manufactories* (1816), p.374
8. *Reports of Inspectors of Factories, half year ending 31 October 1856* (1857), p.30
9. *Second Report of the Children's Employment Commission 1862: Lace, Hosiery etc.* [3414], XXII, 1864, Appendix, p.8
10. *Second Report of the Children's Employment Commission: Trades and Manufactures*, 1843, p.176; *Appendix to the* Second Report *of the Children's Employment Commission: Trades and Manufactures: Part 1*, XIII, 1842, Evidence F, pp.131–2
11. *Third Report of the Children's Employment Commission: Metal Manufactures*, [3414–1], XXII, 1864, Appendix p.100
12. Dickens, Charles, *The Writings of Charles Dickens: Life, Letters and Speeches, Vol. XXX* (Houghton, Mifflin, 1894), Vol.1, p.9
13. Hanway, Jonas, *An Earnest Appeal for Mercy to the Children of the Poor* (London, 1766), p.96
14. Trimmer, Sarah, *The Oeconomy of Charity, Or an Address to Ladies, 2 Vols* (1801), pp.168, 194
15. More, Hannah, *The Complete Works Vol. I* (New York, 1847), p.283
16. Cobbett, William, *Weekly Political Register, Vol. XXXII*, 1817, p.83

17. Malthus, Thomas R., *Essay on the Principle of Population, 2 vols.* Vol II, (London, 1807), p.323
18. Southey, C.C. (ed.), *Life and Correspondence of Robert Southey* (Harper & Brothers, 1855), p.515
19. Chadwick, Edwin, *Inquiry into The Sanitary Condition of the Labouring Population of Great Britain (1842)*, pp. 8, 133, 263
20. *Gentleman's Magazine*, December 1824, Supplement, p.648
21. *Reports of Inspectors of Factories, half year ending 31 October 1875*, (1876), p.83
22. Cooke-Taylor, William, *Notes of a Tour in the Manufacturing Districts of Lancashire* (London, 1842), pp.233, 235–7, 239
23. *Third Report of the Children's Employment Commission: Metal Manufactures* [3414–1], XXII, 1864, Appendix p.15
24. Conway, Katherine St. John (Katherine Bruce Glasier), *The Cry of the Children*, (Manchester Labour Press, 1894), p.7
25. Cooke-Taylor, William, *Notes of a Tour in the Manufacturing Districts of Lancashire* (London, 1842), p.236
26. *Third Report of the Children's Employment Commission: Metal Manufactures* [3414–1], XXII, 1864, Appendix p.87
27. *First Report of the Commissioners, Children's Employment Commission* (1862) [3170], XVIII, 1863, Appendix p.307
28. *Third Report of the Children's Employment Commission: Metal Manufactures* [3414–1], XXII, 1864, Appendix and Evidence, p.139

Chapter 2: Learning a Trade

1. Hansard T.C., *Parliamentary Debates from the Year 1803 to the Present Time*, Vol. XXV (London, 1813) 28 April 1813, p.1094
2. Tuckett, John Debell, *A History of the Past and Present State of the Labouring Population*, Vol.1 (London, 1816), pp.495–6
3. White, George Savage, *Memoir of Samuel Slater, Father of American Manufactures* (Philadelphia, 1836), pp.32–3
4. *The Times*, 9 Sept 1789
5. *Dodsley's Annual Register of the Year 1762* (London, 1763), p.133
6. *Annual Register for the Year 1796*, Vol. XXXVIII (London, 1800), p.29
7. *Annual Register of the Year 1767* (J. Dodsley, London, 1768), pp.140, 190–197
8. Pugh, John, *Remarkable Occurrences in the life of Jonas Hanway*, 3rd edition (London, 1798), p.147
9. Smith, Adam, *An Inquiry into the Nature and Causes of the Wealth of Nations*, 6th edn, vol.1 (Dublin 1801), p.125
10. *25th Report of the Society for Bettering the Condition of the Poor* (London, 1805), pp.135, 156
11. Wood, Isaac, *Some Account of the Shrewsbury House of Industry* (Shrewsbury, 1795), p.26
12. *Report from Her Majesty's Commissioners into the Administration and Practical Operation of the Poor Laws* (1834), p.309

13. Webb, Beatrice and Webb, Sidney, *English Local Government: English Poor Law History* Vol. 2, (Longmans, 1927), p.258
14. Hutton, William, *Life of William Hutton* (Charles Knight, 1841), p.3–4
15. Ure, Andrew, *The Philosophy of Manufactures* (Charles Knight, 1835), p.23

Chapter 3: Unknown, Unprotected and Forgotten

1. *Ashton Chronicle*, 23 June 1849
2. *Gentleman's Magazine*, November 1828, pp.469–70
3. *Report from the Select Committee on the State and Condition of Children Employed in Manufactories* (1819), p.338
4. *Gentleman's Magazine*, November 1828, p.470
5. *Second Report on the Employment of Children in Factories* [519], XXI, (1833) D3, p.8
6. 'The Factory System', no author, *Quarterly Review, Vol. 57* (John Murray, 1836), p.400
7. *Report from the Select Committee on the State and Condition of Children Employed in Manufactories* (1819), p.176, pp.181–186
8. Pennant, Thomas, *History of the Parishes of Whiteford and Holywell* (London, 1796), p.215
9. *Report on the State and Condition of Children Employed in Manufactories* (1819), p.320
10. Jones, John, *Poems* (Manchester, 1856), p.66
11. *25th Report of the Society for Bettering the Condition of the Poor* (London, 1805), p.180
12. Chapman, Stanley D, *The Early Factory Masters*, (David & Charles, 1967), p.170
13. *Report from the Select Committee on the State and Condition of Children Employed in Manufactories* (1819), p.65
14. *Memoirs of the Literary and Philosophical Society of Manchester Vol. II*, no author (London, 1785), pp.499–503
15. *Report from the Committee on Parish Apprentices*, 1815, in Hansard, Thomas Curson, *Parliamentary Debates*, Vol. XXX (1815), p.540
16. John Aikin, *A Description of the Country from Thirty or Forty Miles Round Manchester* (John Stockdale, 1795,) p219
17. Gisborne, Thomas, *An Enquiry into the Duties of Men, Vol. II* (London, 1824), pp.393–5
18. *Anti-Jacobin Review, Vol. XXVIII*, no author (London, 1808), p.401
19. *Report from the Select Committee on the State of Children Employed in Manufactories* (1816), p.132
20. *Report from the Select Committee on the State of Children Employed in Manufactories* (1816), p.133
21. *Report from the Select Committee on the State and Condition of Children Employed in Manufactories* (1819), pp.280–1
22. *Second Report on the Employment of Children in Factories* [519], XXI, (1833) D3, pp.17–18

23. Kydd, Samuel, *History of the Factory Movement Vol. 1* (Simpkin, Marshall & Co., 1857), p.24
24. *Ashton Chronicle*, 19 May 1849
25. *Gentleman's Magazine*, July 1824, p.49
26. *Ashton Chronicle*, 2 June 1849
27. *Ashton Chronicle*, 23 June 1849
28. *Report from the Committee on Parish Apprentices* (1815) in *Hansard's Parliamentary Debates, Vol. XXX* (1815), pp.534–41
29. *Report from the Select Committee on the State of Children Employed in Manufactories* (1816), pp. 316–19
30. *Report from the Select Committee on the State of Children Employed in Manufactories* (1816), p291
31. *Report from the Select Committee on the State of Children Employed in Manufactories* (1816), pp.180–1
32. *Report from the Select Committee on the State of Children Employed in Manufactories* (1816), p210
33. *Ashton Chronicle*, 23 June 1849
34. Owen, Robert, *The Life of Robert Owen Written by Himself* (London, 1857), pp.22, 32, 60
35. *Report from the Select Committee on the State of Children Employed in Manufactories* (1816), p.20
36. Owen, Robert, *The Life of Robert Owen Written by Himself* (London, 1857), p.60
37. *Report from the Select Committee on the State of Children Employed in Manufactories*, (1816), p.20
38. *Report from the Select Committee on the State of Children Employed in Manufactories*, (1816), pp.6–7, p.217
39. *Minutes of Evidence... from the Select Committee on the State and Condition of Children Employed in Manufactories* (1819, Appendix no.12, p45

Chapter 4: Battle Begins

1. Sinclair, John, *The Statistical Account of Scotland, Vol. 15* (Edinburgh, 1795), p.41
2. *Report from the Select Committee on the State of Children Employed in Manufactories* (1816), p.217
3. Gaskell, Peter, *Prospects of Industry* (Smith, Elder & Co., 1835), p.23
4. Simond, Louis, *Journal of a Tour, Vol.1* (Edinburgh, 1815), p.278
5. *Report from the Select Committee on the State of Children Employed in Manufactories* (1816), p.167
6. Kydd, Samuel, *History of the Factory Movement Vol.1* (Simpkin, Marshall & Co., 1857), p.38
7. *Report from the Select Committee on the State of Children Employed in Manufactories* (1816), p.344
8. Hansard, Thomas Curson, *Hansard's Parliamentary Debates Vol. XXXVII* (1818), p.557
9. Harris, R.W., *Romanticism and the Social Order* (Blandford Press, 1969), p.225

10. *An Inquiry into the Principle and Tendency of the Bill now Pending in Parliament for Imposing Certain Restrictions on Cotton Factories*, no author (London, 1818), p.30
11. *Edinburgh Annual Register for 1818, Vol. XI* (Edinburgh, 1822), p.104
12. Kydd, Samuel, *History of the Factory Movement Vol.1* (Simpkin, Marshall & Co., 1857), pp.75–7
13. *Report from the Select Committee on the State and Condition of Children Employed in Manufactories* (1819), p.303
14. *Report from the Select Committee on the State of Children Employed in Manufactories* (1816), p.74
15. *Report from the Select Committee on the State of Children Employed in Manufactories* (1816), p.79
16. *Report from the Select Committee on the State and Condition of Children Employed in Manufactories* (1819), Appendix 34, p.112
17. *Report from the Select Committee on the State and Condition of Children Employed in Manufactories* (1819), Appendix 34, p.113
18. Baines, Thomas, *Yorkshire Past and Present* Vol. II (William Mackenzie, c.1869), p.155
19. *Mechanics Magazine Vol.* 4, no author (London 1825), p.122
20. Kydd, Samuel, *History of the Factory Movement, Vol.1* (Simpkin, Marshall & Co., 1857), pp.97
21. Kydd, Samuel, *History of the Factory Movement, Vol.1* (Simpkin, Marshall & Co., 1857), pp.99–100, 106, 121–2, 226
22. *Report from the Select Committee on Hand-Loom Weavers' Petitions* (341), XIII (1835), p.5
23. Butterworth, Edwin, *An Historical Account of the Towns of Ashton-under-Lyne, Stalybridge, and Dukinfield* (Ashton, 1842), p.147
24. *Speech by Michael Thomas Sadler in the House of Commons*, no author, Friday 16 March 1832 (Seeley & Sons, 1832), 3rd edition, p.28
25. Kydd, Samuel, *History of the Factory Movement Vol.1* (Simpkin, Marshall & Co., 1857), p.209
26. Thompson, E.P., *The Making of the English Working Class* (Pantheon Books, 1964), p.337
27. Kydd, Samuel, *History of the Factory Movement Vol.1* (Simpkin, Marshall & Co., 1857), pp.297–8, 300–2
28. *Speech of Michael Thomas Sadler in the House of Commons*, no author, Friday March 1832 (Seeley & Sons, 1832), 3rd edn, p.28
29. Greg, Robert Hyde, *The Factory Question* (James Ridgeway & Son, 1837), p.7

Chapter 5: Time to Sleep and Time to Play

1. *Blackwood's Edinburgh Magazine*, July 1836, New American Edition Vol. 3 (New York, 1836), p.114
2. Grant, Philip, *The Ten Hours Bill: The History of Factory Legislation* (Manchester, 1866), p.35
3. Grant, Philip, *The Ten Hours Bill: The History of Factory Legislation* (Manchester, 1866), pp38,39, The Times 25 February 1833

4. *The Times*, 28 May 1833
5. Grant, Philip, *The Ten Hours Bill: The History of Factory Legislation* (Manchester, 1866), pp.47
6. Grant, Philip, *The Ten Hours Bill: The History of Factory Legislation* (Manchester, 1866), pp.48–49
7. Kydd, Samuel, *History of the Factory Movement Vol.1* (Simpkin, Marshall & Co., 1857), p.47
8. *The Times*, 10 June 1833
9. *Second Report on the Employment of Children in Factories* [519], XXI (1833) C3, p.22
10. *Second Report on the Employment of Children in Factories* [519], XXI (1833), p.8
11. *Second Report on the Employment of Children in Factories* [519], XXI (1833) D3, p.18
12. *Second Report on the Employment of Children in Factories* [519], XXI (1833), p.1
13. *Second Report on the Employment of Children in Factories* [519], XXI (1833), p.6
14. *Second Report on the Employment of Children in Factories* [519], XXI (1833), p.9
15. *Second Report on the Employment of Children in Factories* [519], XXI (1833), p14
16. *Second Report on the Employment of Children in Factories* [519], XXI (1833) A3, pp. 14– 15
17. *Second Report on the Employment of Children in Factories* [519], XXI (1833) A3, pp.11–12
18. *Second Report on the Employment of Children in Factories* [519], XXI (1833) A3, p.15
19. *Second Report on the Employment of Children in Factories* [519], XXI (1833) A3, pp.1–2
20. *Second Report on the Employment of Children in Factories* [519], XXI (1833) A3, p.3
21. *Second Report on the Employment of Children in Factories* [519], XXI (1833) A3, p.7
22. *Second Report on the Employment of Children in Factories* [519], XXI (1833) C3, p.7
23. *Second Report on the Employment of Children in Factories* [519], XXI (1833) C3, p.8
24. *Second Report on the Employment of Children in Factories* [519], XXI (1833) C3, p.24
25. *Second Report on the Employment of Children in Factories* [519], XXI (1833), C3, p.14
26. *Second Report on the Employment of Children in Factories* [519], XXI (1833) C3, pp.22–23
27. Kydd, Samuel, *History of the Factory Movement Vol.2* (Simpkin, Marshall & Co., 1857), p.52
28. Buckingham, J.S. (ed.), *Parliamentary Review and Family Magazine Vol.3* (London 1833), p.263, *The Times*, 19 July 1833
29. Tapping, Thomas, *The Factory Acts* (Shaw & Sons, 1856), pp.17, 13

30. *Second Report on the Employment of Children in Factories* [519], XXI (1833) C3, p.12, D3, p.18

Chapter 6: Fight the Good Fight

1. Cooper, Lord Anthony Ashley, *Speeches of the Earl of Shaftesbury K.G.* (Chapman & Hall, 1868), p.v
2. *Pictorial History of the County of Lancaster*, no author (London, 1844), p.10
3. *Reports of the Inspectors of Factories for the half year ending 31 December 1840* (1841), p.4
4. *Reports of the Inspectors of Factories for the half year ending 31 December 1840* (1841), p.9
5. Greg, Robert Hyde, *The Factory Question* (James Ridgeway & Son, 1837), pp.12–13, 16
6. Head, Sir George, *A Home Tour through the Manufacturing Districts of England* (John Murray, 1836), p.187
7. Head, Sir George, *A Home Tour through the Manufacturing Districts of England* (John Murray, 1836), pp.146–7
8. Barrow, John Henry (ed.), *Mirror of Parliament Vol. 7* (1838), pp.5673–4
9. Horner, Leonard, *On the Employment of Children in Factories* (London, 1840), p.3
10. Greg, Robert Hyde, *The Factory Question* (James Ridgeway & Son, 1837), pp.18,19
11. Oastler, Richard, *The Fleet Papers Vol. 1* (London, 1841), pp.29, 91
12. *Second Annual Report of the Poor Law Commissioners (1836) Appendix B*, pp. 472, 454, 457
13. *Reports of the Inspectors of Factories for the half year ending 31 December 1840*, (1841), pp.22–3
14. *Minutes of the Committee of Council of Education, 1839–40* (London, 1840), p.182–3
15. Horner, Leonard, *On the Employment of Children in Factories* (London, 1840), pp. 1, v, 16
16. Horner, Leonard, *On the Employment of Children in Factories* (London, 1840), pp. 15, 18
17. Kydd, Samuel, *History of the Factory Movement Vol. 1* (Simpkin, Marshall & Co., 1857), p.108
18. Cooper, Lord Anthony Ashley, *Speeches of the Earl of Shaftesbury K.G.* (Chapman & Hall, 1868), p.91
19. *The Times*, 16 March 1844.
20. Horner, Leonard, *On the Employment of Children in Factories* (London, 1840), p.6
21. Cooper, Lord Anthony Ashley, *Speeches of the Earl of Shaftesbury K.G.* (Chapman & Hall, 1868), p.vi
22. Horner, Leonard, *On the Employment of Children in Factories* (London, 1840), pp.14–15
23. Cooper, Lord Anthony Ashley, *Speeches of the Earl of Shaftesbury K.G.* (Chapman & Hall, 1868), pp.17, 23, 153

Chapter 7: Overburdened: Life Down the Pit

1. Ayton, Richard, *Essays and Sketches of Character* (London, 1825), pp.258, 260–1, 271, 274
2. *A Letter from the Dead to the Living: Or, the Colliery Boy and His Mother*, no author, North of England Institute of Mining and Mechanical Engineers Tracts, Vol.102, pp.95–112
3. *Report from the Select Committee on the State and Condition of Children Employed in Manufactories* (1819) Appendix 34, pp.113–4
4. Sykes, John, *Local Records or Historical Register … of Northumberland and Durham*, Vol. II (1833), p.294
5. Horner, Leonard, *On the Employment of Children in Factories* (London, 1840), pp.126–8, 134–5
6. Martineau, Harriet, *History of the Peace* (W. & R. Chambers, 1858), p.653
7. *First Report of the Children's Employment Commission: Mines, XV* (1842), pp.13
8. *First Report of the Children's Employment Commission: Mines, XV* (1842), pp.31
9. *First Report of the Children's Employment Commission: Mines, XV* (1842), pp.71
10. *First Report of the Children's Employment Commission: Mines, XV* (1842), pp.20–1
11. *First Report of the Children's Employment Commission: Mines, XV* (1842), p.98
12. Vane, C.W. (Third Marquess of Londonderry), *A Letter to Lord Ashley on the Mines and Collieries' Bill* (London, 1842), p.77
13. *First Report of the Children's Employment Commission: Mines, XV* (1842), pp.64, 259,
14. *First Report of the Children's Employment Commission: Mines, XV* (1842), p.136
15. *First Report of the Children's Employment Commission: Mines, XV* (1842), pp.41–43
16. *First Report of the Children's Employment Commission: Mines, XV* (1842), p.130
17. *First Report of the Children's Employment Commission: Mines, XV* (1842), pp. 171–2
18. *First Report of the Children's Employment Commission: Mines, XV* (1842), p.28
19. *First Report of the Children's Employment Commission: Mines, XV* (1842), pp. 91, 93, 96
20. *First Report of the Children's Employment Commission: Mines, XV* (1842), pp.20
21. *First Report of the Children's Employment Commission: Mines, XV* (1842), p.32
22. *First Report of the Children's Employment Commission: Mines, XV* (1842), p.31
23. Cooper, Lord Anthony Ashley, *Speeches of the Earl of Shaftesbury K.G.* (Chapman & Hall, 1868), p.32
24. Martineau, Harriet, *History of the Peace* (W. & R. Chambers, 1858), p.653
25. *Speeches of the Earl of Shaftesbury K.G.* (Chapman & Hall, 1868), p.48
26. Vane, C.W. (Third Marquess of Londonderry*), A Letter to Lord Ashley on the Mines and Collieries' Bill* (London, 1842), pp. 29, 36, 97
27. *Illustrated London News*, 22 March 1851
28. 'Dickens, Charles (ed.), The Cost of Coal', *All The Year Round, Vol. VI* (London 1862), p.495
29. *The Labour Gazette*, (April 1895) *Volume 3, January–December 1895*, HMSO, p.116

Chapter 8: The Devil's Nursery

1. *First Report of the Children's Employment Commission: Mines, XV* (1842), p.3

2. White, William, *History, Gazetteer & Directory of Staffordshire* (Sheffield, 1834), p.527
3. *Report from the Select Committee on the State of Children Employed in Manufactories* (1816), pp.60, 65
4. *Report from the Select Committee on the State of Children Employed in Manufactories* (1816), p.64
5. White, William, *History, Gazetteer & Directory of Staffordshire* (1834), p.522
6. *Second Report of the Children's Employment Commission: Trades and Manufactures XIII*, [430], (1843), p.20
7. *Reports from Commissioners: 1844, Occupation Abstract, 1841*, Vol. 27, [587], 1843, pp.170–4
8. *Second Report of the Children's Employment Commission: Trades and Manufactures XII,I* [430], (1843), p.35
9. *Second Report of the Children's Employment Commission: Trades and Manufactures XIII*, [430], (1843), p.31
10. *Second Report of the Children's Employment Commission: Trades and Manufactures XIII* [430], (1843), p.108
11. *Second Report of the Children's Employment Commission: Trades and Manufactures XIII* [430], (1843), p.8
12. *First Report of the Commissioners, Children's Employment Commission* (1862) [3170], XVIII, 1863, p.xxvi
13. *Second Report of the Children's Employment Commission: Trades and Manufactures XIII* [430], (1843), p.85
14. *Second Report of the Children's Employment Commission: Trades and Manufactures XIII* [430], (1843), p.45
15. *Second Report of the Children's Employment Commission: Trades and Manufactures XIII* [430], (1843), p.85
16. *Second Report of the Children's Employment Commission: Trades and Manufactures XIII* [430], (1843), p.172
17. *Cooper, Lord Anthony Ashley, Speeches of the Earl of Shaftesbury K.G.* (Chapman & Hall, 1868), p.21
18. *Second Report on the Employment of Children in Factories* [519], XXI (1833) D2, p.43
19. *Second Report of the Children's Employment Commission: Trades and Manufactures, XIII* [430], (1843), p.79–80
20. West, William, *The History, Topography and Directory of Warwickshire* (Birmingham, 1830), p.255
21. Espriella, Don, (Southey, Robert) *Letters from England* (1836), p.71
22. *Second Report of the Children's Employment Commission: Trades and Manufactures XIII* [430], (1843), p.16
23. *Second Report of the Children's Employment Commission: Trades and Manufactures XIII* [430], (1843), p.7
24. *Second Report of the Children's Employment Commission: Trades and Manufactures XIII* [430], (1843), pp. 80, 84

25. *Second Report of the Children's Employment Commission: Trades and Manufactures XIII* [430], (1843), p.44
26. *Second Report of the Children's Employment Commission: Trades and Manufactures XIII* [430], (1843), pp.105–6
27. Mackenzie, E., *Descriptive and Historical Account ... of Newcastle upon Tyne* (Mackenzie & Dent, 1827), p.716
28. *Second Report of the Children's Employment Commission: Trades and Manufactures XIII* [430], (1843), p.109
29. *Second Report of the Children's Employment Commission: Trades and Manufactures XIII* [430], (1843), p.86
30. *Second Report of the Children's Employment Commission: Trades and Manufactures XIII* [430], (1843), pp.114, 122
31. *Second Report of the Children's Employment Commission: Trades and Manufactures XIII* [430], (1843), pp.116, 117
32. *Second Report of the Children's Employment Commission: Trades and Manufactures XIII* [430], (1843), pp.119
33. *Second Report of the Children's Employment Commission: Trades and Manufactures XIII* [430], (1843), pp.116, 119, 120, 122
34. *Second Report of the Children's Employment Commission: Trades and Manufactures XIII* [430], (1843), pp.122–123
35. *The Times*, 7 November 1843
36. *The Times*, 21 April 1843
37. Dickens, Charles (ed.), *Household Narrative of Current Events for the Year 1850* (London, 1850), p.228
38. *Second Report of the Children's Employment Commission: Trades and Manufactures XIII*, [430], (1843), pp.57, 68
39. *Second Report of the Children's Employment Commission: Trades and Manufactures XIII*, [430], (1843), pp.10, 11
40. *Second Report of the Children's Employment Commission: Trades and Manufactures XIII*, [430], (1843), p110
41. *Cooper, Lord Anthony Ashley Speeches of the Earl of Shaftesbury K.G.* (Chapman & Hall, 1868), p.vii
42. *Second Report of the Children's Employment Commission: Trades and Manufactures XIII* [430], (1843), p.84
43. *Second Report of the Children's Employment Commission: Trades and Manufactures XIII*, [430], (1843), pp.104,177, 178–9, 199
44. *Second Report of the Children's Employment Commission: Trades and Manufactures XIII*, [430], (1843), p.206
45. *The Physical and Moral Condition of Children and Young Persons Employed in Mines and Manufactures* (London, 1843), pp.266–7
46. Cooper, Lord Anthony Ashley, *Speeches of the Earl of Shaftesbury K.G.* (Chapman & Hall, 1868), p.vii

Chapter 9: Rural Bliss

1. McCulloch, J.R., *Statistical Account of the British Empire, Vol.1* (London, 1839), p.550.
2. Horn, Pamela, *Children's Work and Welfare 1780–1890* (Cambridge University Press, 1995), pp.72–73; Horn, Pamela, *The Victorian Country Child* (Sutton Publishing, 1974), p.107
3. *Reports of Special Assistant Poor Law Commissioners on the Employment of Women and Children in Agriculture XII* (1843), p.31
4. *Reports of Special Assistant Poor Law Commissioners on the Employment of Women and Children in Agriculture XII* (1843), p.123
5. *Reports of Special Assistant Poor Law Commissioners on the Employment of Women and Children in Agriculture XII* (1843), p.82
6. *Reports of Special Assistant Poor Law Commissioners on the Employment of Women and Children in Agriculture XII* (1843), p.113
7. *Reports of Special Assistant Poor Law Commissioners on the Employment of Women and Children in Agriculture XII* (1843), p.7
8. Winstanley, Roy, 'Skip-Jacks', *Parson Woodforde Society Journal Vol. XIX*, Spring 1986, p.8
9. Beresford, John (ed.), *The Diary of a Country Parson Vol. II* (Oxford University Press, 1926), p.155
10. Winstanley, Roy, 'Skip-Jacks', *Parson Woodforde Society Journal Vol. XIX*, Spring 1986, pp.10, 12
11. Jameson, Peter (ed.), *The Diary of James Woodforde Volume 15 1796–7* (Parson Woodforde Society, 2004), pp.36, 38, 47, 86, 55
12. Cobbett, William, *Rural Rides* (London, 1853), p.93
13. *Reports of Special Assistant Poor Law Commissioners on the Employment of Women and Children in Agriculture XII* (1843), pp.44, 45–6
14. *Reports of Special Assistant Poor Law Commissioners on the Employment of Women and Children in Agriculture XII* (1843), p.99–100
15. *Reports of Special Assistant Poor Law Commissioners on the Employment of Women and Children in Agriculture XII* (1843), p.95
16. *Reports of Special Assistant Poor Law Commissioners on the Employment of Women and Children in Agriculture XII* (1843), pp.112–113
17. *The Times*, 2 February 1850
18. *Annual Register of the Year 1850 Vol. 92*, no author, March 1850 (London, 1851), p.42
19. *The Times*, 25 March 1850
20. *The Times*, 27 March 1850
21. Somerville, Alexander, *The Whistler at the Plough, Vol. 1* (Manchester, 1852), p.38
22. Trevelyan, George Macaulay, *Life of John Bright* (Constable & Co., 1913), p.47
23. *Report from the Select Committee into the State of Agriculture, V* [464] 1837, p.96
24. *Report from the Select Committee into the State of Agriculture, V* [464] 1837, p.56
25. *Reports of Special Assistant Poor Law Commissioners on the Employment of Women and Children in Agriculture XII* (1843), p.83

26. Gregg, Pauline, *A Social and Economic History of Britain, 1760–1970* (G. Harrap & Co. Ltd., 6th edn, 1971), p.177
27. *Report from the Select Committee into the State of Agriculture, V* [464] (1837), p.180
28. *Index to the Reports... on the Poor Law Amendment Act,* [97, 45], (1838), p.24
29. *Seventeenth Report from the Select Committee on the Poor Law Amendment Act: Minutes of Evidence and Appendix* [222], 1838, p.4
30. *Second Annual Report of the Poor Law Commissioners, together with Appendices,* [320.1], (1836), p.224
31. Cobbett, William, *Legacy to Labourers* (London, 1835), p.122
32. *The Times*, 17 May 1844
33. *Reports of Special Assistant Poor Law Commissioners on the Employment of Women and Children in Agriculture XII* (1843), pp.222–3, 224, 275, 277
34. *The Times*, 13 March 1844
35. Somerville, Alexander, *The Whistler at the Plough, Vol.1* (Manchester, 1852), pp.32, 34
36. Cooper, Lord Anthony Ashley, *Speeches of the Earl of Shaftesbury K.G.* (Chapman & Hall, 1868), p.90
37. *The Times*, 1 December 1843
38. Engels, Friedrich, (ed. D. McLellan) *The Condition of the Working Class in England* (Oxford University Press, 1993), p.202
39. *Second Report of the Children's Employment Commission: Trades and Manufactures, XIII* (1843), p.129
40. Cooke Taylor, William, *Factories and the Factory System* (London, 1844), p.26

Chapter 10: Sweeps and Slaveys

1. *Report from the Committee on Employment of Boys in Sweeping Chimnies* (1817), p.41
2. *Reports of the Society for Bettering... The Condition of the Poor, Vol.1*, (London, 1798) p.108
3. *Edinburgh Annual Register*, August 1809
4. *The Examiner*, Sunday 23 April 1815, (London, 1815), p.272
5. *The Times*, 28 August 1811; *Report from the Committee on Employment of Boys in Sweeping Chimnies* (1817), p.38
6. *Report from the Committee on Employment of Boys in Sweeping Chimnies* (1817), pp.50–1
7. *Gentleman's Magazine*, March 1819
8. Official name 'The Society for Superseding the Necessity of Climbing Boys by encouraging a New Method of Sweeping Chimneys and for Improving the Condition of Children and Others Employed by Chimney Sweepers', *Annual Subscription Charities and Public Charities in London*, no author (John Murray, 1823), p.140
9. Ayton, Richard, *Essays and Sketches of Character* (London, 1825), pp.273–4
10. *British Magazine and Monthly Register Vol. 8*, no author (London, 1835), p.117
11. *First Report of the Commissioners, Children's Employment Commission* (1862) [3170], XVIII (1863) Evidence, p.308

12. *First Report of the Commissioners, Children's Employment Commission* (1862) [3170], XVIII (1863), p.lxxxvii
13. Hammond, J.L. and Barbara, *Lord Shaftesbury*, 2nd ed (Constable & Co., 1923), pp.221–2
14. *First Report of the Commissioners, Children's Employment Commission* (1862) [3170], XVIII (1863), pp.lxxxiii, lxxxvi, 298, 302
15. *First Report of the Commissioners, Children's Employment Commission* (1862) [3170], XVIII (1863), pp.lxxxiv, 297, 300
16. Hansard, Thomas Curson, *Hansard's Parliamentary Debates, Third Series Vol. CLCCV* (London, 1864), p.1130
17. *Fifth Report of the Children's Employment Commission (1862): Printing and Miscellaneous Trades*, XXIV (1866), p.xxii
18. *The Times*, 6 March 1873; 24 March 1875
19. Booth, Charles, *Occupations of the People: England, Scotland, Ireland, 1841–1881*, London, 1886, pp.20, 41, 62
20. *Reports from Commissioners: 1844, Occupation Abstract, 1841*, Vol. 27, [587], 1843, p.120
21. Horn, Pamela, *Children's Work and Welfare 1780–1890* (Cambridge University Press, 1995), p.72
22. Cobbett, William, *Advice to Young Men* (New York, 1831), 'Letter IV', p.123
23. Porter, George Richardson, *The Progress of the Nation* (John Murray, 1851), p.530
24. Beeton, Isabella, *The Book of Household Management* (London, 1861), p.1001
25. Parkes, Mrs William, *Domestic Duties; Or Instructions to Young Married Ladies* (New York, 1829), p.51
26. Wood, Isaac, *Some Account of the Shrewsbury House of Industry* (Shrewsbury, 1795), p.107
27. *Report from the Select Committee … into the Education of the Lower Orders* (1816), pp.432–3
28. *Second Report of the Children's Employment Commission: Trades and Manufactures XIII* (1843), pp.27, 193
29. Rose, Lionel, *The Erosion of Childhood: Child Oppression in Britain 1860–1918*, (Routledge, 1991), p.36
30. *The Times* 29 January 1851, *Illustrated London News*, 1 February 1851
31. *The Times* 4 December, 9 December, 28 December 1850; *Punch, Vol. XX* (1851), p.72
32. *The Times*, 11 February 1851
33. Gaskell, Elizabeth Cleghorn, *North and South* (Bernhard Tauchnitz, 1855), p.70
34. Rose, Lionel, *The Erosion of Childhood: Child Oppression in Britain 1860–1918*, (Routledge, 1991), p.36

Chapter 11: Candles of Hope

1. *Children's Magazine, Vol. 2* (New York, 1830), p.14
2. *Reports of the Society for Bettering the Condition of the Poor Vol. I* (London, 1798), p.153
3. *Journal of the Statistical Society of London*, Vol. IV, (Charles Knight & Co., 1841), p.251

4. *Report from the Select Committee … into the Education of the Lower Orders* (1816), pp.425, 429
5. *Reports of the Inspectors of Factories for the half-year ending 31 October 1856*, [2153], 1857, p.30
6. *Journal of the Royal Statistical Society of London, Vol. 2* (1839), pp.177–179
7. *Second Annual Report of the Poor Law Commissioners* (1836), p.529
8. *Reports of the Inspectors of Factories for the half year ending 31 December 1842*, (1843), pp.4–5
9. *Second Report of the Children's Employment Commission: Trades and Manufactures XIII* (1843), pp.201–2
10. *Second Report of the Children's Employment Commission: Trades and Manufactures XIII* (1843), p. 167
11. *Second Report of the Children's Employment Commission: Trades and Manufactures XIII* (1843), p.202
12. *Second Report of the Children's Employment Commission: Trades and Manufactures XIII* (1843), pp155–6, 171, 202
13. *Second Report of the Children's Employment Commission: Trades and Manufactures XIII* (1843), p.201
14. *Second Report of the Children's Employment Commission: Trades and Manufactures XIII* (1843), p.194
15. *Second Report of the Children's Employment Commission: Trades and Manufactures XIII* (1843), p.172
16. *Second Report of the Children's Employment Commission: Trades and Manufactures XIII* (1843), pp. 149–50
17. *Second Report of the Children's Employment Commission: Trades and Manufactures XIII* (1843), p. 148
18. *The Physical and Moral Condition of Children and Young Persons Employed in Mines and Manufactures* (London, 1843), p.256
19. *Second Report of the Children's Employment Commission: Trades and Manufactures XIII* (1843), pp.161, 162, 165
20. *Reports of the Inspectors of Factories for the half year ending 30 June 1843*, (1843) pp.10, 12–13
21. Cooper, Lord Anthony Ashley, *Speeches of the Earl of Shaftesbury, K.G.* (Chapman & Hall, 1868), pp.73, 86
22. Tapping, Thomas, *The Factory Acts* (Shaw & Sons, 1856), p.64
23. *Reports of the Inspectors of Factories for the half year ending 31 October 1845* (1846), pp.7, 9, 10–11
24. *Appendix to the Reports … On Public Petitions: Appendix to the Tenth Report, Petitions against adopting the Principles in Mr Horner's Report*, Session 1846, p.107
25. *Irish Quarterly Review, Vol V,* Part 1 (Dublin, 1855), p.80
26. *Fraser's Magazine for Town and Country* (London, 1852), pp.106–112
27. *Irish Quarterly Review, Vol V,* Part 1 (Dublin, 1855), p.87
28. *Irish Quarterly Review, Vol V,* Part 1 (Dublin, 1855), pp.123–4,: *North British Review*, LXXXII (November) 1864, p.136

29. Jevons, William Stanley, *The Coal Question* (Macmillan & Co., 1866), pp. xxiv-xxv

Chapter 12: Mangling the Operatives

1. Horner, Leonard, *On the Employment of Children in Factories* (London, 1840), pp.121–124
2. *Second Report of the Children's Employment Commission: Trades and Manufactures*, [430], XIII (1843), p.21
3. Cooper, Lord Anthony Ashley, *Speeches of the Earl of Shaftesbury, K.G.* (Chapman & Hall, 1868), pp.153, 166
4. *Reports of Inspectors of Factories for the half year ending 30 April 1846* (1846), p.7
5. Lord Anthony Ashley, *Speeches of the Earl of Shaftesbury, K.G.* (Chapman & Hall, 1868), p.vi
6. *Reports of the Inspectors of Factories for the Half-Year ending 31 October 1856*, (1857), pp.30, 31
7. *Report of the Commissioner appointed to inquire … Better Regulation of Mills and Factories to Bleaching Works Evidence and Appendix*, (1855), pp.235, 300
8. *Reports of the Inspectors of Factories for the Half-Year ending 31 December 1838*, (1839), pp.74, 75; *Reports of the Inspectors of Factories for the Half-Year ending 31 December 1840*, (1841), p.25
9. Engels, Friedrich, (ed. D. McLellan) *The Condition of the Working Class in England* (Oxford University Press, 1993), p.173
10. *The Times*, 30 September 1840
11. *Reports of the Inspectors of Factories for the Half-Year ending 31 December 1840*, (1841), p.7–8
12. R.B. Seeley, *The Perils of the Nation*, (Seeley, Burnside & Seeley, 1843), pp.262–3
13. *Reports of the Inspectors of Factories for the half year ending 30 June 1844*, (1844), pp.3–4
14. *Special Reports of the Inspectors of Factories On the Practicability of Legislative Interference to Diminish the Frequency of Accidents* (1841), p.56
15. *Reports of the Inspectors of Factories for the Half-Year ending 30 April 1849*, (1849), pp.10, 14
16. *Reports of the Inspectors of Factories for the Half-Year ending 31 October 1851*, (1852), pp.33, 35
17. *Mechanics' Magazine Vol. LX*, no author (London, 1854), p.555; *Journal of the Society of Arts*, Vol. II, London, 1854, p.493
18. *Reports of the Inspectors of Factories for the half year ending 31 October 1854* (1855), p.21
19. *Reports of the Inspectors of Factories for the half year ending 31 October 1854* (1855), pp.6–7
20. Tapping, Thomas, *The Factory Acts* (Shaw & Sons, 1856), p.vi
21. 'Ground in the Mill' in Dickens, Charles (ed.), *Household Words Vol. IX* (London, 1854), p.224
22. 'Deadly Shafts' in Dickens, Charles (ed.), *Household Words Vol. XI* (London, 1855), p.495

23. Martineau, Harriet, *The Factory Controversy: A Warning Against Meddling Legislation* (Manchester, 1855), pp. 34, 25, 27
24. 'Our Wicked Mis-Statements', in Dickens, Charles, *Household Words Vol. XIII*, (London, 1856), p.18
25. *Reports of the Inspectors of Factories for the half year ending 31 October 1856* (1857), p.40
26. *Fifth Report of the Children's Employment Commission (1862): Printing and Miscellaneous Trades, XXIV*, p.35
27. *The Times*, 29 November 1850
28. *The Times*, 2 December, 16 December 1850
29. *The Times*, 21 March, 27 March, 11 April 1851
30. *Illustrated London News*, 5 April 1851
31. *Fifth Report of the Children's Employment Commission (1862): Printing and Miscellaneous Trades, XXIV* (1866), pp. xv,.35, 123, 124
32. *Reports of the Inspectors of Factories for the half year ending April 1868* (1868), pp.38–9

Chapter 13: A Change of Heart

1. *Report from the Select Committee on the State of Children Employed in Manufactories* (1816), p.64
2. *First Report of the Commissioners, Children's Employment Commission (1862)* [3170], XVIII (1863), p.322
3. *Second Report of the Children's Employment Commission: Trades and Manufactures XIII* (1843), p.141
4. *First Report of the Commissioners, Children's Employment Commission (1862)* [3170], XVIII (1863), pp.xlviii, 49, 52–3, 57
5. *Third Report of the Children's Employment Commission: Metal Manufactures*, [3414–1], XXII (1864), Evidence, p.88
6. *Third Report of the Children's Employment Commission: Metal Manufactures*, [3414–1], XXII (1864), Evidence, pp.86, 89–90
7. *Fourth Report of the Commissioners, Children's Employment Commission (1862)*, [8357], XX (1865), pp.215–6, 217
8. *Third Report of the Children's Employment Commission: Metal Manufactures*, [3414–1], XXII (1864) Evidence, p.145
9. *Fourth Report of the Commissioners, Children's Employment Commission (1862)*, [8357], XX (1865), pp.258–9
10. *Fourth Report of the Commissioners, Children's Employment Commission (1862)*, [8357], XX (1865), p.210
11. *Fifth Report of the Commissioners, Children's Employment Commission, (1862), with Appendix*, [3678], 1866, p.xxiii
12. *Second Report of the Children's Employment Commission 1862: Lace, Hosiery etc.*, [3414], XXII (1864), Evidence, p.100
13. *Second Report of the Children's Employment Commission 1862: Lace, Hosiery etc.*, [3414], XXII (1864), Evidence, pp. lix, 122

14. Carlyle, Thomas, *Past and Present* (Chapman & Hall, 1840), pp.211, 265
15. Disraeli, Benjamin, *Sybil or The Two Nations* (Leipzig, 1845), p.68
16. Dickens, Charles, *The Old Curiosity Shop* (Chapman & Hall, 1841), p.269
17. *Boy's Book of Trades*, no author (George Routledge and Sons, London, c.1890), p.iii
18. *Third Report of the Children's Employment Commission: Metal Manufac*tures [3414–1] XXII (1864) Evidence, pp.188
19. *Third Report of the Children's Employment Commission: Metal Manufac*tures [3414–1] XXII (1864) Evidence, p.30
20. *Reports of the Inspectors of Factories for the half year ending 31st October 1854* (1855), p.62
21. Cooke-Taylor, R. Whately, *The Factory System and the Factory Acts* (Methuen & Co., 1894), pp.90, 400
22. *Reports of the Inspectors of Factories for the Quarter Ending September 1844*, (London, 1845), pp.19–22
23. *The Times*, 10 May 1860
24. *Reports of Inspectors of Factories for the half year ending 31 October 1865* (1866), p.12
25. Whately Cooke-Taylor, R, *The Factory System and the Factory Acts* (Methuen & Co., 1894), p.95
26. *Fifth Report of the Children's Employment Commission (1862): Printing and Miscellaneous Trades, XXIV* (1866), p.xxv
27. *Second Report of the Children's Employment Commission 1862: Lace, Hosiery etc.*, [3414], XXII (1864) Evidence, p.201
28. Cooper, Lord Anthony Ashley, *Speeches of the Earl of Shaftesbury, K.G.* (Chapman & Hall, 1868), p.xii
29. *The Graphic*, 10 June 1871
30. *Second Report of the Children's Employment Commission: Trades and Manufactures XIII* (1843), p.138
31. *Third Report of the Children's Employment Commission: Metal Manufactures*, [3414–1], XXII (1864) Evidence, pp.56, 138, 139
32. *Fifth Report of the Children's Employment Commission (1862): Printing and Miscellaneous Trades, XXIV* (1866) Evidence, pp. xvii, 130, 152, 154
33. *Reports of the Inspectors of Factories for the half year ending 31 October 1864*, (1865) pp.120–3
34. *Fifth Report of the Children's Employment Commission (1862): Printing and Miscellaneous Trades, XXIV* (1866) Evidence, pp.133
35. *Third Report of the Children's Employment Commission: Metal Manufactures*, [3414–1], XXII (1864) Evidence, pp.39
36. Smith, George, *The Cry of the Children From the Brick-yards of England*, (London, 1879), pp.34,191
37. *Report of the Commissioners … into the State of Popular Education in England, Vol. 1* (1861), p.181
38. Cooper, Lord Anthony Ashley, *Speeches of the Earl of Shaftesbury, K.G.* (Chapman & Hall, 1868), pp.411–2

39. *First Report of the Commission into the Employment of Children, Young Persons and Women in Agriculture*, [21157] (1868), pp.ix, 178

Chapter 14: Empire Builders

1. Conway, Katherine St. John (Katherine Bruce Glasier), *The Cry of the Children* (Manchester Labour Press, 1894), p.13
2. Mayhew, Henry, *London Labour and the London Poor, Vol. II* (London, 1861), p.480
3. *Illustrated London News*, 11 January 1851
4. *Illustrated London News*, 14 June 1851
5. *Illustrated London News*, 8 March 1851
6. *Illustrated London News*, 15 March 1851
7. Levi, Leone, *Annals of British Legislation*, Vol. XIII, (Smith, Elder, & Co.,) 1864, p.317
8. *Correspondence ... relating to the Emigration of Children to Bermuda* [243], (1851), pp.3, 7
9. *Correspondence ... relating to the Emigration of Children to Bermuda* [243], (1851), pp.11, 14
10. *Correspondence ... relating to the Emigration of Children to Bermuda* [243], (1851), p.7
11. Webb, Beatrice and Webb, Sidney, *English Local Government (Vol. 8): English Poor Law History Part II, The Last Hundred Years, Vol. I*, (Longmans, 1927) p.295
12. *Report of the Commissioners ... into the State of Popular Education in England, Vol. 1* (1861), p.29
13. *Report of the Commissioners ... into the State of Popular Education in England, Vol. 1* (1861), p.35,
14. *Report of the Commissioners ... into the State of Popular Education in England, Vol. 1* (1861), pp.79, 80, 81
15. *Report of the Commissioners ... into the State of Popular Education in England, Vol. 1* (1861), p.85
16. *Report of the Commissioners ... into the State of Popular Education in England, Vol. 1* (1861), p.93
17. *Report of the Commissioners ... into the State of Popular Education in England, Vol. 1* (1861), p.185
18. *Report of the Commissioners ... into the State of Popular Education in England, Vol. 1* (1861), p.188–9
19. Mill, John Stuart, *On Liberty* (London, 1859), p.189
20. Gregg, Pauline, *A Social and Economic History of Britain, 1760–1970*, 6th edition, (G. Harrap & Co. Ltd., 1971), p.513
21. Bagley, J.J. and A.J., *The State of Education in England and Wales, 1833–1968* (Macmillan, 1969), p.25
22. Whately Cooke-Taylor, R, *The Factory System and the Factory Acts* (Methuen & Co., 1894), p.104
23. *Reports of the Inspectors of Factories for the half year ending 30 April 1872* (1872), pp.134–9

24. *Reports of the Inspectors of Factories for the half year ending 30 April 1872* (1872), p.139
25. *Reports of the Inspectors of Factories for the half year ending 31 October 1872* (1873), pp.7–8
26. *Reports of the Inspectors of Factories for the half year ending 31 October 1870* (1871), p.58
27. *Reports of the Inspectors of Factories for the half year ending 30 April 1875* (1875), pp.76–7, 79, 80
28. *Reports of the Inspectors of Factories for the half year ending 30 April 1875* (1875), p.78
29. Conway, Katherine St. John (Katherine Bruce Glasier), *The Cry of the Children* (Manchester Labour Press, 1894), p.13
30. McLeod, Donald, (ed.), 'Bundlewood Work and Workers', *Good Words*, London, 1879, pp.781–5
31. Conway, Katherine St. John (Katherine Bruce Glasier), *The Cry of the Children* (Manchester Labour Press, 1894), p.12
32. *Reports of the Inspectors of Factories for the half year ending 30 April 1875* (1875), p.166
33. *Reports of the Inspectors of Factories for the half year ending October 1875* (1876), p.81
34. *Reports of the Inspectors of Factories for the half year ending October 1879*, (1880), p.68
35. *Reports of the Inspectors of Factories for the half year ending 30 April 1875* (1875), p.11
36. *Reports of the Inspectors of Factories for the half year ending 30 April 1875* (1875), p12
37. *Reports of the Inspectors of Factories for the half year ending 31 October 1872* (1873), p.132
38. Hirst, F.W. (ed.), Porter, George R., *The Progress of the Nation* (London, 1912), p.25–6
39. *Parliamentary Debates*, 59 Victoriae, Fourth Series, Vol. XL, Waterlow & Sons, 1896, p.552
40. *Reports of the Inspectors of Factories for the half year ending 31 October 1877* (1878), p.9
41. *Reports of the Inspectors of Factories for the year ending 31 October 1879* (1880), p.93
42. *The Times*, 2 October 1885
43. Lavalette, Michael, *Child Labour: A Thing of the Past?* (Liverpool University Press, 1999), pp.130, 133

Select Bibliography

Contemporary Works

Newspapers, Periodicals, Pamphlets etc.

25th Report of the Society for Bettering the Condition of the Poor (London, 1805)

A Letter from the Dead to the Living: Or, the Colliery Boy and His Mother, no author, North of England Institute of Mining and Mechanical Engineers Tracts, Vol.102, pp.95–112.

An Inquiry into the Principle and Tendency of the Bill now Pending in Parliament for Imposing Certain Restrictions on Cotton Factories, no author, (London, 1818)

Transactions, Vol. XI, Northumberland Institute of Mining Engineers, (Newcastle-on-Tyne, 1862)

Annual Register of the Year 1767 (J. Dodsley, London, 1768)

Annual Register for the Year 1796, Vol.XXXVIII, no author, London, (1800)

Annual Register of the Year 1850 Vol.92, no author, March 1850 (London, 1851)

Annual Subscription Charities and Public Charities in London, no author (John Murray, 1823)

Anti-Jacobin Review Vol. XXVIII (London,1808)

Ashton Chronicle 19 May 1849, 2 June 1849, 23 June 1849

Blackwood's Edinburgh Magazine July 1836 New American Edition Vol. 3 (New York, 1836)

British Magazine and Monthly Register Vol.8, no author, (London, 1835)

Children's Magazine Vol. 2 no author (New York, 1830)

Dodsley's Annual Register of the Year 1762 (London, 1763)

Dodsley's Annual Register of the Year 1767 (London, 1768)

Edinburgh Annual Register, August 1809

Edinburgh Annual Register for 1818 Vol. XI, no author (Edinburgh,1822)

Fraser's Magazine for Town and Country no author (London, 1852)

Gentleman's Magazine March 1819, July 1824, December 1824, November 1828

Illustrated London News 11 January 1851, 11 February 1851, 8 March 1851, 15 March 1851, 5 April 1851, 22 March 1851, 5 April 1851, 14 June 1851

Irish Quarterly Review, Vol. V, Part 1 no author (Dublin, 1855)

Mechanics Magazine Vol 4 28 May 1825 no author (London 1825) p.122

Mechanics' Magazine Vol. LX, no author (London, 1854)

North British Review, November, New York, 1864

Punch Vol. XX (1851)

Quarterly Review, Vol. 57 no author (John Murray, 1836)

Reports of the Society for Bettering the Condition of the Poor (London, 1797, 1798, & 1805)
The Examiner, Sunday 23 April 1815, (London, 1815)
The Graphic, 10 June 1871
The Times, 9 September 1789, 28 August 1811, 10 June 1833, 28 May 1833, 19 July 1833, 30 September 1840, 21 April 1843, 7 November 1843, 1 December 1843, 13 March 1844, 16 March 1844, 17 May 1844, 2 February 1850, 25 March 1850, 27 March 1850, 29 November 1850, 2 December 1850, 4 December 1850, 9 December 1850, 16 December 1850, 28 December 1850, 29 January 1851, 1 February 1851, 11 Feb 1851, 21 March 1851, 11 April 1851, 10 May 1860, 2 October 1885

Parliamentary Papers
Abstract of Answers and Returns under the Population Act 1841 (1844)
Appendix to the Reports... On Public Petitions: Appendix to the Tenth Report, Petitions against adopting the Principles in Mr Horner's Report, Session 1846, p.107
Appendix to the Second Report of the Children's Employment Commission: Trades and Manufactures: Part 1, XIII, 1842
Children's Employment Commission: Report on Mines, XV, 1842.
Condition and Treatment of Children Employed in the Mines and Collieries of the United Kingdom, (William Strange, London, 1842).
Condition of the Framework Knitters, Appendix Part I, XXIV, 1845.
Correspondence between the Poor Law Board and Guardians...Pauper Children to the Factory Districts, [259], House of Lords, 1861.
Correspondence... relating to the Emigration of Children to Bermuda, [243], 1851.
Fifth Report of the Children's Employment Commission (1862): Printing and Miscellaneous Trades, XXIV, 1866.
First Annual Report of the Poor Law Commissioners (1835)
First Report of the Children's Employment Commission: Mines, XV (1842)
First Report of the Commission into the Employment of Children, Young Persons and Women in Agriculture, [21157] (1868)
First Report of the Commissioners, Children's Employment Commission (1862) [3170], XVIII, 1863.
Fourth Report of the Commissioners, Children's Employment Commission (1862), [8357], XX, (1865)
Hansard, Thomas Curson, *Parliamentary Debates from the Year 1803 to the Present Time*, Vol. XXV (London, 1813)
Hansard Thomas Curson, *Parliamentary Debates, Vol. XXX* (1815)
Hansard Thomas Curson, *Hansard's Parliamentary Debates Vol.XXXVII* (1818)
Hansard, Thomas Curson, *Hansard's Parliamentary Debates, Third Series Vol. CLCCV*, (London, 1864)
Index to the Reports... on the Poor Law Amendment Act, [97, 45], (1838)
Minutes of Evidence: Act for the Better Regulation of Chimney Sweepers and their Apprentices (1818)

Minutes of Evidence: Act for the Better Regulation of Chimney Sweepers and their Apprentices, XXIII (1834)
Minutes of Evidence…from the Select Committee on the State and Condition of Children Employed in Manufactories (1819)
Minutes of the Committee of Council of Education, 1839–40, (London, 1840).
Report from Her Majesty's Commissioners into the Administration and Practical Operation of the Poor Laws (1834)
Report from the Committee on Employment of Boys in Sweeping Chimnies (1817)
Report from the Committee on Parish Apprentices (1815)
Report from the Select Committee…into the Education of the Lower Orders (1816)
Report from the Select Committee into the State of Agriculture, V, [464] (1837)
Report from the Select Committee on Coal Mines, [509] (1852)
Report from the Select Committee on Hand-Loom Weavers' Petitions, [341], XIII, 1835.
Report from the Select Committee on the Education of the Poorer Classes, VII, (1837–8)
Report from the Select Committee on the Poor Law Amendment Act, XXXII (1838)
Report from the Select Committee on the Regulation of Mills and Factories (1841)
Report from the Select Committee on the State and Condition of Children Employed in Manufactories (1819)
Report from the Select Committee on the State of Children Employed in Manufactories (1816)
Report…into the State of Popular Education in England, Vol. I, XXI (1861)
Report…into the State of the Population in Mining Districts, XLV (1855)
Report on the Establishment of Schools in the Factory Districts (1843)
Reports by H.M. Inspectors of Schools, Minutes of the Committee of Council on Education, Vol.1, LXXIX (1852–3)
Reports from Commissioners: 1844, Occupation Abstract, 1841, Vol. 27, [587], 1843
Reports of Special Assistant Poor Law Commissioners on the Employment of Women and Children in Agriculture XII (1843)
Report of the Commissioner appointed to inquire… Better Regulation of Mills and Factories to Bleaching Works Evidence and Appendix, (1855)
Reports of the Inspectors of Factories (1839, 1840–9, 1852, 1854–6, 1864–5, 1868–79)
Second Annual Report of the Poor Law Commissioners (1836)
Second Report of the Children's Employment Commission 1862: Lace, Hosiery &c., [3414], XXII (1864)
Second Report of the Children's Employment Commission: Trades and Manufactures, [430], XIII (1843)
Second Report on the Employment of Children in Factories [519], XXI (1833)
Seventeenth Report from the Select Committee on the Poor Law Amendment Act: Minutes of Evidence and Appendix [222], 1838
Special Reports of the Inspectors of Factories On the Practicability of Legislative Interference to Diminish the Frequency of Accidents (1841)
The Labour Gazette, (April 1895) *Volume 3, January–December 1895*, HMSO
Third Report of the Children's Employment Commission: Metal Manufactures [3414–1], XXII (1864)

Books

Boy's Book of Trades, (no author), (George Routledge and Sons, London, no date. c.1890).

Journal of the Royal Statistical Society of London, Vol. 2, no author (1839)

Journal of the Society of Arts, Vol. II, (London, 1854)

Journal of the Statistical Society of London, Vol. IV, (Charles Knight & Co., 1841)

Memoirs of the Literary and Philosophical Society of Manchester Vol. II (no author), (1785)

Speech of Michael Thomas Sadler in the House of Commons (no author) (Seeley & Son, 1832)

The Physical and Moral Condition of Children and Young Persons Employed in Mines and Manufactures (no author), (London, 1843)

Topographical, Statistical and Historical Account of Scotland (no author), (A. Fullarton & Co. 1853)

Acton, Thomas A., *Gypsy Politics and Social Change* (Routledge & Kegan Paul, 1974)

Adams, Samuel and Adams, Sarah, *The Complete Servant*, (London, 1825)

Aikin, John, *A Description of the Country from Thirty or Forty Miles Round Manchester*, (John Stockdale, 1795)

Anderson, Michael: *Family Structure in 19th Century Lancashire* (Cambridge University Press, 1971)

Archer, Stewart, 'The Servants of Parson Woodforde', *Parson Woodforde Society Journal Vol XLVII* (Spring 2009)

Ashmore, Owen, *A Brief Account of the Early Textile Industry in Derbyshire* (Derbyshire Archaeological Society, Supplement No.10, 1966)

Ashmore, Owen, *The Industrial Archaeology of North-West England* (1982)

Ashton, T.S. and Hayek, F.A., *Capitalism and the Historians* (Routledge, 2003)

Aspin, Chris, *Lancashire: The First Industrial Society* (Carnegie, 1995)

Atkinson, Glen, *The Canal Duke's Collieries* (2nd edition, Neil Richardson, 1998)

Ayton, Richard, *Essays and Sketches of Character* (London, 1825)

Bagley, J.J. and A.J., *The State of Education in England and Wales, 1833–1968* (Macmillan, 1969)

Baines, Edward, *History of the Cotton Manufacture* (H. Fisher, R. Fisher & P. Jackson, London, 1835)

Baines, Thomas, *Yorkshire Past and Present*, 4 vols., (William Mackenzie, c.1875)

Barker, T.C., *Pilkington Brothers and the Glass Industry* (George Allen & Unwin Ltd, 1960)

Barrow, John Henry (ed) *Mirror of Parliament Vol.7* (1838)

Beeton, Isabella, *The Book of Household Management* (London, 1861)

Behlmer, George K., 'Smith, George (1831–1895)', *Oxford Dictionary of National Biography* (Oxford University Press, 2004)

[http://www.oxforddnb.com/view/article/25807, accessed 2 Sept 2009]

Benson, John. *British Coalminers in the Nineteenth Century*, (Gill and Macmillan, 1980)

Beresford, John, *Diary of a Country Parson*, 5 vols. (Oxford University Press, 1924–1931)

Bindman, David, *Hogarth* (Thames & Hudson, 1981)

Blackburn, Sheila, *A Fair Day's Wage for a Fair Day's Work*? (Ashgate Publishing, 2007)

Blaikie, William Garden, *Heads and Hands in the World of Labour* (Alexander Strahan, 1865)

Booth, Charles, *Occupations of the People: England, Scotland, Ireland, 1841–1881*, London, 1886

Bray, Reginald Arthur, *Boy Labour and Apprenticeship* (Constable & Co., 1912)

Buckingham, J. S. (ed)*Parliamentary Review and Family Magazine Vol.3* (London 1833)

Burke, Thomas, *Catholic History of Liverpool* (Liverpool, 1910)

Butterworth, Edwin, *An Historical Account of the Towns of Ashton-under-Lyne, Stalybridge, and Dukinfield, Ashton* (1842)

Butterworth, Edwin, *Historical Sketches of Oldham* (Oldham, 1856)

Campbell, George Douglas (Eighth Duke of Argyll) *The Reign of Law*, 5th edition (London, 1868)

Carlyle, Thomas, *Past and Present* (Chapman & Hall, 1840)

Chadwick, Edwin, *Inquiry into The Sanitary Condition of the Labouring Population of Great Britain* (London, 1842)

Chadwick, Edwin, *The Sanitary Population of the Labouring Population of Great Britain (1842)*, (ed. by M. W. Flinn) (Edinburgh University Press, 1965)

Challinor, Raymond, *The Lancashire and Cheshire Miners* (Frank Graham, 1972)

Chaloner, W. H., *People and Industries* (Frank Cass & Co., 1963)

Chaloner, W. H., and Redford, Arthur, *Labour Migration in England 1800–1850* (Manchester University Press, 1976)

Chambers, J.D. and Mingay, G. E., *The Agricultural Revolution 1750–1880* (B. T. Batsford Ltd, 1970)

Chapman, Stanley D., *The Early Factory Masters* (David & Charles, 1967)

Chapman, Sydney J., *The Lancashire Cotton Industry* (Manchester University Press, 1904)

Cobbett, William, *Advice to Young Men* (New York, 1831)

Cobbett, William, *Legacy to Labourers* (London, 1835)

Cobbett, William, *Rural Rides* (London, 1853)

Cobbett, William, *Weekly Political Register, Vol .XXXII*, 1817

Collier, Frances, *The Family Economy of the Working Classes in the Cotton Industry 1784–1833* (Manchester University Press, 1964)

Conway, Katherine St John (Katherine Bruce Glasier), *The Cry of the Children* (Manchester Labour Press, 1894)

Cooke, George Alexander, *Topographical and Statistical Description of the County of Stafford* (London, no date, c.1803)

Cooke-Taylor, R.Whately, *The Factory System and the Factory Acts*, (Methuen & Co., 1894)

Cooke-Taylor, R.Whately, *The Modern Factory System* (London, 1891)

Cooke-Taylor, William, *Factories and the Factory System*, (London, 1844).

Cooke-Taylor, William, *Notes of a Tour in the Manufacturing Districts of Lancashire* (London, 1842)

Cooper, Lord Anthony Ashley, *Speeches of the Earl of Shaftesbury, K.G.* (Chapman & Hall, 1868)

Cooper, Thomas, and Coxe, J. R., *Emporium of Arts and Sciences, Vol.II* (Kimberley & Richardson, Philadelphia, 1813)
Corbould, Richard and Springsguth, Samuel, *Juvenile Philosophy* (London, 1801)
Cottle, Joseph, *Early Recollections, chiefly relating to the late Samuel Taylor Coleridge*, 2 Vols, (Longman, Rees & Co., 1837)
Crossick, Geoffrey, *An Artisan Elite in Victorian Society: Kentish London 1840–1880* (Taylor & Francis, 1978)
Cunningham, Hugh, *The Invention of Childhood* (BBC Books, 2006)
Dickens, Charles (ed) *All The Year Round Vol. VI* (London 1862)
Dickens, Charles, (ed) *Household Narrative of Current Events for the Year 1850* (London, 1850)
Dickens, Charles, (ed) *Household Words Vol. IX* (London, 1854)
Dickens, Charles, (ed) *Household Words Vol. XI* (London, 1855)
Dickens, Charles, (ed) *Household Words Vol. XIII*, (London, 1856)
Dickens, Charles, *The Old Curiosity Shop* (Chapman & Hall, 1841)
Dickens, Charles, *The Writings of Charles Dickens: Life, Letters and Speeches Vol* XXX (Houghton, Mifflin, 1894), vol. 1, p9
Dickens, Charles, and Law, Graham (ed.), *Hard Times* (Broadview Press, 2000)
Disraeli, Benjamin, *Sybil or The Two Nations* (Leipzig, 1845)
Dunlop, Olive Jocelyn and Denman, Sir Richard D., *English Apprenticeship and Child Labour* (T. Fisher Unwin, 1912)
Engels, Friedrich, (ed. D. McLellan), *The Condition of the Working Class in England* (Oxford University Press, 1993)
Espriella, Don (Southey, Robert) *Letters from England*, (1836)
Evans, Eric J., *The Forging of the Modern State* (Longman, 1993)
Finlayson, Geoffrey B.A.M., *Seventh Earl of Shaftesbury 1801–1885* (Eyre Methuen, 1981)
Forster, John, *The Life of Charles Dickens Vol. I* (Boston, 1872).
Gaskell, Elizabeth Cleghorn, *North and South* (Bernhard Tauchnitz, 1855)
Gaskell, Peter, *The Manufacturing Population of England* (London, 1833)
Gaskell, Peter, *Prospects of Industry* (Smith, Elder & Co., 1835)
Gibbins, Henry de Beltgens, *English Social Reformers* (Methuen & Co., 1892)
Gisborne, Thomas, *An Enquiry into the Duties of Men, Vol. II* (London, 1824)
Grant, Philip, *The Ten Hours Bill: The History of Factory Legislation* (Manchester, 1866)
Greg, Robert Hyde, *The Factory Question* (James Ridgeway & Son, 1837)
Gregg, Pauline, *A Social and Economic History of Britain, 1760–1970* 6th edition, (G. Harrap & Co. Ltd., 1971)
Guest, Richard, *A Compendious History of the Cotton Manufacture* (Manchester, 1823)
Hammond, J.L. and Barbara, *Lord Shaftesbury*, 2nd ed (Constable & Co., 1923)
Hammond, J.L. and Barbara, *The Bleak Age* (Pelican Books, 1947)
Hammond, J.L. and Barbara, *The Skilled Labourer* (Allan Sutton Publishing, 1995)
Hammond, J.L. and Barbara, *The Town Labourer* (Longman, 1978)
Hanson, Harry, *The Canal Boat-Men 1760–1914* (Manchester University Press, 1975)
Hanway, Jonas, *An Earnest Appeal for Mercy to the Children of the Poor* (London, 1766)
Harris, R.W., *Romanticism and the Social Order 1780–1830*, (Blandford Press, 1969).

Harrison, Brian, 'Blincoe, Robert (*c.*1792–1860)', *Oxford Dictionary of National Biography*, Oxford University Press (Sept 2004) [http://www.oxforddnb.com/view/article/52805, accessed 17 June 2010]

Head, Sir George, *A Home Tour through the Manufacturing Districts of England* (John Murray, 1836)

Higgs, Edward, *A Clearer Sense of the Census* (HMSO, 1996)

Hirst, F.W. (ed), Porter, George R., *The Progress of the Nation* (London, 1912)

Hobsbawm, E.J., and Rudé, George, *Captain Swing* (Penguin Books, 1969)

Holmes, J. H. H., *A Treatise on the Mines of Durham and Northumberland* (London, 1816)

Honeyman, Katrina, *Child Workers in England 1780–1820* (Ashgate Publishing Ltd, 2007)

Horn, Pamela, *Children's Work and Welfare 1780–1890* (Cambridge University Press, 1995)

Hopkins, Eric, *Childhood Transformed: Working Class Children in Nineteenth Century England* (Manchester University Press, 1994)

Horn, Pamela, *Labouring Life in the Victorian Countryside* (Gill and Macmillan, 1976)

Horn, Pamela, *The Victorian Country Child* (Sutton Publishing, 1974)

Horner, Leonard, *On the Employment of Children in Factories* (London, 1840)

Hutchins, B.L., and Harrison, A., *A History of Factory Legislation* (Frank Cass & Co. Ltd, 1966)

Hutton, William, *History of Derby* (London, 1817)

Hutton, William, *Life of William Hutton*, (Charles Knight & Co., 1841)

Jackson, Patrick, *Education Act Forster: A Political Biography* (Associated University Presses, 1997)

Jameson, Peter (ed.), *The Diary of James Woodforde Volume 15 1796–7* (Parson Woodforde Society, 2004)

Jevons, William Stanley, *The Coal Question*, (Macmillan & Co., 1866)

Jones, John, *Poems* (1856)

Kay, James Phillips, *Moral and Physical Condition of the Working Classes* (1832)

Kirby, Peter, *Child Labour in Britain 1750–1870* (Palgrave Macmillan, 2003)

Kirby, Peter, *Child Labour, Public Decency and the Iconography of the Children's Employment Commission of 1842, Manchester Papers in Economic and Social History No. 62* (October 2007)

Knight, Charles, *Pictorial Gallery of Arts: Vol. I, Useful Arts* (London Printing and Publishing Company, c.1860)

Knowles, L.C.A., *Industrial and Commercial Revolutions* (George Routledge & Sons, 1937)

Kydd, Samuel, *History of the Factory Movement*, 2 vols (Simpkin, Marshall & Co., 1857)

Landscape of Industry: an industrial history of the Blackstone Valley, (no author), Worcester Historical Museum, (UPNE, 2009)

Langford, John Alfred, *Staffordshire and Warwickshire Past and Present* Vols 1–3, (William Mackenzie)

Lavalette, Michael, *Child Labour: A Thing of the Past?* (Liverpool University Press, 1999)
Law, Brian R., *The Fieldens of Todmorden* (George Kelsall, 1995)
Lazarus, Mary, *Victorian Social Conditions and Attitudes 1837–71* (Macmillan and Co., 1969)
Lee, Sidney (ed.), *Dictionary of National Biography*, (Adamant Media Corporation, 2001).
Le Faye, Deirdre, *Jane Austen: A Family Record* (Cambridge University Press, 2004)
Levi, Leone, *Annals of British Legislation*, Vol. XIII, (Smith, Elder, & Co.,) 1864
Lightwood, Rev. Edward, *The Good Earl* (London, 1886)
Macaulay, Thomas Babington, *Works of Lord Macaulay*, (London, 1866).
Mackenzie, E., *Descriptive and Historical Account… of Newcastle upon Tyne* (Mackenzie & Dent, 1827)
Malthus, Thomas R., *Essay on the Principle of Population*, 2 vols. (London, 1807)
Mantoux, Paul, *The Industrial Revolution in the Eighteenth Century* (Routledge, 2006)
Martineau, Harriet (ed. M. W. Chapman), *Autobiography, Vol. I* (Boston, 1877)
Martineau, Harriet, *History of the Peace* (W. & R. Chambers, 1858)
Martineau, Harriet, *The Factory Controversy: A Warning Against Meddling Legislation* (Manchester, 1855)
Matsumura, Takao, *The Labour Aristocracy Revisited: Victorian Flint Glassmakers 1850–80* (Manchester University Press, 1983)
May, Trevor, *The Victorian Schoolroom* (Shire Publications, 2006)
Mayhew, Henry, *London Labour and the London Poor, Vol. II* (London, 1861)
McCulloch, J.R., *Statistical Account of the British Empire*, 2 vols. (London, 1839)
McLeod, Donald, (ed.), *Good Words*, London, 1879
Mill, John Stuart, *On Liberty* (London, 1859)
More, Hannah, *The Complete Works Vol. I* (New York, 1847)
Moritz, Carl P., *Travels, Chiefly on Foot Through Several Parts of England in 1782* (London, 1797)
Musson, A.E., *An Introductory Note on Robert Blincoe and the Early Factory System* (Derbyshire Archaeological Society, Supplement No.10, 1966)
Nardinelli, Clark, *Child Labor and the Industrial Revolution*, Indiana University Press, 1990.
Oastler, Richard, *The Fleet Papers Vol. 1* (London, 1841)
Owen, Robert, *The Life of Robert Owen Written by Himself* (London, 1857)
Palmer, F.P., and Crowquill, Arthur, *Wanderings of a Pen and Pencil* (London, 1846)
Palmer, Marilyn, & Neaverson, Peter, *Industrial Archaeology* (Routledge, 1998)
Parkes, Mrs William, *Domestic Duties; Or Instructions to Young Married Ladies* (New York, 1829)
Parton, John, *Captains of Industry* (Kaydreams, 1910)
Pennant, Thomas, *History of the Parishes of Whiteford and Holywell* (London, 1796)
Pictorial History of the County of Lancaster, no author, (London, 1844)
Pierce, Gilbert Ashville, *Writings of Charles Dickens Vol. XXX* (Houghton, Mifflin, 1894)

Pike, E. Royston, *Human Documents of the Industrial Revolution in Britain* (George Allen & Unwin, 1978)

Pike, E. Royston, *Human Documents of the Victorian Golden Age* (George Allen & Unwin, 1967)

Pinchbeck, Ivy, *Women Workers and the Industrial Revolution 1750–1830* (Virago Press, 1981)

Porter, George Richardson, *The Progress of the Nation* (John Murray, 1851)

Prentice, Archibald, *Historical Sketches and Personal Recollections of Manchester*, (London, 1851).

Pugh, John, *Remarkable Occurrences in the life of Jonas Hanway*, 3rd edition (London, 1798)

Redford, Arthur, *Labour Migration in England 1800–1850* (Manchester University Press, 1976)

Rose, Lionel, *The Erosion of Childhood: Child Oppression in Britain 1860–1918* (Routledge, 1991)

Sargant, William Lucas, *Robert Owen and his Social Philosophy* (Smith, Elder & Co., 1860)

Sarget, Epes, (ed.), *The Works of Thomas Hood Vol. I* (George P. Putnam, 1864)

Seely, Robert Benton, *Memoirs of the Life and Writings of Michael Thomas Sadler* (Seeley & Burnside, 1848)

Seely, Robert Benton, *The Perils of the Nation* (Seeley & Burnside & Seeley, 1844)

Simmons, James R., *Factory Lives: Four Nineteenth Century Working Class Autobiographies* (Broadview Press, 2007)

Simond, Louis, *Journal of a Tour*, 2 vols (Edinburgh, 1815)

Simpson, A.W. Brian, *Leading Cases in the Common Law* (Oxford University Press, 2001)

Sinclair, John, *The Statistical Account of Scotland, Vol. 15* (Edinburgh, 1795)

Smiles, Samuel, *Lives of the Engineers: Boulton and Watt* (John Murray, 1874)

Smiles, Samuel, *Self-Help: with Illustrations of Character and Conduct* (New York, 1860)

Smiles, Samuel, *Thrift* (Chicago, 1890)

Smith, Adam, *An Inquiry into the Nature and Causes of the Wealth of Nations* (A. & C. Black, 1863)

Smith, George, *A Cry From the Brick-yards of England*, (London, 1879)

Smith, George, *Our Canal Population* (London, 1878)

Snell, K.D.M., *Annals of the Labouring Poor* (Cambridge University Press, 1992)

Somerville, Alexander, *The Whistler at the Plough* (Manchester, 1852)

Southey, C.C. (ed.), *Life and Correspondence of Robert Southey* (Harper & Brothers, 1855)

Spackman, William Frederick, *An Analysis of the Occupations of the People* (London, 1842)

Sykes, John, *Local Records or Historical Register… of Northumberland and Durham*, Vol. II (1833)

Tapping, Thomas, *The Factory Acts* (Shaw & Sons, 1856)

Thompson, E. P., *The Making of the English Working Class* (Pantheon Books, 1964)

Trevelyan, George Macaulay, *Life of John Bright* (Constable & Co., 1913)
Trimmer, Sarah, *The Oeconomy of Charity, Or an Address to Ladies,* 2 vols (1801)
Trinder, Barrie, *The Making of the Industrial Landscape* (J. M. Dent & Sons Ltd., 1982)
Tuckett, John Debell, *A History of the Past and Present State of the Labouring Population, Vol.1*, London, 1816)
Unwin, George, *Samuel Oldknow and the Arkwrights* (Manchester University Press, 1924)
Ure, Andrew, *The Philosophy of Manufactures* (Charles Knight, 1835)
Vane, C.W., *A Letter to Lord Ashley on the Mines and Collieries' Bill* (London, 1842)
Wade, John, *History and Political Philosophy of the Middle and Working Classes* (William and Robert Chambers, 1842)
Weaver, Stewart A., 'Sadler, Michael Thomas (1780–1835)', *Oxford Dictionary of National Biography* (Oxford University Press, 2004) [http://www.oxforddnb.com/view/article/24461, accessed 6 May 2010].
Webb, Beatrice and Webb, Sidney, *English Local Government: English Poor Law History* (2 Vols) (Longmans, 1927)
Webb, Beatrice and Webb, Sidney, *English Local Government (Vol. 8): English Poor Law History Part II, The Last Hundred Years, Vol. I*, (Longmans, 1927)
West, William, *The History, Topography and Directory of Warwickshire* (Birmingham, 1830)
White, George Savage, *Memoir of Samuel Slater, Father of American Manufactures*, Philadelphia, 1836)
White, William, *History, Gazetteer & Directory of Staffordshire* (Sheffield, 1834)
Wilkes, Sue, *A Visitor's Guide to Jane Austen's England*, (Pen and Sword, 2015)
Wilkes, Sue, *Narrow Windows, Narrow Lives: The Industrial Revolution in Lancashire* (History Press, 2008)
Wilkes, Sue, *Regency Cheshire* (Robert Hale, 2009)
Wilkes, Sue, *Tracing Your Ancestors' Childhood*, (Pen and Sword, 2020)
Winstanley, Roy, '*Skip-Jacks*', *Parson Woodforde Society Journal XIX No.1*, Spring 1986
Wolffe, John 'Cooper, Anthony Ashley-, seventh earl of Shaftesbury (1801–1885)', *Oxford Dictionary of National Biography*, Oxford University Press, Sept 2004; online edn, Jan 2008 [http://www.oxforddnb.com/view/article/6210, accessed 27 Oct 2009].
Wood, Isaac, *Some Account of the Shrewsbury House of Industry* (Shrewsbury, 1795)
Woodward, Donald, *Early Modern Servants in Husbandry Revisited, Agricultural History Review*, (2000), pp.141–150
Woodward, E.L., *The Age of Reform* (Oxford University Press, 1954)

Index